B L O O M S B U R Y
LONDON · OXFORD · NEW YORK · NEW DELHI · SYDNEY

River
Cottage

LOVE YOUR
LEFTOVERS

Recipes for the resourceful cook

Hugh Fearnley-Whittingstall

Photography by Simon Wheeler   Illustrations by Tim Hopgood

Contents

Some of the most satisfying meals of my life have been created, seemingly, from almost nothing. Planned and carefully shopped-for feasts, such as Christmas dinner and elaborate parties, can be great fun and delicious. But it's those seat-of-the-pants, spur-of-the-moment dishes, rustled up from odds and ends loitering in the fridge or cupboards, that often bring me the greatest pleasure.

Winging it with what's to hand can be so liberating – flinging in this or that with the joyful abandon that comes from not trying too hard or expecting too much. Before you know it, you can produce a plateful that has you thinking, 'Why haven't I tried this before?' And, more importantly, 'I'll definitely make this again,' to which, by the very nature of leftovers, you have to add, 'Or something a bit like it.'

This book represents the scribbling-down of my most cheerful and satisfying experiments, the ones that turned a few, simple, pre-loved ingredients into memorable meals. I've hugely enjoyed writing it. And I'm sure that's because it's really the story of how I cook at home most of the time. Not with a list or even much of a plan, but standing in front of the fridge scanning for possibilities.

A few dried-up odds and ends of cheese, a bit of leftover meat, a dab of cream in dignified old age, the remains of an excellent loaf and some seasonings rummaged out from the back of the storecupboard, can create a rarebit that will beat the world – or at least a raging hunger. And such a dish is always, in my experience, made more scrumptious by the knowledge of its unpromising beginnings.

It's the sort of cooking that allows the cook, quite justifiably, to feel rather pleased with themselves. And it's as efficient as it is tasty. Not only is it thrifty in a financial sense, the work you do for one meal pays dividends because subsequent meals are easier. Often, they are just simple assemblies of meals that have gone before. Or they might flow pleasingly into whole new dishes, significantly different from, though indebted to, the 'original'. A roast chicken might become a fricassée that then turns into a pie (see page 70). Surplus cannellini beans may be destined for a robust soup, salad or cassoulet (see page 192). Bolognese makes its debut with pasta but might then fill an omelette (see page 180), stuff a pepper, or top a baked potato.

It's always hugely pleasing to save money, of course, but the drive to waste nothing is not about parsimony. It's emphatically joyful, a way to honour your food and yourself. When you've sought out and paid for something wonderful, or tended it in your garden, why wouldn't you want to relish it down to the very last morsel? You'd be mad not to.

I do sometimes toss a mouldy apple or some yellowing cabbage onto the compost. I don't beat myself up about that. But I like to think that not much hits the bin unless it's really irretrievable. And I would certainly feel guilty about not eating every last scrap of meat or fish that makes its way into my kitchen. Nothing less than my kitchen honour is at stake here. When an animal has died to feed me, that's quite a thing. And no part of it that can be made tasty should ever go to waste.

I admit that such careful cooking can become something of an obsession. In the course of creating this book, I've turned my naturally competitive eye to those things I might previously have cast compost-wards or fed to my pigs, and asked myself if I could get a bit more out of them first.

I've given fresh thought to the skeletal remains of roast dinners and to slightly past-it veg and reconsidered the bendy, the floppy and the slightly tired to see what can be done with them. I've come up with some answers too – from crispy fish skeletons (see page 104) and chicken skin crackling (see page 79) to roast root peelings (see page 130), which are better than any you can buy in a packet. There's a soul-feeding pleasure to be had from dishing up something tasty from such unprepossessing raw materials.

There's no need to see leftovers cooking as a constant challenge, however. At its heart, it's about simplicity. Sometimes, you just want to reheat and eat, without feeling you should be doing more. There are days when merely tucking that leftover roast ham into a sandwich, rather than turning it into a soup or a pie, is what fits the bill. The former option isn't a compromise – it all comes down to the time and energy you have available.

When I looked at each recipe for this book, the first question I asked myself was not, 'Is it speedy?' Or 'Is it thrifty?' But, 'Would I be delighted to have that for my supper (or lunch, or tea) today?' If I couldn't answer that question with a resounding 'Yes!' the recipe didn't make the cut.

Of course, there is a deeper issue at play here: in this country, we waste a shocking amount of food. Although recent campaigns, such as the one run by the Waste and Resources Action Programme (WRAP), are helping to reduce our profligacy a little, we still throw out some seven million tonnes of food every year. That is scandalous, particularly in a world where scarcity is the norm for so many people. And all that wasted food took energy and resources to produce and transport – putting less in the bin means easing the pressure on our planet too.

Thrifty cooking is hardly a new idea, of course. Many people enjoy lovingly re-invented leftovers as part of their daily diet already. But as with any cooking, we all get stuck in ruts, often returning to the same tried-and-tested dishes and techniques. I want to show you that leftovers cuisine is an area as broad and exciting as any other. You can be just as creative and inventive with ingredients you have dabbled with already as with pristine items freshly bought. Probably more so, since they encourage you to stretch boundaries, take a few chances, and be a bit left-field with your combinations and seasonings.

So set your expectations high and take a new look at how you cook and what you cook. You'll discover that you absolutely can make meals from peels, and snacks from skin and bone. You can take the surplus and the borderline and cook them back to sparkling originality, roasting and simmering, frying and blending your way to a sense of deep satisfaction that is very sweet indeed.

Planning for leftovers

If you embrace leftovers as a central part of your daily cooking and a wellspring for culinary creativity, you will change not just the way you eat, but also the way you buy food and the way you manage both your kitchen and the time you spend in it. This is because all your food plans will be made – consciously at first but soon pretty much without thinking – with leftovers in mind.

The business of getting food on to the table can be split into three broad stages: shopping, storing and cooking. All of those stages can be quite stressful if you imagine each meal must be a self-contained unit – you are constantly trying to calculate quantities, always planning to end up with zero when the meal is done.

Take a more leftovers-centred approach and the entire process becomes more relaxed and flexible because each meal can beget another, or part of another, with precise amounts mattering very little, if at all. I'm reminded of a line from the American writer Calvin Trillin, 'The most remarkable thing about my mother is that for 30 years she served the family nothing but leftovers. The original meal has never been found.'

I love this quote. And I aspire to be more like Calvin's mother! I do still cook a few 'original meals' but I like to think of each one as the beginning of a daisy chain of deliciousness. Sometimes it's a short chain – leftover meat and veg into a simple hash (see page 50). Sometimes a meal keeps giving all week, as is often the case with big roast joints of meat or hearty feed-a-crowd stews and curries.

So I'm going to outline what I think is the best approach to establishing and maintaining a glorious, belly-filling procession of lovely, leftover-y meals.

SHOPPING

Why talk about shopping in a book about leftovers, you may ask? Leftovers just happen, don't they, whatever you buy? Well, yes and no. You will always find yourself with some wild-card ingredients to hand, the result of unexpected under-consumption. But, as I explain more fully later, clever cooks can (and I think should) deliberately create leftovers.

And it pays also to keep a pretty good stock of leftovers-friendly complementary ingredients. All of which means shopping with a modicum of foresight.

For me, shopping starts before I leave the house, with a cursory check of the fridge and cupboards to see what's running low and what I have in abundance. I then note the things I might want to turn into meals in the next few days and the kind of ingredients necessary to complete those dishes. But I also make sure there's a good amount of play in the plan and plenty of blank space on my mental list so that I can take advantage of what I find when I hit the shops.

When I say 'hit the shops', that's a pretty flexible term. Actually we order quite a bit of our fresh food from a local organic delivery service – especially in the winter when our own veg garden is less productive. But I also regularly visit my favourite local delis, health food shops and farmers' markets. I like to see what's new in store, what's coming in with the seasons, who's making a quirky new cheese... And I like to chat with people who are roughly in the same business as I am – the business of feeding people. I have to admit that for me, food shopping is kind of a hobby.

Of course it's not like that for everyone, and how you shop depends very much on how, and where, you live. Perhaps you like to buy a week's groceries from an out-of-town store in one trip, though there is some evidence that 'the big shop' is falling out of favour and being replaced by smaller, more frequent trips. I do think that shopping widely, fairly often, in multiple retailers, at least some of whom are independent, pays off – because it makes you more adventurous, more savvy and more likely to take advantage of seasonally plentiful foods.

I make the point several times in this book that it's nearly always worth cooking more of something than you need. However, this approach does not neatly translate into a shopping strategy. It's not always a good idea to buy more than you need, if what you are buying is fresh produce.

Be wary of the BOGOF (buy one, get one free). One of the biggest causes of food waste in recent years has been the increase of supermarket two-for-one or three-for-two deals: seemingly irresistible offers on fresh food which tempt us to buy more than we can possibly eat in the time before it goes off.

Having said that, if you see a brilliant offer on fresh produce in your supermarket or farmers' market, you have space in your freezer and, more importantly, you have space in your diary, it is a great opportunity to get ahead, to stock up on what I think of as 'forethought leftovers' (as opposed to afterthought ones).

Prepping a big stash of fruit or veg doesn't have to mean the time-consuming making of whole meals. It can simply be blanching or roasting ingredients and/or freezing them in portion-sized bags, ready for when you need a handful of broad beans to toss into a soup or some raspberries for a smoothie. So, although it may sound a little paradoxical, my advice is not to buy too much but to buy as much as you can for the resources (in terms of time and space) that you have.

If you hunt down the plumpest and perkiest produce, it will keep well and see you through the next few days or even weeks, broadening your options when it comes to using it. At the same time, bruised, blemished and even slightly mouldy fruit and veg don't need to be thrown away, they just need to be used up first and trimmed as necessary. (Whatever The Osmonds may have told you, one bad apple can spoil the whole bunch, girl.)

While quality is important, bear in mind that appearances aren't everything (it's a lot like falling in love). Try to see past lumps and bumps and less-than-perfect skins, and think about flavour. Sometimes it's the less buffed

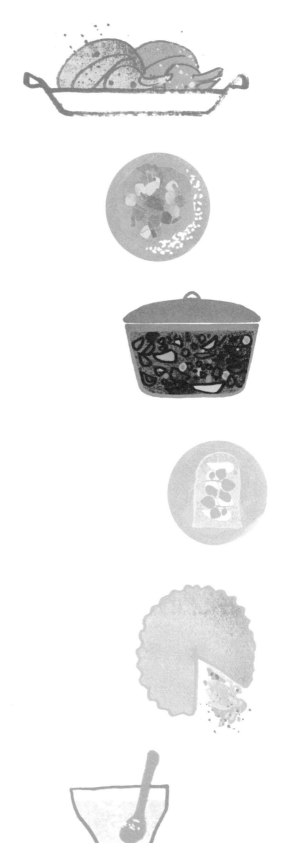

and alluring-looking fresh fruit and veg – that are, crucially, in season – which taste the best.

And if you can get a great deal and you have a little time, do consider produce that's past the first flush of youth, especially if it's at a reduced price (often the case at the end of the day in street markets selling fresh produce). Slightly bendy carrots can be roasted, soft tomatoes turned into soup, tired parsnips puréed and stirred into cakes (see page 146). Bargain.

When shopping for meat and fish, however you intend to cook it, bring home as much of the beast as you can. If you get your fishmonger to clean and fillet your fish, ask them to wrap up the bones and heads for you too, because they make great soup (page 116) or even an unusual and tasty light meal (see spicy crispy fish skeletons, page 104).

If you're planning a chicken dish which only uses parts of the bird, you may be better off buying a whole chicken and cutting it into portions – or have the butcher do it for you – rather than choosing the portion pack in the first place. Then you have the bones to make stock and the skin for delicious crackling (see page 79). In fact, it's worth building up a good relationship with your butcher so they're more inclined to pass along the bounty of free bones for stocks (see page 28), and who knows what other perks, next time you're buying a more substantial cut.

Buy eggs when they're good and fresh and they will keep for a couple of weeks at room temperature (see page 21), no problem. With milk, try to pay the best price for the best quality you can find. Supermarket price wars have had a catastrophic effect on the British dairy industry, so seeking out more ethical suppliers is a long-term investment in our farmers.

Your storecupboard is the single greatest weapon in your leftovers-to-dinner arsenal. So it's really worthwhile keeping it well stocked with tinned and dry goods, useful condiments and seasonings (see pages 318–21). Pulses and lentils, tins of tomatoes or passata, jars of capers and cornichons, packets of rice and pasta, spices, good oil and mustard – these are the things that will stretch what remains of your Sunday lunch into Monday dinner for four or more. But keep a brisk eye on them. There is a balance to be kept between having enough to make whipping up meals a cinch, and having so much crammed in there that you don't know what you've got and end up repeat-buying things that are lingering out of sight at the back of the shelf.

Internet shopping is the friend of the thrifty cook, allowing you to select just what you need without having to leave the house and subjecting yourself to the varied temptations of the supermarket. It also opens the door to some particularly interesting and unusual ingredients, including the sort of fantastic spices and seasonings that can really lift your daily cooking.

Box schemes, meanwhile, are an excellent way of discovering fresh seasonal produce you might not otherwise come across. They also encourage just the kind of 'what-have-I-got-in-here' spontaneity that is the life and soul of leftovers-friendly cooking.

The more you embrace your food shopping as a wily, strategic-minded adventure, the less of a chore it will seem.

COOKING

The cooking in this book is based around two key groups of ingredients: leftovers of a single product nearing the conclusion of its useful life (the half-tub of cream, the last few slightly soft digestives), and leftovers that are the remnants of prepared meals (the chicken carcass, the roast potatoes, the excess tomato sauce, etc.). Generally, I try to shop in a way that minimises the former and cook in a way that maximises the latter. But great leftovers cooking is really about bringing the two together, taking whatever good things you find when you open the fridge door and re-combining them in delicious, neat, waste-busting harmony.

If you understand the immense satisfaction that's to be got from leftovers, you may well find yourself, as I do, deliberately creating them. In fact, I'd urge you to do so. For me, cooking more than I need for one particular meal is just as likely to be a deliberate act as a fortuitous accident. These 'planned overs', the leftovers you know about in advance, are perhaps the most valuable of all.

If I get a leg of lamb out of the freezer to roast for a family Sunday lunch, it doesn't bother me in the slightest to know that the six of us won't eat it all. In fact, I'd be consternated if we *did* eat it all – partly because that would mean we were being exceptionally greedy, but more because I'd feel robbed of 2 or 3 days' worth of gorgeous cold meat sitting in the fridge tempting me to make shepherd's pie (see page 90) or a Middle Eastern-inspired lamb and chickpea thing-in-a-pan with spices and raita (see page 88).

Likewise, these days, I rarely roast just one chicken. I can get two into my oven, which means a great feast for the family plus plenty of leftover meat and a couple of lovely carcasses ready to be simmered down into a litre or more of fine stock.

The creation of 'planned-overs' doesn't even have to be linked to the meal you're making. If I'm in the kitchen anyway, roasting vegetables or stirring a soup, I'll often throw half a box of Puy lentils into a pan with a bay leaf, half an onion and a kettleful of water, and get them cooked. It's almost no work, and while I might not have a specific plan for their use, I know that tub of pulses in the fridge will see me right for some mouth-watering, substantial salads over the next few days, with crumbled cheese, crisp leaves – and perhaps some of those roasted roots.

Another canny cook's trick is to double-up (or triple-up) recipes. With one-pot dishes in particular, such as casseroles, soups, chillies, pasta sauces and curries, twice as much food can be produced with only a little more effort, ready to be bagged up and chilled or frozen for a rainy, or a lazy, day. These stewy, 'wet' dishes are prime candidates for making in advance anyway – they taste even better after a day or two's maturing. And they lend themselves to further additions from the larder or fridge: Sunday's stew gains a pastry lid and becomes Tuesday's pie; a bolognese, with kidney beans and spices, becomes a chilli con carne; a veg curry becomes... another veg curry, with more and different veg added, and maybe a dash of coconut milk second time around.

And those pockets of the day when you are naturally kitchen-centred and food-focused are also a good opportunity to deal with the unplanned kind of leftover. So, while I'm boiling pasta or frying onions for tonight's supper, I might also quickly melt some slightly aged butter into longer-lasting ghee (see page 108), suspend some mature yoghurt in muslin to make a batch of labneh (see page 218) or bake some stale bread into croûtons (see page 39), which will keep in an airtight jar for a week or so and crunchily enhance the appeal of any soup or salad they're added to.

The key to using such opportunistically created items is to be relaxed about quantities. Go with what you have. In my ingredients lists, you'll notice quite a few 'abouts', 'handfuls', 'bits' and 'splashes'. That's because I don't want you to be put off trying a dish because you're 50g short of something. There are almost always very good potential swap-ins anyway (you'll find myriad suggestions for such in the recipes). Why not throw some cooked pulses or sautéed mushrooms in a pie or casserole to make up for not having quite enough meat? No one will berate you – though they may hassle you for the recipe after they've tasted it.

Being a successful leftovers cook is not labour-intensive. Quite the reverse. The joy of using leftovers is that you've already done most of the work – why create more? The ideas in this book are as quick and straightforward as I could make them. Use a bit of nous when it comes to maximising the quality and usability of your leftovers, and you'll find life in the kitchen just gets easier and easier.

Here's a bunch of tips that might just speed up your leftovers hit rate:

Go easy on the seasoning at first if you are doubling, tripling or even quadrupling the quantities of a recipe – and taste, taste, taste. You may not need to add seasoning in the same multiples as the rest of the ingredients. For example, a recipe that calls for a couple of chopped fresh chillies may be volcanic if you triple it up and add six.

Add veg late on to a soup or stew and stop simmering when the veg are still slightly underdone. They will continue to cook when you reheat them and this precaution avoids mushiness.

Cool cooked food that you're not going to eat straight away (and so is destined to become 'leftover') as quickly as possible. Rinse it in cold water, if that's practical (e.g. with just-cooked veg) or stand the saucepan in a sink of cold water (for a stew or sauce). You'll preserve better flavour and colour this way – and it's good food hygiene too.

Minimise the risk of freezer burn (which taints and gives an unpleasant flavour to foods) by getting rid of as much air as possible before you freeze things. Either carefully press air out of the freezer bag before sealing or, if you're freezing in a plastic container, cover the surface of the food with baking parchment before you put the lid on. And label it. You may think you'll remember what's in there but you won't. Don't forget to put the date on too.

Pick meat off bones from a chicken carcass, or flesh off a fish skeleton at the end of a meal, while you have a glass of wine beside you and a conversation on the go, rather than leave it until tomorrow. Finding a plastic tub of tidily torn cooked chicken or nicely flaked fish in the fridge, without remembering precisely how it got there, is one of the great treats of being a leftover-mindful cook.

Once you get the hang of it you will find that leftovers are the oil that greases the wheels of a well-run kitchen. And I don't mean a Michelin-starred enterprise ruled by a tyrant. I mean a happy-go-lucky family kitchen that pootles along merrily, satisfyingly and sustainably, with one tasty meal being carried over into another, the week's shopping all happily and frugally used up (except for the bits that aren't yet, but are about to be). That's the kind of kitchen we all want to be in, isn't it?

STORING

If you cleave to the virtuous goal of turning leftovers into great meals, one thing that will boost your success rate more than anything else is proper storage. If your ingredients are in good nick to start with, you're halfway there.

Storage isn't just about maintaining food quality, it's also about food safety. The older the food, the more chances of it becoming home to some nasty microbe or other. Happily, the bacteria that cause food poisoning can be assailed in a two-pronged attack.

Firstly, there is cold. These days, we are blessed with superb, efficient fridge and freezer technology, which is something previous generations didn't have – and an enormous boon to the leftovers cook. It's one of the reasons I am very much in the laid-back camp when it comes to how long you keep things for. I now maintain my fridge at a rather chilly 3°C – and it's remarkable how well, and how long, many foods keep at that temperature, even when compared to, say, 5°C. A fish I've caught myself, for instance, will be perfectly good after 4 or even 5 days at the bottom of my fridge – a less fresh but still respectable specimen from the fishmonger will be ok for 2 or 3 days.

And the other powerful tool is, conversely, heat. Although some bugs can withstand cooking (see rice, below), generally, if you heat something high enough for long enough, it will be safe to eat. The official guidelines are that food reheated so that the internal temperature reaches 75°C or more for at least 1 minute is safe to eat.

This is not completely fail-safe. Rice (see page 19) and peanuts can both grow moulds that produce dangerous toxins not destroyed by cooking. And botulism toxin requires a more prolonged, hotter treatment in order to be destroyed. But these are rare exceptions to a rule on which the food safety of the entire catering industry depends, and which will also stand you in good stead in your kitchen at home: heat something until piping hot all the way through, and it is safe to eat. Soups, stews and saucy dishes should be stirred during the process so that heat is distributed throughout.

It is prolonged mild warmth that should be resolutely avoided: keeping fresh food at room temperature for hours, not reheating things thoroughly, or simply leaving the door of the fridge open on a hot day, are all invitations to bacteria that can make you ill.

I hope these points make it clear that I absolutely do not advocate a cavalier approach to food safety. However, it could certainly be argued that these days we have become a little too fearful. Almost everything we buy is plastered with scary-looking dates, suggesting that ill will befall anyone who doesn't heed them. The result is that many of us are chucking out food that is perfectly good to eat. Let's take a look at those dates:

'Use-by' date This appears on perishable fresh foods like fresh meat, fish and dairy products, prepared veg, some deli items, and chilled ready meals. You'll see it mostly on things you would put in your fridge. These dates are conservative and make some allowance for inconsistent fridge temperatures and storage habits of the general public.

A use-by date sounds a note of caution, certainly, but it doesn't mean it's necessarily risky to consume a product after that date. If your nose, and a cautious taste, tells you that yoghurt or cream or milk or cheese, or veg or salad, is still good a few days out of date, then go for it. Even meat and fish, provided it is smelling fine, and thoroughly cooked before eating, could be safely consumed a day or two out of date. A lot of people are throwing away food religiously on the day it hits the use-by date. And that means we are wasting a lot of good food.

'Best-before' date Whereas 'use-by' relates to food safety, 'best-before' simply relates to food quality. It applies mainly to 'ambient foods' – tinned foods and dry-store goods, such as pulses, rice, biscuits, cereals, etc., that do not require refrigeration. It's a manufacturer's way of saying that flavour or texture may diminish after this time. But the food can be safe to eat for weeks after that. Trust your eyes, your nose and your good sense.

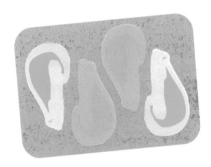

Getting the most out of your fridge

It won't suspend the deleterious effects of time indefinitely, but an efficiently working fridge gives you a lot of control when it comes to meal management. Try to perform a brief fridge survey about once a week so you can remove anything that is beyond redemption, clear up any spills and bring to the fore those things that most urgently require the cook's attention. Beyond that, simply love your fridge for the magnificent leftovers-marshalling machine it is.

Meat

It's important to store meat safely in the fridge to prevent the spread of any bacteria it might contain. Chicken and pork are the most likely to harbour harmful bugs, so take particular care in storing them. (And always make sure they are cooked right through, never left pink.)

Keep raw meat at the bottom of the fridge so it can't touch or drip onto other food. I ring-fence the salad drawer for this since it's self-contained at the bottom and is easy to remove and wash.

Keep raw and cooked or cured meat apart.

Leftover cooked meat, carefully sealed in a plastic container or wrapped in several layers of cling film, will keep for 3 or 4 days. If it was thoroughly cooked to begin with (i.e. not pink in the middle), it may still be good to go for a couple more days if it smells fine and is free from mould and you are going to thoroughly reheat it. I have roasted a shoulder of lamb on a Sunday, fridged the leftover joint, and made a shepherd's pie the next Friday. But I should add that I trust my fridge and my judgement.

Fish

Fish is particularly susceptible to deterioration at room temperature, so it is essential to get it into the fridge as soon as possible after buying.

Smoked fish in vacuum-packs may last a week or so beyond its 'use-by' date in the fridge. Once opened, keep it sealed in cling film and eat it within a few days.

Shellfish should be bought live and kept damp – not soaking in water, but wrapped in clean, wet tea towels (or under a few handfuls of fresh seaweed if you can get them) in the fridge. Most shellfish will keep for a couple of days like this, but the usual caveats for checking clams, mussels and oysters apply.

Cooked leftover fish or shellfish should be sealed in glass or plastic containers and used within 24 hours if eating cold (in salads, for example), or 48 hours if being thoroughly reheated (in fishcakes, kedgeree, soups, etc.).

Dairy

Some dairy products, particularly cultured ones like cheeses, yoghurt and crème fraîche, can keep for several days past their 'use-by' date, especially in a very cold fridge. Fresh whole milk is not so obliging, especially once opened. But unopened, it's probably good for a couple more days than advised on the carton.

It's best not to keep dairy items for extended periods in those handy compartments in the fridge door, though. Frequent opening and closing of the door means that the temperature there fluctuates too much for delicate dairy: keep it at the back of the fridge.

Safe storage of cooked meat

Some recipes in this book suggest that meat can be used and reheated several times over: the roast that becomes a curry, the remains of which end up in a pasty or wonton. This is acceptable practice, provided you are being sensible about how long you keep the meat at each stage, and provided you heat thoroughly to bug-killing temperature every time. It's also good practice to cool anything that is surplus to the meal rapidly – or at the very least decant and refrigerate as soon as the meal is over. This level of vigilance means you can safely keep a stew, curry or bolognese on the go for up to a week, serving it in three or even more incarnations.

Yoghurt keeps well in the fridge, often for a couple of weeks or more but, like crème fraîche, cream cheese, cottage cheeses and some soft cheeses, it should be discarded as soon as it shows any sign of microbial growth, i.e. if it is fizzy or the carton has blown, or if it doesn't smell fresh.

Hard 'dry' cheeses such as Parmesan or Cheddar keep much better than soft ones. If you find a bit of mould around the edges, it's perfectly safe simply to cut it off and eat what remains. Don't throw out the thick rind left at the end of a wedge of Parmesan – keep it in the fridge or freezer ready to toss into simmering soups and stocks to add a rich umami flavour.

Milk that is just on the turn, and so just a bit too sour for your cornflakes or tea, can still be used for pancakes, breads, béchamel etc., or for making simple cheeses (see page 216).

Butter that has seen slightly better days, and smells just a touch cheesy, can still be used for savoury cooking, or to make some ghee (see page 108) to extend its life.

Rice and pulses

Cooked rice and pulses, including opened tinned pulses, should be cooled quickly, stored in a covered container in the fridge and eaten within a day or two.

Safe storage of cooked rice

As cooked rice cools down, the spores of a harmful bacteria, *bacillus cereus*, can germinate on it and produce a toxin that causes food poisoning, particularly if the rice is left standing at room temperature. The toxin is not killed by reheating, no matter how hot you get it, so it's important not to let the bacteria grow in the first place. Cool leftover rice down as rapidly as you can so the spores don't get a chance to proliferate. Either rinse the rice under cold water and drain it well or spread it out on a plate to cool rapidly. Either way, get it into the fridge within an hour of cooking. Even cooled efficiently and stored safely in the fridge, you should use it within a day or two.

Fruit and veg

Many fruits and vegetables can be kept quite successfully in the fridge to prolong their lives, although any you want to serve raw should be returned to room temperature before eating, for the best flavour. Others, however, are spoilt by such low temperatures.

Fridge-friendly ingredients include the following:

Apples stay plump, firm and crisp at low temperatures (industrial scale refrigeration is how the season is extended commercially). I keep mine in the fridge (including my own orchard windfalls), releasing a few every couple of days into the family fruit bowl.

Bananas ripen very fast in a warm kitchen. You can halt this by refrigerating them once they have reached the point of ripeness you like. The cold will hold them there for a few more days. The skins will blacken but the flesh will be fine. Fridge-cold ripe bananas are great for smoothies.

Celery can last for a week or so if it is kept upright in a jug of water in the fridge. Wrapping it in a wet tea towel is a good alternative if vertical storage is not practical. You can revive wilted celery in this way too.

Herbs such as parsley and coriander can be stored in bunches in water in the fridge, as for celery, or wrapped in a wet cloth.

Raspberries, blackberries and blueberries are delicate and turn bad very quickly if they are not kept chilled.

Root veg such as carrots, parsnips, celeriac and swede do well for at least 2 weeks in the fridge, loosely wrapped in whatever packaging you bought them in.

Salad leaves and leafy greens such as lettuce, rocket and spinach are best kept in the fridge in the packaging you bought them in or loosely wrapped in a roomy plastic bag to hold in some moisture, otherwise they are liable to wilt if they dehydrate. The salad drawer is the obvious place to store them unless, like me, you save

this for meat, in which case keep them on the shelf above. Avoid placing them in the coldest part of the fridge (usually the back) as they might get frost damage.

Fridge-phobic ingredients include the following:

Aubergines and courgettes both go a bit soft and wrinkly in either warm kitchens or cold fridges. A cool larder is the best place for these.

Garlic is likely to develop those dreaded green shoots in the fridge, as low temperatures stimulate germination. Ideally, keep your garlic in a cool, well-ventilated place. However, if the only other option is a warm, humid kitchen, your fridge probably is the best bet – just use up the garlic quickly.

Onions soften in the relative humidity of the fridge and their aroma can permeate other foods stored in close proximity.

Peas and beans – once picked – convert their sugars to starches rapidly. While refrigeration slows the process down a little, it's really best to cook and freeze those you're not eating straight away.

Potatoes are best kept in a dark cool larder. Fridge temperatures encourage potatoes to turn their starches into sugars and develop an odd, sweet taste. These sugars can also convert into a potentially harmful chemical called acrylamide when the potatoes are cooked at high temperatures.

Squashes and pumpkins can keep for a month or longer in a dry and well-ventilated place between 10°C and 15°C. They deteriorate more quickly in the fridge.

Tomatoes lose their aroma and flavour and become mealy when chilled, so store them at cool room temperature. Or keep at warm room temperature if you want them to ripen – but be vigilant, as they will go OTT in a couple of days.

Eggs

Use your eggs as soon as you can after buying (or gathering) for optimum texture and flavour. The exception to this is using egg whites for meringues – older, thinner egg whites are more stable and foam up more quickly and easily. Use the freshest eggs you can in things like mayonnaise where they'll be eaten raw. Older eggs can be used in baking, or in any recipe where they are cooked through completely.

Store eggs somewhere cool and away from other strong-smelling foods, as their porous shells mean they absorb other flavours. They don't need to be kept in the fridge.

—

Break eggs separately into a bowl, not straight into a mixture, so you know they are fresh and don't risk wasting the whole dish.

—

Leftover egg whites can be kept in a sealed, scrupulously clean, container in the fridge for a week or so. They also freeze very well, indeed some cooks claim defrosted egg whites make the best meringues. A batch of 4–6 egg whites will make a decent pavlova or roulade – make sure you note the number of whites in the container so you know how much sugar to add.

—

Leftover egg yolks keep well in a sealed small container in the fridge for up to 3 days; cover the surface with cling film to prevent them drying out. They freeze successfully if you take steps to prevent them becoming gelatinous:

beat in a good pinch of salt or 1½ teaspoons sugar to every 4 yolks. Remember to scribble 'savoury' or 'sweet' on the bag.

To test for freshness If you've lost track of your eggs' age, lower them into a bowl of cold water. If the egg lies on its side at the bottom, it's fresh. If it stands on its end, it's less fresh, and needs eating (but crack into a cup first and check). If it floats, it's a bad 'un. Don't crack it, chuck it!

Bready things

Bread should never be kept in the fridge as it will quickly go hard and stale. Keep it in a bread bin and use it within 3 days or so. If you do have stale bread on your hands, there are loads of things you can do with it, from croûtons and seasoned breadcrumbs (see page 39) to classic stale bread dishes like eggy bread (see page 174) and bread and butter pudding (see page 176). But bread *freezes* very well: if you freeze it ready-sliced, you can take out just what you need. A word of caution: don't eat bread that has gone mouldy: the spores may have travelled well into the loaf without you being able to see them, and some bread moulds – specifically black ones – are harmful.

Crackers and biscuits should be kept in airtight tins or plastic containers. If soft they can be revived for a final outing by baking briefly in the oven to crisp them up: 5 minutes at 180°C/ Fan 160°C/Gas 4 should do it.

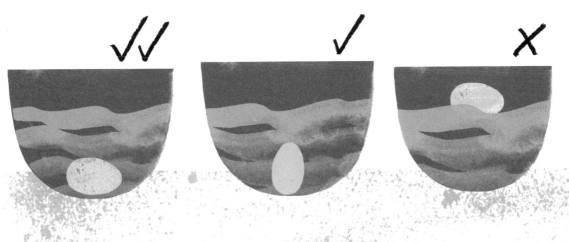

Storecupboard

Keeping a well-stocked larder will help you create the sort of flavourful and filling meals that are the joy of leftovers cooking. In a sense, the sealed, tinned, bagged, dried or preserved ingredients we fill our cupboards with are permanent leftovers – ready to be pressed into service alongside fresh bits and pieces. Most of these ingredients keep very well for over a year in a cool and dark place: try to locate your main food storage cupboard(s) away from the warmest, brightest part of the kitchen.

Chocolate that is coated with a white bloom is fine to use. The bloom develops when cocoa fats are exposed to air. You can still cook with the chocolate quite happily, and deliciously.

Chutneys and jams sealed in jars will keep for a year or so, but inspect the lids and the surface on opening for any taint or sign of mould. Once opened, store the jars in the fridge and use within a month or two. In the case of the usual bluey-green-whitish mould that often appears on jams (usually after opening and keeping in a warm kitchen), I am happy to scrape off the mould and keep using the jam.

Flour can deteriorate more quickly than other storecupboard items. All wheat flours contain some oil and so have the potential to turn rancid (particularly at warm temperatures), but the risk is much higher for wholemeal flours, which are richer in oil. Keep them cool and use within 3 months of buying. White wheat flours usually keep very well for several months. Some very sweet and/or oil-rich flours, such as chestnut flour, do better in the fridge.

Honey keeps almost indefinitely, although it may crystallise. This is nothing to worry about: just stand the jar in a bowl of hot water or remove the lid and warm the honey jar gently in the microwave to re-liquefy.

Mustard keeps very well unopened for several years. Once opened keep it in the fridge to preserve its flavour and colour.

Nuts and seeds will keep in sealed packets for up to a year, but once opened, they should be used up fairly quickly as they can go rancid. Never eat nuts that are mouldy – some nut moulds are dangerous.

Pasta in its dried form will keep, unopened, for a couple of years. Once opened and resealed (or transferred to a jar), it should be used within 3 months.

Pulses in their dried form keep for several years but they will become tougher and require more soaking and simmering to get them soft the older they are. To get the best out of them, try to buy them from somewhere with a brisk turnover and use them up at a steady rate. This shouldn't be difficult as they are one of the mainstays of leftover cooking.

Rice will keep for several years if it is white rice, but brown or wild rice spoils more quickly and should be used within 6–8 months.

Tinned goods can last for years as long as the tins aren't dented or damaged in any way.

Frequently occurring leftovers

As a nation, we follow distinct patterns when it comes to food waste, binning certain ingredients such as bread, potatoes, milk, fresh fruit and salad in enormous quantities. We could banish the huge bulk of that waste, partly by more savvy shopping and better portion control, but also by having some super-simple strategies for these FOLs (frequently occurring leftovers).

These common leftovers are all celebrated more fully, via many delicious recipes, in the chapters that follow – but this handy list is a first-stop, quick-fire guide to help you buck the chuck-it-out trend.

Marmalade pudding (page 178)

Bruschetta (page 301)

Croûtons (page 39)

Bread

Breadcrumbs (page 39)

Egg fried rice (page 196)

Bread and butter pudding (page 176)

Eggy bread (page 174)

Ricey pudding (page 210)

Ricey pancakes (page 198)

Cooked rice

Rice veggie burgers (page 208)

Risottover (page 204)

Bubble and squeak (page 50)

Gnocchi (page 134)

Stuffed vegetables (page 202)

Potatoes

Potato cakes (page 132)

Paneer (page 216)

Fishcakes (page 102)

Soups (pages 126–8)

Smoothies (page 252)

Cheese sauce (page 228)

Salads (page 37)

Milk

Drop scones (page 264)

Ricey pudding (page 210)

Clafoutis (page 262)

Cheese

Cheesy biscuits (page 49)

Rarebits (page 232)

Cheese straws (page 226)

Cheese sauce (page 228)

Potted cheese (page 230)

Cheesy egg custards (page 240)

Cucumbers

Chilled soup (page 156)

Sautéed cucumbers (page 158)

Smoothies (page 252)

Raita (page 88)

Cucumber-infused water (page 158)

Chicken

Soups (page 68)

Stew enchiladas (page 72)

Salads (pages 74–6)

Fricassée (page 70)

Turkish chicken (page 78)

Curry (page 284)

Bananas

Drop scones (page 264)

Smoothies (page 252)

Ice cream (page 254)

Trifle (page 59)

Teabread (page 266)

Bread and butter pudding (page 176)

Salad leaves

Soups (page 156)

Pasta (page 160)

Chilli beef noodles (page 94)

Toasties (page 42)

Frittata (page 44)

Vietnamese wilted greens (page 164)

Berries

Crumbles and fumbles (page 62)

Trifles and messes (pages 59–61)

Lollies (page 258)

Smoothies (page 252)

Granita (page 256)

Frozen yoghurt (page 254)

LAUNCHPADS FOR LEFTOVERS

Whether it's a simple snack or a full-on family dinner, most of us, most of the time, rely on a repertoire of trusted dishes. We might ransack cookbooks or magazines for new ideas at the weekend, or have a go at approximating something we've enjoyed in a restaurant, but most cooking is based around a core of reliable favourites that we know and love, and that have already achieved cross-party approval at the family dinner table.

There's nothing wrong with that. But if you can be a bit more flexible – loosen the culinary stays, as it were – you will be able to use those faithful recipes to accommodate almost anything that you have in the fridge or kitchen cupboards. A shepherd's pie (see page 90) for instance, can be a receptacle not just for your leftover leg of lamb, but also for veg that needs using up, such as courgettes, peppers, sweet potatoes and carrots. A good flapjack recipe (see page 308) will welcome oddments of dried fruit, seeds, nuts and nut butters, crushed biscuits or breakfast cereal, as well as spices, ripe bananas or citrus zest: a real cupboard clear-out transformed into a sustaining snack.

Some of my bases are even more elemental, and flexible. Things like good stocks, bread (fresh or slightly stale), eggs and salad leaves are blank canvases, crying out for the colour, not to mention the flavour and texture, of your finest leftovers. So this section contains my own cache of fail-safe 'leftover launchpads': formulations based on the most adaptable of primary ingredients and staples.

These are not recipes exactly but outlines, templates or blueprints that willingly receive all manner of leftovers with a good heart and a generous spirit. They are the ideas I come back to almost daily when I'm working out what I'd like to eat, the things that enable me to transform what might at first glance be an unpromising array of random ingredients into a deliciously satisfying meal.

So here you'll find guidelines for omelettes and frittatas that you might not call authentic but that I defy anyone to resist – basic, eggy mixes that will deliciously enfold and enhance leftover veg, trimmings of smoked fish, snippets of bacon or ham, and all kinds of cheese.

And I'm sharing some of my all-time favourite puddings, which happily take in all manner of leftovers. These are all based on a much-loved trinity formula of three simple components: something fruity, something creamy and something crisp or cakey.

Along with some classic ways to use up yesterday's dinner, such as curries, hashes, sandwiches and soups, you'll also find 'launchpads' you may not have thought of before – like wontons (try them filled with sausage and brown sauce – it's a revelation), my favourite noodle salads (flexible enough to take all manner of leftovers and flavourings) and Bloody Mary broth (great if hungover, equally good if not).

These are the sort of concepts that inspire me in those moments when I'm standing in front of the open fridge, with my tummy rumbling audibly and/or several other family members demanding dinner. I hope they will become the kind of go-to, dependably delicious starting points in your house that they are in mine.

Stocks

Stock. It's where it all starts really. If you make your own, there's hardly a better expression of your commitment to kitchen thrift, and judicious recycling of viable leftovers. And the rewards are great. A rich, flavoursome stock can turn the simplest of leftovers – some shredded chicken, a few greens, a handful of frozen peas – into supper in a matter of seconds. Any effort you put into saving some bones and simmering them up will be amply rewarded later, with an umami-rich broth, soup, curry or stew. Used like this – and I trot out a version almost every week – stocks are one of the finest and most versatile leftovers templates.

Save the bones from virtually everything you cook if you can: raw carcasses and bones from deboning before cooking, as well as those left over after roast dinners. Use them straight away or store them in plastic tubs or self-sealing bags in the freezer until you're ready to simmer up a batch. You will need a good-sized chicken carcass or around 700g meat bones to make 1–1.5 litres well-flavoured stock.

CHICKEN STOCK

This also works with game birds and other types of poultry. Break any bits of carcass into smallish bits. Add them to a large pan with the giblets if you have them, and any bits of skin and jellied juices left over from a roast. Add a couple of chopped carrots, a couple of celery stalks and an onion or some leek tops. Toss in a couple of bay leaves and a few peppercorns, then pour in enough water to cover everything. Cook at a bare simmer for at least 3 hours, skimming off any scum from time to time. Strain, cool and refrigerate or freeze.

If you're low on freezer space, after straining, you can simmer the stock to reduce the amount of liquid, until it's quite concentrated, before cooling and freezing. Remember to dilute it with boiling water before using.

Beef stock Ask your butcher for a marrowbone sawed into about five bits so they will fit in your stockpot, and a few more random beef bones. Keep the marrowbones raw. Roast the other bones, including any left from a roast (fore rib or sirloin, for example), in a hot oven until well browned, then proceed as for chicken stock. Simmer for longer if you like (up to 6 hours).

Venison stock You can use venison bones (or a combination of beef and venison) to make a particularly full-flavoured, lightly gamey stock. Proceed as for beef stock.

Lamb stock Use any leftover bones and gravy or juices and proceed as for chicken stock. Save and freeze the bones from a Sunday roast (leg or shoulder), even from chops, until you have enough. This strongly flavoured stock is best used in lamb dishes such as hot pot, moussaka or shepherd's pie. And of course it makes a classic Scotch broth (see page 31).

Pork stock Roast the bones until just browned before proceeding as for chicken stock. In fact, you can combine pork and chicken bones to make a tasty stock – ideal for oriental soups.

Ham stock The stock left over from boiling a ham is of course the beginnings of a great pea and ham soup, but it's also good in some vegetable soups as long as it's not too salty.

QUICK VEG STOCK

I make this a lot. It's easy and speedy and can happily be made with carrots, celery and onions not in the first snap of youth, if you peel or trim off any dark spots. You can also use peelings here, provided they are well scrubbed first.

Coarsely grate an onion, a carrot and a couple of celery stalks. Warm 1 tablespoon sunflower or rapeseed oil in a saucepan over a medium heat. Add the veg and a bay leaf, plus a peeled garlic clove, if you like. Cover and sweat for 5 minutes. Pour 1 litre boiling water from the kettle over the vegetables and simmer, uncovered, for 5 minutes. Strain and either use straight away or cool and refrigerate or freeze.

READY-MADE STOCK

All of us reach for a stock cube or a tub of bouillon powder from time to time and there's no shame in that. It can be a short cut to a great dinner. At home, I keep a stash of organic stock cubes (I use the yeast-free veg stock the most) for those days when I don't have time to make or defrost fresh stock, or for when I'm making strongly flavoured dishes such as curries where the delicacy of a carefully made stock isn't paramount. One word of caution about stock cubes or powders is that they can be salty, so taste the made stock before adding to a recipe and adjust the seasoning accordingly; you may not need to add extra salt at all. Of course, you can vary the strength of a stock by the amount of water you use, but a more flavoursome stock will be a saltier one too.

DO YOU ALWAYS NEED STOCK?

If you're working with full-flavoured ingredients in your soups and stews, you don't always need stock. Sometimes water will do just fine. If, for example, you are making a soup based on the slow sautéeing of a mirepoix of veg (diced onion, carrot and celery), thinning with water may be enough, especially if you are adding celeriac, turnip or swede and a bit of garlic and/or bacon or ham to your soup base.

   If you're going the no-stock route, here are a few things you can do to maximise flavour:

Use butter or rendered fat from chicken (see page 79), or beef or bacon, or a good rapeseed oil, rather than a flavourless vegetable oil to sauté the vegetables.

Add a pinch of salt when sautéeing the onions. It helps to draw out the liquid and speeds their cooking, as well as enhancing the flavour. Season well with freshly ground pepper, too.

Add a bay leaf and/or thyme sprigs when you're sautéeing the onions and any other veg. This gives a more rounded flavour than a bouquet garni added later with the liquid.

Be generous with herbs at the end of cooking. Freshly chopped herbs add vitality and flavour.

Soups

Some days, only soup will do. A steaming bowl of broth is just the thing for a solitary lunch at home or, with some bread and salad, for an easy-going family supper. When I'm in a hurry or feeling under the weather, it's often soup I crave. Just as well, then, that it's one of the most versatile, multi-faceted, and yet often straightforward dishes there is.

Some of my favourite soups – those I make time and again – are the serendipitous results of speedy rummaging about in the fridge or kitchen cupboards or, of course, the veg garden. They'll happily accommodate gluts of tomatoes, courgettes, lettuces and other veg plot excesses. And they seldom demand the most picture-perfect produce either.

Even if you only have time to make the simplest of soups, they are very amenable to being dolled up with finishes and garnishes in an almost infinite variety of combinations. Of course, most fantastic soups start with a great stock (see page 28).

BROTHS

As far as I'm concerned, a stock becomes a broth when it has the depth of flavour to stand up as a clear soup base – and once you have the intention to use it in this way.

Some of the finest concoctions are very simple and light combinations, involving just a few ingredients: a well-flavoured stock with a handful of vegetables and herbs thrown in. But the generally productive business of throwing good things into good broths can be taken to complex and substantial levels too.

Once you have a stock, whether lovingly simmered or made in haste from a cube, powder or paste, and you've decided that some lurking leftovers will turn it into supper, you have the option to tweak it into a broth in various directions. The idea is to add a bit of extra zing that will make the most of what you're about to fling into it.

Tweaking stocks into broths

There are so many ways to enhance a broth with things you've probably already got in your cupboards or fridge. Here are some ideas to get you started:

Hot and sour broth A dash of soy sauce, a squeeze of lemon or lime, a good pinch of dried chilli flakes and a few thin slices of fresh ginger, or a sprinkling of ground ginger. This works particularly well with chicken and pork stock.

Piquant Bloody Mary broth A spoonful of ketchup, a dash of Worcestershire sauce and a few drops of Tabasco. A great way to tweak a beef or game stock.

Herby broth A teaspoon of dried mixed herbs or herbes de Provence, or a small handful of fresh herbs, freshly chopped. Great for chicken, game or veg stock.

Mushroom broth A mere handful of dried mushrooms, added to piping hot stock and left for half an hour, will add great depth of flavour to almost any stock. Strain through a muslin-lined sieve before using, to remove any grit. You'll almost certainly want to add the soaked mushrooms back in to your finished dish – rinse well after straining out and sauté until tender before adding back in.

Seaweed broth Dried seaweed, in flakes or strips, is an exciting way to add texture and flavour to a stock. Especially good for chicken, fish or veg stock. There are more and more types available, including some excellent British ones, so stock up (ha!) and have a play.

BROTHS WITH BITS

Once you have your designated broth (whether tweaked or deemed delicious in its own right), you're just a handful of leftovers (and/or storecupboard stand-bys) away from a great, substantial soup. Here are some of my favourite improvisations:

Hot and sour noodle soup Hot and sour broth (see left) with shredded cooked chicken, or tofu, or strips of omelette, plus noodles or pasta and shredded greens (fresh or leftover) or seaweed.

Herby summer broth Herby broth (see left) with a handful of peas, a little gem lettuce or two (quartered lengthways) and some freshly chopped herbs (chervil, tarragon and/or parsley), plus a dollop of crème fraîche or trickle of extra virgin oil if you like.

Scotch broth Lamb stock (see page 28), plus a handful of pearl barley or spelt, shreds of leftover lamb, diced carrots, parsnips or turnips, a handful of peas and/or shredded or leftover greens, flavoured with plenty of black pepper and chopped parsley.

Bloody beetroot 'borscht' Piquant Bloody Mary broth (see left) with some diced cooked beetroot, shredded spring onions, any leftover meat and some cooked pasta, pearl barley or spelt.

Thai mushroom broth Mushroom broth (see left) flavoured with 1 tablespoon Thai curry paste, plus thinly sliced mushrooms, shredded cooked chicken if you have some, roughly chopped coriander and a squeeze of lime.

Spanish broth Beef, chicken or pork stock (see page 28), or mushroom broth (see left) enriched with quickly sautéed chunks of chorizo and a handful of cooked Puy lentils or chickpeas. Finish with chopped parsley.

THICKENING A SOUP

If you want a heartier, homier feel to your soup, you might want to thicken it up a bit. The best way to do this will depend partly on what's in it. In order of simplicity, here are the best options:

Bash it a bit Assuming the soup contains at least some starchy ingredients (roots, potato, pulses, for example), whisking or mashing it a bit with a potato masher will often break these up enough to turn a 'clear broth with bits in' into a rougher, cloudier, more peasant-y concoction. A soup that contains lots of vegetables and pulses will usually thicken all on its own if left for a few hours or overnight, then reheated.

Whiz it a bit A more sure-fire technique for thickening a veg soup, without blending it until completely smooth, is to remove a couple of ladlefuls and whiz them in a blender, then return the purée to the soup, stirring it in well. Alternatively, just use a stick blender to partially blend the soup in the saucepan. If your soup is lacking in naturally starchy elements, a clever trick is to add a rice cake or two to the portion you are blending.

Make a beurre manié This old-school method of thickening a stock can also be used to thicken up a soup. Work some flour and butter together to a paste with your fingertips – about one-third flour to two-thirds butter. Add the beurre manié to the soup a little at a time, in bits about the size of a hazelnut, towards the end of the cooking time, whisking in each addition until fully absorbed before adding more.

Add breadcrumbs A handful of breadcrumbs sprinkled into the soup towards the end of simmering will help thicken it.

Add egg yolk Allow 1 egg yolk to about every 500ml soup. Remove the pot from the hob and let the soup cool slightly. Whisk the egg yolk in a small bowl with 60ml of the broth and return it slowly to the soup, stirring as you go and making sure you don't let it boil again.

Note If you're adding meaty leftovers to your hearty soup, do so after you've thickened the basic broth.

CREAMY SMOOTH SOUPS

Sometimes the best thing you can do with an improvised vegetable soup is to whiz it up into creamy, velvety loveliness. This is particularly the case for soups where one particular veg, or family of veg, is dominant – for example a soup that's mainly peas, or mainly cauliflower, or mainly roasted roots. Add everything to your blender (or use a stick blender in the pan) and whiz until smooth. Check the seasoning and texture, and add more of what you need – including stock or water if it's too thick – then whiz again. You can make it even creamier by adding, naturally enough, cream, crème fraîche or a knob of butter. And if your veg are mostly leafy, not starchy, adding a rice cake or a little leftover cooked rice to the blender is a good trick for getting it creamy and smooth.

ROOTY TOMATO SOUP BASE

This is a handy base for many a hearty soup. Take any leftover roasted roots, such as carrots, parsnips and celeriac, and whiz in a food processor with some tinned tomatoes or passata. Thin to the consistency you like with water or stock and use this as a base for thick wintry soups, adding in more leftover veg or meat, tinned pulses, cooked pasta or rice, etc.

DUMPLINGS

Dumplings transform the most straightforward of soups into a comforting, hearty meal. For 12–16 dumplings, allow 100g self-raising flour to 50g suet. Add any flavouring ingredients (see below), season with salt and pepper and mix in enough cold water to make a fairly stiff dough. With floured hands, roll into balls about the size of walnuts. Drop into the simmering soup, cover and cook for about 15 minutes.

Try flavouring your dumpling mixture with any of the following:

A handful of finely grated cheese.

A little English mustard powder.

Chopped herbs: parsley, chives, thyme, sage, rosemary and/or dill depending on the soup.

A little horseradish, especially if the soup includes beef, tomato or beetroot.

Some finely chopped spring onion.

FINISHING TOUCHES

All it may take to transform a fairly simple soup into a special event – or a stand-alone supper at least – is a sprinkling or trickle of something added at the last minute.

Croûtons Made with good leftover bread (see page 39).

Toasted nuts and seeds Flaked almonds, pine nuts, pumpkin seeds or whatever you have.

Herbs A generous sprinkling of fresh herbs.

Pesto A dollop added to each portion.

Spice A sprinkling of smoked paprika or other earthy spices, such as cumin.

Leftover fish Flakes of smoked fish, especially, or even mussels are good in creamy, leeky or rooty soups.

Leftover meat Scraps of ham, or shards of pork, beef or chicken fried until crispy.

Dairy A few dollops of yoghurt, crème fraîche or cream – this can be quite mature.

Poached egg Allow one per portion. Poach in water first, then gently lower into the bowl of soup.

Extra virgin oil A trickle of rapeseed or olive, or a nut oil such as hazelnut or walnut.

Spiced butter Melt some butter with some dried chilli flakes or chilli powder and trickle it over the soup.

And of course you can make a soup super-special by adding two or more of the above. Did I just spot you finishing a smooth, creamy soup (made from leftover roasted carrots and parsnips, blended with a good veg stock and a knob of butter) with a swirl of natural yoghurt, a trickle of spicy oil, *and* a sprinkling of toasted pumpkin seeds? *Nice one!* You are well on your way to earning your soup stripes...

Salads

There's seldom a day in my life when I don't eat something that can loosely be described as a 'salad'. It could be as simple as a few leaves glistening in a sharp vinaigrette, or a pile of lovingly prepared veg, raw or cooked or both, garnished and sprinkled and seasoned into a state of high beauty. Long gone are the days when a salad meant dreary wedges of tomato and cucumber nestled on the limpest and most naked leaf of lettuce, a tut on a plate. These days, salads are stars. They're colourful, clever and above all, enticing, exciting combinations of texture and flavour that tempt the eye and the palate.

I like to think of the new non-conformist salads as 'playful', as they frolic with the full spectrum of tastes and textures:

Bitter

Bland

Caramelised

Charred

Cool

Creamy

Crisp

Crunchy

Earthy

Fresh

Granular

Hot

Juicy

Meaty

Mild

Nutty

Piquant

Salty

Sharp

Silky

Slippery

Smoky

Spicy

Sweet

Tangy

Tart

Waxy

STRUCTURE YOUR SALADS

For a great salad, you probably need at least three of these taste/texture elements to be present. It is entirely possible to create a world-beating salad with the humblest of ingredients and many of my favourites begin with FOLs (Frequently Occurring Leftovers). To enhance an ingredient's core flavour, often all it needs is a clever, contrasting ingredient. You have stale bread for **crunchy** croûtons? Combine them with **crisp** leaves and **creamy** hard-boiled egg... You get the idea. And just in case you don't, here are some more winning salads, based on three or four elements (to which you could easily add and swap):

Smoky trout, **hot** rocket and **sweet** roasted beetroot.

Cool, **crunchy** cucumbers, **hot, sweet** chilli dressing and **crunchy** toasted seeds or nuts.

Silky, creamy avocado, **crisp** lettuce, **bitter, sharp, charred** lemons and **smoky** tahini dressing.

Sweet, crisp grated carrot, **creamy** chickpeas, beans or other pulses and **creamy, nutty** lentils.

Crisp kohlrabi, **hot** mustardy dressing, **meaty** rare roast beef and **tart** lemony vinaigrette.

Hot, **crunchy** radishes, **cool** parsley, **creamy** hard-boiled egg and **salty** olives.

Caramelised roots, **tart, sweet, juicy** blood oranges or grapefruit and **smoky** fish.

Creamy pulses, **sharp** vinaigrette, **crisp** leaves and **salty** anchovies or bacon.

Crunchy croûtons, **creamy** hard-boiled egg, **crisp** lettuce and **creamy, nutty** lentils or beans.

Sweet butternut squash, **tangy** goat's or blue cheese and **creamy, nutty** lentils or beans.

BUILD ON CORE INGREDIENTS

The business of building a salad begins with all kinds of ingredients, but there are a few dependable bases on which you can build. Here I'm outlining some of my favourite everyday inspirations – and passing on some of the FOLs I love to fling on them.

Leaves

Often I start with leaves. If you have any in the fridge, the time to use them is now. If you have any in the garden, you'll want to use them as often as possible. Try these leafy favourites:

Robust winter salad Toss sharp winter leaves (chicory, mizuna, watercress) and caramelised roasted roots (beetroot, carrot, Jerusalem artichokes, parsnip), with creamy blue cheese and crunchy toasted walnuts.

Caesar plus Combine crisp leaves, such as romaine, with meaty chicken, pork, beef or even fish and a creamy lemony mustardy vinaigrette. Finish with shavings of salty Parmesan and crunchy croûtons.

Waldorf take Combine crisp apple and celery, crunchy walnuts, sweet raisins or grapes and salty cubes of Cheddar, crumbled Stilton or goat's cheese with a creamy dressing of mayonnaise mixed with yoghurt.

Revved-up niçoise Combine robust fish (especially mackerel, but also bass, bream and mullet), creamy boiled egg, waxy potatoes, crisp lettuce, crunchy green beans, salty black olives and sharp vinaigrette.

Partial niçoise Combine any three or four of the above revved-up niçoise ingredients, including the dressing.

Roots and bulbs

Crunchy grated, julienned or mandolined roots and bulbs add freshness to scraps of leftover meats. A little goes a long way – toss them all together or if you have only a few meaty or fishy scraps, sprinkle them over the top for optimum impact. Play around with the following ideas:

Carrot and chickpea Toss sweet grated carrots with spicy chickpeas and dress with a sharp lemony vinaigrette.

Rémoulade take Toss julienned or grated celeriac in a sharp mustardy vinaigrette with crisp shards of roast pork.

Fennel and citrus Finely slice sweet aniseedy fennel and combine with tart, sweet, juicy orange or grapefruit segments and flakes of charred barbecued fish or shredded meaty pork, duck or goose.

Spuds

Cold new potatoes make one of the finest leftover salads of all, with nothing but good mayonnaise and a snip of chives. But they are also ripe for absorbing the flavours of other salady things. These are some of my favourite combinations:

Piquant potato Waxy potatoes with sharp cornichons, crisp red onion and capers, plus mild mustardy vinaigrette and earthy, sweet dill.

Minted potato Waxy potatoes tossed in tangy crème fraîche with chopped fresh mint, tart lemon juice and black pepper.

Potato, celery and bacon Waxy potatoes, crumbled, salty cooked bacon and crunchy diced celery dressed with an earthy, sharp wholegrain mustard vinaigrette.

Pulses

Pulses are an excellent way to add instant, inexpensive substance to simple salads and they carry the flavour of dressings, herbs and spices brilliantly. Tins of chickpeas and lentils are great standbys but I also create deliberate leftovers of Puy lentils – they are so useful to have hanging around in the fridge. I'll either cook more than I need for a recipe, or simmer half a pack on a whim, knowing they will be deployed in salads – or soups, or stews – in the coming days. They also freeze really well. Combined with other leftovers and store-cupboard staples they offer endless salad possibilities. Try these for starters:

Lentil, onion and rare beef Earthy Puy lentils, crisp spring onions and strips of meaty rare roast beef, plus sharp mustardy vinaigrette.

Pulses with meaty leftovers Earthy chickpeas or Puy lentils, meaty leftover sausages, ham, chorizo or tongue and cool chopped parsley, tossed in earthy, sharp mustardy vinaigrette.

Bean and artichoke Creamy cannellini beans, crisp green beans, silky artichoke hearts, creamy boiled egg and sharp shallot, tossed in sharp red wine vinaigrette.

FIVE JAM JAR DRESSINGS

Sometimes it's all in the dressing. A really good dressing can elevate the humblest of ingredients or the simplest of fridge-foraged combinations into a really special salad. For each of the following, simply tip the ingredients into a jam jar, seal and shake, shake, shake! until deliciously emulsified:

Vinaigrette

Combine 6 tablespoons oil (rapeseed, olive, or a combination), 2 tablespoons vinegar (red wine, white wine or cider) or lemon juice with ½–1 tablespoon Dijon or wholegrain mustard and a pinch each of sugar, salt and pepper.
Add fresh herbs at the end, an egg yolk for creaminess and/or grated cheese such as Parmesan for a Caesar-salad-style dressing. Up the lemon juice, add grated lemon zest, or use more mustard, for a sharper, more punchy dressing.
Try with any green salad, warm new potatoes or roasted vegetables.

Pomegranate dressing

Combine 6 tablespoons rapeseed or olive oil, 2 tablespoons pomegranate molasses, 1 finely grated garlic clove and a squeeze of lemon juice.
Add crumbled feta or other salty cheese and/ or a sprinkling of sumac if you have it.
Try with leftover roast aubergines or thick slices of almost-too-ripe tomatoes.

Tahini dressing

Combine 3 tablespoons tahini, 2 tablespoons lemon juice, 2 tablespoons rapeseed or olive oil and a pinch of salt with a little hot water to thin to the consistency of double cream.
Add any combination of garlic, dried chilli flakes, ground coriander, cumin, cayenne and/ or turmeric. Add lemon zest as well as juice, or orange juice as well as lemon, or chopped preserved lemons.
Substitute the tahini for peanut butter or any other nut butter – a good way to use up the final bits clinging to the jar.
Try with roasted squash or carrots, or salads which contain pulses or grains. Finish with a sprinkling of toasted sesame seeds if you like.

Thai-style sweet sour dressing

Combine 2 tablespoons groundnut or sesame oil, the juice of 1 lime (about 1 tablespoon), 1 teaspoon finely grated ginger, 1 finely grated garlic clove, ½–1 very finely diced red or green chilli and a pinch of sugar.
Add toasted, chopped peanuts.
Try with leftover chicken or pork salad, crunchy cucumbers or noodles tossed with leftover veg.

Yoghurt dressing

Combine 4 tablespoons wholemilk yoghurt, 1–2 tablespoons rapeseed or olive oil, 1 finely grated small garlic clove, a good pinch of flaky sea salt and a few twists of black pepper.
Add chopped herbs to suit. Mint is an obvious one, but chervil and parsley are also very good. If you have a bit of soft goat's cheese or creamy blue cheese hanging around, whisk a spoonful or two into the dressing for a tangy dip.
Try with crudités, pittas or flatbreads, roasted courgettes or charred lamb chops.

ENHANCING SALADS

The idea here is to boost your confidence and broaden your concept of an improvised salad put together with what's to hand. Many of the finest family meals are presented under the blissfully broad banner of 'salad'. Here are a few final tips and pointers to hone your leftover-enhanced assemblies:

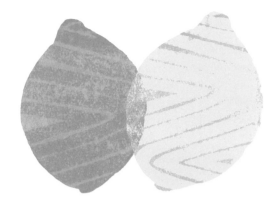

Be generous with herbs Think of them as an ingredient, not a garnish. Be generous, thread their flavour throughout the dish; don't just sprinkle them on top. Use especially: whole flat-leaf parsley and coriander leaves, sprigs of chervil and dill.

Freshen with citrus If your salad tastes a bit 'muddy' and indistinct, try adding a fine grating of citrus zest or a squeeze of juice, right at the end, to lift it. Lemon is the obvious choice, but orange, clementine, satsuma, lime, even grapefruit can all bring welcome zest and unexpected new flavours to your salads.

Add a little cheese To pep up the flavour of a salad, pare hard cheese with a vegetable peeler into the thinnest of strips or crumble soft cheese into rough little chunks and scatter over your salad. Those nuggets of cheese that have been lurking too long in the fridge are perfect for this.

Scatter on toasted seeds or nuts This will lend extra flavour and texture, and boost the nutritional value of a salad. Of course, you can use any combination of nuts and seeds you like, including pumpkin, sunflower and sesame seeds, pine nuts, pistachios and cashews. To toast seeds, dry-fry them in a pan until fragrant and tip them onto a plate to cool. To toast nuts, roast them on a baking sheet in a preheated oven at 180°C/Fan 160°C/Gas 4

for 6–10 minutes until they are fragrant and just take on some colour. Set a timer... you'll forget they're in there.

Throw on croûtons A great way to use leftover bread. Cut into cubes, then toss in rapeseed or olive oil, season with salt and pepper and bake in a preheated oven at 180°C/Fan 160°C/Gas 4 for about 10 minutes until golden. Let cool completely, then seal in an airtight container where they will keep quite happily for a couple of weeks.

Sprinkle on seasoned breadcrumbs Crumbed leftover bread adds a great crunch to salads. Whiz stale bread in a food processor to fine crumbs, spread on a baking tray and bake in a preheated oven at 180°C/Fan 160°C/Gas 4 for 8–10 minutes, stirring halfway through. Cool and then add whatever dried seasonings you like: chilli powder, garlic powder, ground cumin or coriander, dried herbs or lemon zest all work well. The breadcrumbs keep well in a jar for around a month, or sealed in a bag in the freezer for 3 months. To use, fry in a little butter or oil until crisp and golden, then sprinkle over your salads at the last minute. (Or use as they are to coat fishcakes etc., before frying.)

Sandwiches

Sometimes I think we can all measure our lives in sandwiches. There is a carb-and-filling combo for every age and occasion: the energy-boosting school lunchbox, hangover-banishing bacon sarnie, lunch-at-your desk time-saver, summer picnic stalwart and that late-night indulgence hastily scrambled together from the remains of dinner. And one of the best things about having a rich array of leftovers at your disposal is the opportunity it gives for the construction of top-drawer sandwiches.

SIMPLE CLASSICS

It's worth emphasising that a good sandwich doesn't have to try too hard. The French station café stalwart – 25cm of meagrely buttered baguette containing nothing more than a not-too-generous slice of Emmenthal cheese – is the salutary lesson here in perfection-by-restraint. Sometimes, bread, butter, a fine filling from the pantheon of great leftovers and perhaps a dash of the right condiment are all that's needed.

By all means create all manner of piled-high, multiple-filling, experimental Scooby snacks on your own time. Here I'd like to share with you my pared-back, leftover favourites which, done right, will never lose their charm.

Start with good bread and a slick of butter and keep the filling simple:

Ham A single, fat slice of great ham and a whisper of mustard.

Cheese A perfectly ripe slice of Cheddar and a dollop of chutney.

Tomato Thick slices of ripe tomato plus salt and pepper.

Cucumber Thin slices (from the knobbly end), peeled and overlapping, plus salt and pepper.

Chicken Torn up leftover chicken from the Sunday roast, good mayonnaise and a twist of black pepper.

Rare beef Sliced or shredded rare roast beef with a good smear of mustard or horseradish.

Salami When there isn't enough left to slice and hand around, but just enough to go in your sandwich. Just bread, butter and thin slices of salami.

Fish Flaked leftover fish, especially mackerel, with mayonnaise and capers.

Since that last example has unwittingly strayed into double condiments territory I will show restraint and stop there.

THE OPEN TOP SANDWICH

Odd as it may sound, I would argue that you don't even need good fresh bread to make a great sandwich. For example, if you have slightly stale bread hanging about, toasting it gives it another opportunity to become a respectable sandwich. Often, a nice thick slice of toast, buttered or oiled, works better cold as the base for a classic open sandwich, or hot as a base for all kinds of things you might scatter over it. We're in the realms of bruschetta and even pizzas here.

And we can push deeper into this territory beyond the limits of bread, if we consider what else might do the job equally well. Essentially, the bread is a texture, the gentle background to showcase entertaining fillings and toppings. You can recreate this with other soothing carbs you might have hanging about the place, or can put together easily, from oatcakes to pancakes (see page 166), potato cakes (see page 132) to my omelettey ricey pancakes (see page 198). Okay, it's a stretch to call such a gregariously garnished base an actual sandwich, but these are definitely good launching pads for a similar kind of business, and that's the business of topping and filling.

What's on first

Once you have chosen your base, there are various ways you can customise it. Start with:

A trickle of good oil or smear of butter (one or other is probably a given).

A slick of tomato sauce or purée, pizza style.

A smear of pesto.

A spoonful of nut butter.

A dollop of hummus.

To top it

Scatter on top the best pre-loved morsels your fridge and larder have to offer. The temptation may be to load it up with all your favourite things, but it's often best to stick to a few well-chosen compatible ingredients to enjoy their distinct flavours and textures at their best.

Here's some open-top inspiration for you:

Thinly sliced vegetables Mushrooms, peppers, fennel, red or yellow onion, shallots, spring onions and courgettes can be deployed raw or cooked. If they are a bit tired, a quick shake in a hot pan with a dash of oil, some salt and pepper, and maybe a pinch of curry powder, will re-motivate them most effectively.

Shredded meat Small bits of shredded meat leftover from the Sunday roast, or crumbled cooked sausages or bacon, scraps of ham, salami or other charcuterie.

Flaked fish Use leftovers from cooked fresh fish or hot or cold smoked fish, or crumbled tinned fish such as sardines and anchovies.

Condiments Raid your cupboard and add whatever appeals. Could be some capers, sun-dried tomatoes, flame-grilled peppers, olives, preserved artichoke hearts and/or pine nuts.

Cheese Top with grated hard cheese, or crumbled blue cheese or feta. Or introduce other dairy, such as a few dollops of crème fraîche or thick cream (this can be quite ripe, almost to the point of cheese itself).

To bake or not to bake

I'm not saying your lovingly adorned base won't be delicious cold – especially if you are working in the realms of Italian bruschetta or the Danish open sandwich. But you will probably know by now if it's shaping up to be the kind of thing that might be improved by flashing in a fierce oven or under a hot grill. Do you want those crumbled cheesy ends to go all melty? As pizzas and toasties tell us, molten cheese is one of the best unifying elements for other ingredients. Do you want the meaty or veggie bits to get caramelised and crusty-topped? Or are there too many fresh, crunchy, salad-y elements going on that would wilt and wither under the heat? With that in mind, you can always add some fresh chopped or torn herbs, a scattering of rocket, watercress or other greens after removing from the oven.

TOASTED GLORIES

I want to run with the irresistible subject of molten cheese for a moment – into rarebit and toastie territory. For the classic, sauce-based Welsh rarebit, and some leftover enhanced variations, see page 232.

For simple, fridge-rummaged variations on the theme, I work on the principle of some cooked veg and/or leftover cooked meat plus a handful of grated or crumbled cheese with a little cream or crème fraîche to lighten, and some seasoning. Piled onto a thick slice of toast and flashed under a hot grill, that equals a pretty delicious and almost instant lunch, snack or supper.

You'll find the cream or crème fraîche a particularly useful binder and mollifier of such concoctions, but if it isn't to hand, then a dash of milk, olive oil, mayonnaise or even beer can provide just enough lubrication to bring the rest together, and help your chosen filling sit up on its toastie base.

Here are some trusty toastie combinations to get you started:

Leek and ham Sautéed leeks or onions and some snippets of cooked ham, plus a little cream or crème fraîche and grated Cheddar, or crumbled Wensleydale.

Cheesy potato and greens Leftover cooked potatoes, crème fraîche and a handful of greens such as leftover spinach, watercress or rocket, plus some creamy cheese such as soft goat's cheese, Stinking Bishop, Camembert or brie.

Spinach and pine nut Cooked spinach tossed with crème fraîche, pine nuts and raisins, if you like, plus grated hard goat's cheese, Parmesan or Cheddar.

Mushroom or squash Either grilled or fried mushrooms or cubes of roasted squash (or indeed both), plus some chopped spring onions and crumbled blue cheese.

Roasted veg Any combination of roasted (or fried) peppers, courgettes and/or aubergines plus chopped olives and capers, topped with slices of good melting cheese such as Taleggio, Reblochon, Camembert or Stinking Bishop.

Omelettes & Frittatas

Eggs are one of the finest fast foods around. Enormously versatile and terrific carriers of flavour, they are supreme vehicles for giving last night's dinner a second great outing. And the movable eggy feasts that can repackage leftovers most brilliantly are those continental favourites that we've come to know and love: the omelette, the frittata and the tortilla. I'd put in a shout for the 'crustless tart' (see page 45) too. These eggy launchpads are endlessly customisable, so play around with the fillings, making the most of your leftovers.

FILLED OMELETTE

Lightly whisk together 3–4 large eggs and season with salt and pepper. Melt a generous knob of butter in a 23–25cm frying pan until foaming, then tip some of the butter into the eggs (this spreads the lovely, buttery flavour throughout the omelette and also helps to stop it sticking). Whisk the eggs again and pour into the pan. Allow to set for 20–30 seconds, then use a spatula to pull the set outer edges into the middle, swirling the pan to let the runny egg mixture flow onto the surface of the pan. When the omelette is almost set (you still want it to be a bit runny on top at this point), sprinkle over your chosen filling ingredient(s), alone or in any combination (see below). Cook for a minute just to heat through, then fold your omelette and tip onto a warm plate. SERVES 2

Note Allowing the butter to brown to a nutty richness before adding it to the eggs gives a richer flavour. This is particularly good if the butter is slightly past its cow-fresh best.

Filling options

The potential for deploying leftovers here is pretty much unlimited. Here are a few simple suggestions for you to expand on:

Cheese Almost much any kind, alone or in combination, can be grated or crumbled onto an omelette. It's a great way of using up the tiniest scraps, the thinnest and driest ends of the wedge.

Potato Chopped-up leftover roast or sautéed potatoes, tossed with a good sprinkling of chopped parsley and/or snipped chives if you have some to hand.

Ham or bacon Any shards of chopped ham or crumbled cooked bacon.

Chicken Morsels of roast chicken add pleasing texture, especially if crisply fried.

Roasted roots or squash Chopped leftover roasted roots or squash.

Peas or beans A handful of lightly blanched fresh peas and/or broad beans.

Uses for leftover omelette

A plain omelette can be an ingredient, as well as a dish in itself. Whether you've made more than you need, or just have some eggs that need using up, there are several things you can do with it:

Egg fried rice Before the omelette has fully set, toss it with just-cooked or leftover cooked rice. (See also page 196.)

Enriched broth Cut the omelette into strips and drop into a broth, to add texture, flavour and substance.

Wrap Roll a thin omelette around a filling (of leftovers, perhaps). Or spread with some pesto and roll up.

Omelette 'sandwich' Sandwich a hefty slab of omelette (warm or cold) between slices of buttered bread, with or without cheese, or ham, and, in all cases, smeared with ketchup or brown sauce.

FRITTATA

Lightly beat 8–10 eggs in a bowl and season well with salt and pepper. Heat 1–2 tablespoons rapeseed or sunflower oil (or a mix of oil and butter), in a 25–30cm non-stick ovenproof frying pan over a medium-high heat. Stir your chosen additions (except cheese) into the eggs and tip the egg mixture into the pan. Cook gently, letting the eggs set slowly from the base up. After about 5 minutes, give the pan a little shake – the bottom half should be set. Sprinkle over any cheese (crumbled if soft, grated if hard). Put the pan into a preheated oven at 180°C/Fan 160°C/Gas 4 for 7–10 minutes until just set. Alternatively, you can place it under a medium-hot grill for about 5 minutes. Allow to cool slightly or completely before slicing and serving. SERVES 4–6

Frittata additions

All manner of leftovers can be added to a frittata to enhance the flavour and add substance:

Potato Always a great addition to a frittata. You can use chopped chunks of leftover boiled or roast spuds, or even leftover chips from the chip shop.

Onions These are best sliced and sweated until tender and golden before adding to the eggs. Or use fresh, raw chopped spring onions or chives.

Greens Pretty much any green veg – either leftover or blanched to order – can be tossed in. Wilted leafy greens, such as kale, cabbage, chard or spinach, work particularly well; also blanched asparagus and purple sprouting broccoli spears.

Lettuce, rocket and other salad leaves These make surprisingly good 'wilted greens'. If your leftover leaves have been dressed, shake off any extra dressing and coarsely shred before adding to the beaten eggs.

Bacon and ham Leftover scraps or cubes of cooked ham, snippets of bacon, diced pancetta or even the diced tail end of a salami or chorizo all work.

Smoked fish Scraps of smoked fish are great in a frittata. Use trimmings of smoked salmon or trout, smoked mackerel or kippers, or any leftover smoked white fish such as haddock or pollack.

Cheese Use leftover Cheddar, Gruyère, blue cheese or goat's cheese and coarsely grate, cube or crumble, as appropriate. Little blobs of cream cheese, soft cheeses or crème fraîche are great too.

Favourite frittata combinations

Frittatas are endlessly adaptable and happily accommodate seasonal leftovers. Try these delicious combinations:

Summer garden frittata Add sautéed sliced courgettes, a handful of lightly blanched peas, broad beans and/or roughly chopped blanched runner or French beans to the eggs, along with a smaller handful of pitted and chopped green or black olives and a generous scattering of chopped herbs – chervil, tarragon, parsley and/or soft-leaved lemon thyme are all good. Top the frittata with 120–200g crumbled soft or grated hard goat's cheese.

Autumn garden frittata Add chunks of roasted squash, carrot, parsnip, fennel or leek (or any combination) to the eggs with a little dried or chopped fresh oregano and some dried chilli flakes, if you like a bit of heat. Scatter cubes of feta or Cheddar or crumbled goat's cheese on top of the frittata.

Spinach and mushroom frittata Add sliced, sautéed mushrooms, some cooked spinach (squeezed dry) and a few gratings of nutmeg to the eggs. Top the frittata with some crumbled blue cheese, or Cheddar or goat's cheese if you're not a blue cheese fan.

'Quiche Lorraine' frittata Add a dash of cream, crème fraîche or milk to the eggs along with sautéed bacon or chopped ham trimmings, sweated diced onion and a handful of grated Cheddar or some Parmesan. Add a grating or two of nutmeg or a dash of English or French mustard too, if you like.

TORTILLA

This delicious Spanish cousin to the frittata can essentially be made in the same way, with the same fillings, but at the end, instead of placing it in the oven or under the grill, you invert it into another pan – or onto a plate then back, upside down, into the same pan – and return it to the heat to continue cooking.

CRUSTLESS TART

Generously butter a 25cm flan tin (not a loose-bottomed one!) or ceramic quiche dish. Follow the instructions for making a frittata, adding a good splash of milk and/or a dash of cream or crème fraîche to the egg mixture to lighten it – milk or cream that's just on the turn is fine. Add all of your chosen extras to the eggy mix, including any cheese. Pour the mixture into your prepared dish and bake in a preheated oven at 180°C/Fan 160°C/Gas 4 for 25–30 minutes or until just set.

You can also make one-portion crustless tartlets in individual flan tins or dishes. Just reduce the cooking time accordingly, to about 15–20 minutes.

Egg tips and tricks

Don't crack eggs straight into the mixture or pan. Break each into a small bowl first, so you know it's fresh. See also page 21 for the 'floating egg test'.

———

If you have a tub of double cream or crème fraîche that's a bit past its best to use in its raw state, whisk a dollop of it into the egg mixture to add richness and greater depth of flavour before you start cooking.

———

The classic fresh fines herbes mix – parsley, chives, tarragon and chervil – is delicious in omelettes, frittatas, tarts, and egg dishes of all kinds. Use any of these herbs – alone or in combination.

———

Eggs love chilli. A dash or two of Tabasco or other chilli sauce, or a sprinkling of dried chilli flakes, or a very finely diced fresh red or green chilli will lift a simple omelette, frittata or tortilla even if you have no other ingredients to hand.

Pies & Tarts

If there was ever any doubt about the widespread appeal of pie, we only have to look around when we travel abroad. In every country, in every culture, the simplest of ingredients wrapped up in dough are elevated to the sublime. We may differ in many ways and dispute many things, but we agree on this: fold a few good things in a pastry overcoat and the result is a thing of joy. Whether it's a pasty or a pithivier, a wonton or a samosa, a borek or a wellington, a tart or a slice, or indeed an unambiguous good old English, pastry top-and-bottom pie, memories are made of this – or, at the very least, lunch is.

EASY LEFTOVER PIE

When you have a substantial amount of meaty or even veggie leftovers and some pastry on standby in the freezer, a pie is a genuinely quick option as well as a very appealing one. Sometimes all it takes to produce a pie is to tip last night's stew into a pie dish, roll over the pastry and bake until golden. Of course you can line your pie dish with pastry in addition to topping it – then you get the gooey bottom as well as the crispy top; you'll just need to double up the pastry.

Shortcrust pastry

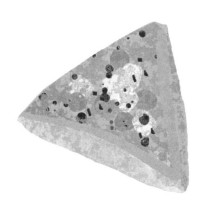

In a large bowl or food processor, mix together 250g plain flour and a pinch of salt.

Add 125g chilled butter, cut into cubes, and rub in (or blitz in the processor, being careful not to overwork) until it resembles coarse breadcrumbs. Work in 1 egg yolk mixed with 2 tablespoons cold milk or iced water to bind the pastry, adding a little extra liquid (up to another tablespoon) if needed.

Turn out onto a lightly floured surface, knead very gently to bring the dough together, wrap in cling film and rest in the fridge for about 30 minutes before rolling out.

Savoury fillings

The possibilities are endless here, but these leftover assemblies work really well:

Chicken pie Reprise the chicken fricassée on page 70, adding mushrooms or leeks sweated to order, and/or any leftover veg.

Beef or lamb pie Combine chopped leftover roast beef or lamb with sautéed or roast onions and garlic, a strong, reduced stock or gravy and a dash of red wine. For a medium pie, you would need 200–400g meat. Add any leftover roast roots, including potatoes, plus a good splash of Worcestershire or horseradish sauce and chopped herbs such as parsley, dill or thyme, if handy.

Veg pie Combine a mix of leftover roast veg with enough cheese sauce (see page 228 – use the smaller amount of cheese) to coat them generously, and add plenty of chopped herbs, such as parsley or chervil.

Curried vegetable and egg pie Sauté a chopped onion with 1 tablespoon curry paste, then mix with a 400g tin chopped tomatoes and leftover roast veg, bulked out with a 400g tin of chickpeas or beans if needed, and a few peeled hard-boiled eggs.

To make your pie

Spoon the filling into a pie dish (a pie funnel or an upturned egg cup in the middle of the dish will help stop the pastry becoming soggy). Brush the rim of the dish with water. Roll out your pastry (home-made shortcrust or bought puff) to make a lid to cover the pie generously. Lay the pastry over the top of the pie dish and press the edges onto the rim. Trim off the excess pastry and brush the top with beaten egg or milk. Bake in a preheated oven at 190°C/ Fan 170°C/Gas 5 for about 30–40 minutes until the filling is bubbling and the top golden.

Pastry tips and tricks

If you're making your own shortcrust pastry you can customise it with odds and ends such as roughly grated cheese, or a sprinkling of spice such as ground cumin, or chopped herbs (thyme, chives, parsley, even sage). If you're freezing it, make sure you label it with its custom ingredient before freezing... in case chive and apple pie doesn't appeal.

FREE-FORM TART

This works well for drier, less saucy fillings that will benefit from browning and blistering and bubbling in a hot oven; not surprisingly, cheese is often involved.

Just roll out some home-made shortcrust or ready-made puff pastry into a circle, place on a parchment-lined baking sheet, spread the filling over the circle, leaving a clear margin, and then roll/fold the marginal edges of the pastry back over the edges of the filling to help retain it – kind of like a raised crust pizza.

Brush the pastry edges with beaten egg or milk. Bake in a preheated oven at 190°C/Fan 170°C/Gas 5 for 30 minutes, or until the filling is piping hot and the pastry rim is golden.

These free-form fillings are particularly good:

Squash and cheese Leftover roast pumpkin or squash, plus crumbled feta or blue cheese or grated Cheddar and a trickle of cream or a few blobs of crème fraîche, if handy.

Tomato and pesto A good smear of pesto and sliced, ripe or overripe tomatoes.

Mushroom and sage Leftover mushroom pilaf or risotto, chopped sage and shavings of Parmesan.

Garlicky courgette Leftover fried or roasted courgettes, garlic and crème fraîche or soft goat's cheese.

Cheesy potato and ham Chunks of cooked potatoes, scraps of ham or bacon, grated Gruyère and chives or spring onions.

Of course, you can buy decent ready-made puff and other pastries of all kinds – look out for 'all butter' on the label. It's always useful to have a pack of good ready-made puff on standby in the freezer.

If you're making pastry for a tart or pie, it takes no more time to double and triple it up to store the other batch(es), well wrapped, in the freezer for another occasion.

PARCELS AND PASTIES

If you only have modest amounts of leftovers, or indeed of pastry, then pretty much all of the leftover pie fillings can be adapted to create simple pasties or turnovers.

Simple pasties

For triangles or semi-circles of plump pasty, put a dollop of well-flavoured filling on a square or circle of pastry (any kind), brush the edges with milk or beaten egg, then fold over and press/crimp the edges to seal. Place on a parchment-lined tray and bake in a preheated oven at 200°C/Fan 180°C/Gas 6 for around 20 minutes until piping hot and golden.

Filo parcels

Fine, delicate filo is great for parcelling up small amounts of leftovers with punchy flavourings. The resultant parcels are great for lunchboxes, picnics and parties. Most supermarkets sell filo – look for it in the chiller cabinet or freezer. Follow the handling instructions on the packet.
To shape For triangular parcels, peel off a square sheet of filo and brush it with melted butter. Fold into thirds lengthways, brushing with butter as you go, so you have a rectangle that is a third of a square. Drop a spoonful of your chosen filling (see left) at one end, a little in from the edges. Take the right corner and

fold it diagonally, enclosing the filling in a little triangle. Fold again, and keep folding on the diagonal, until you reach the end of the strip.
To cook Pop into a preheated oven at 200°C/Fan 180°C/Gas 6 until golden and crisped, about 12–15 minutes. Or, if well sealed, you can deep-fry them in batches for 3 minutes in hot oil at about 160°C (a cube of bread dropped in should turn golden in about 90 seconds).

These leftover-based fillings are particularly successful for simple pasties and filo parcels:

Curry Make sure it's not too wet. Bulk it out with lentils or other pulses if necessary.

Kedgeree Add extra herbs if you like, such as snipped chives or parsley.

Roasted roots Use any combination and spice up with some curry powder or paste.

Wilted spinach Squeeze very dry, then mix with crumbled paneer or curd cheese (see page 216) or other cheesy leftovers, and season to taste with salt, pepper, turmeric, ground cumin and ground coriander.

Cheese and onion Use grated strong cheese, fried onion or chopped fresh spring onion and chopped, cooked potatoes or mash. You can also add scraps of roast chicken or ham.

Wontons

Like filo parcels, these dim sum delights are brilliant for packaging punchy fillings. You can pick up wonton wrappers in any Chinese food shop; many supermarkets stock them now too. You only need a scant tablespoon of highly seasoned filling per dumpling, so they're a great way to use tasty leftovers. Once filled, they freeze brilliantly: freeze on a baking sheet until solid, then seal in a bag, ready to toss into soups from frozen.

To shape Brush the edges of the wonton with water, lay a spoonful of filling in the middle, fold into a half-moon and press to seal, taking care to push out any air bubbles.

To cook Steam the wontons in a basket lined with baking parchment for about 6 minutes, or drop them into a clear broth (see page 30). Or, if well sealed, you can deep-fry them in batches for 3 minutes in hot oil at about 160°C (a cube of bread dropped in should turn golden in about 90 seconds).

Serve with a hot sweet and sour dipping sauce, or lightly warmed redcurrant jelly thinned with a little cider vinegar and spiked with a pinch of dried chilli flakes.

Try filling wontons with any of the following spiced-up leftovers:

Chopped or shredded roast chicken Season generously with grated ginger, grated garlic and finely diced fresh red or green chilli. Add peas or greens or chopped roast veg if you have some.

Flaked fish Mix with peas, chopped spring onions and shredded mint and season with salt and pepper.

Roast pork or sausages Chop and mix with a little chutney or brown sauce. The result tastes surprisingly like an authentic dim sum!

PASTRY PERKS

When I make pies or tarts, I often have scraps of raw pastry left over. It's a shame to waste these, so here are some of my favourite things to do with them:

Cheesy biscuits

Roll out the leftover pastry to a 5mm thickness. Brush lightly with beaten egg white. Sprinkle on some grated cheese and roll lightly with the rolling pin to 'fix' the cheese to the dough, then grind on some black pepper and sprinkle on other seasonings if you like (I like whole cumin seeds, but ground coriander or cumin, cayenne and paprika work well too). Cut out small discs and place on a parchment-lined baking sheet (along with the random-shaped trimmings). Bake in a preheated oven at 180°C/Fan 160°C/Gas 4 for 10–12 minutes until golden.

Turnovers

Roll out pastry scraps to a 5mm thickness and cut into 10–12cm squares. Brush the edges with egg wash or milk, place a couple of spoonfuls of filling (see below) on one half of the square, fold the pastry diagonally over the filling and seal by pressing the edges with a fork. Place on a baking sheet lined with baking parchment. Brush the top with egg wash or milk and sprinkle with sugar if the filling is sweet. Make two small slits in the top and bake at 200°C/Fan 180°C/Gas 6 for 20 minutes, until the pastry is golden.

Try these simple leftover fillings for turnovers:

Ham and baked beans Mix leftover baked beans with shredded bits of ham and some grated cheese, if you like.

Cheesy potato Toss cooked potato, either cubed or mashed, with blue cheese or other strongly flavoured cheese.

Sausage and potato Mix chopped cooked, cooled sausage, haggis or sausage stuffing with potato and loosen with a small amount of stock or gravy.

Hashes & Squeaks

Sometimes you don't have to do much: it's enough to take the remains of one meal, mix it all together, season it up a bit, then pile it into a sizzling pan. And maybe flip a fried egg on top for a feisty finale.

I admit, some of these dishes may not be the most beautiful things you'll ever see on a plate, yet they can be among the most satisfying. They are the sort of trencherman standbys that put an arm round your shoulder, a cold beer in your hand and say, 'You know, it's a not always a bad idea to make a hash of things…'

HASH

Hash is a classic leftover dish. The bits and pieces of a traditional roast dinner – meat, potatoes, cabbage, carrots or anything else you have left over – fried together until the flavours blend and you have some delicious crispy bits around the bottom and sides.

Melt some butter and/or oil or rendered fat in a frying pan, add a chopped onion if you like and let it sweat until softened. Chop bigger pieces of meat and spud up a bit, but keep everything quite chunky. Tip all the vegetables and meat into the pan, increase the heat to medium-high and press everything down with a spatula. Don't be too keen to stir it – you want it to brown on the bottom. As it browns, flip bits over so the other side crisps up too. Add herbs or seasonings such as Worcestershire sauce, mustard or herbs now.

When your hash is golden and delicious, remove from the pan and serve piping hot, with any topping(s) you fancy (see right).

Try these winning hash leftover combinations:

Classic corned beef hash Fry a couple of sliced onions, then add roughly equal amounts of chopped cooked potatoes, tinned corned beef or boiled salt beef or pressed tongue and a good splash of Worcestershire sauce. Finish with chopped parsley if you like.

Red flannel hash Prepare as for the classic corned beef hash (above), adding some roasted or sliced boiled beetroot.

Ham or pork hash Fry a couple of sliced onions, then add roughly equal amounts of chopped boiled potatoes and boiled ham or roast pork, along with a spoonful of mustard and a sprinkling of thyme leaves or chopped sage, if handy. Any greens, peas, carrots or beans can go in too.

Chicken hash Fry a couple of sliced onions, then add 2 sliced red peppers, 2 chopped green chillies and roughly equal amounts of chopped cooked potatoes and shredded cooked chicken.

Stew and mash hash When there's not really enough stew to serve up again, take out the meat and veg, chop them up and fry hard until crisping. Add some mash or chopped cooked spuds and fry some more. Serve with the liquor from the stew as gravy.

Fish hash Mix leftover fish – picked clean off the bones and flaked – with mash and any greens for a really lovely hash that is rather like unformed fishcakes.

BUBBLE AND SQUEAK

So called because of the sound it makes when it's being fried in the pan, this is perhaps the most quintessentially British of all leftover dishes. It's traditionally made with potatoes and sliced cabbage or Brussels sprouts in roughly equal proportions. You can also add whatever other leftover veg you have to hand: peas, chopped carrots, spinach, broccoli and parsnips are all good. No problem to add meat too, but then I would say you are technically back in the world of hash.

Melt some butter and/or oil or rendered fat in a frying pan, add a thinly sliced onion or two if you like and sweat gently until softened. Chop bigger bits of potatoes up a bit, but keep everything quite chunky. Tip all the veg into the pan and add any chopped herbs or seasonings.

Increase the heat to medium-high and press everything down with a spatula. Fry hard until the base is brown and crispy, then flip the cake over. Cook until the underside is brown and crispy, then remove from the pan. Serve as it is, or embellished with a topping (see below).

Curried bubble and squeak This is a lovely variation. Just fry a little curry powder or paste in the pan before you add the other items.

HASH AND SQUEAK TOPPINGS

Often what turns a nicely made hash or bubble and squeak into a near perfect comfort-eating experience is what you choose to top it off with. The obvious candidates more or less select themselves:

Any leftover gravy poured over the top.

Thick slices of ham or bacon.

Poached or fried eggs.

Ketchup or brown sauce.

Baked beans.

Mango chutney (for the curried variation).

HASH AND SQUEAK CAKES

The above hashes and the bubble and squeak can, if you prefer, be pressed into smaller patties before frying. This makes for a neater presentation and they'll also freeze well, ready to be whipped out individually and reheated when you need them.

Chop all of the ingredients up a bit smaller than you would for the one-pan wonder, and crush roast potatoes up a little more if you're using them (a few lumps are fine). Form into two-per-person-size patties, pressing quite firmly with your hands. If the mix is reluctant to come together, a dash of milk and a shake of flour may help – but really just a smidge or the mixture will get gluey.

Dust the formed patties with flour seasoned with salt and pepper. You can then dip the cakes in beaten egg and coat them with breadcrumbs (see page 39), if you like. Lay them on a plate, cover and refrigerate for about an hour. (Or freeze them separately on a tray, and bag up in batches once frozen.)

Heat about a 4mm depth of groundnut or sunflower oil in a pan over a medium heat. Add the hash cakes and fry for about 3–4 minutes each side until nicely golden brown and crispy.

Pasta & Noodles

The starchy character of pasta makes it a great carrier of flavour and an obvious foil for leftovers. When you have a rich endowment of leftovers – veggie, meaty, fishy or cheesy – cooking up a panful of pasta (or noodles) to turn them into a meal is often the best way to go.

COOKING THE PASTA

Whether you're cooking up pasta from scratch or you've overestimated how much to cook and have some left over for another meal, it's important to keep it in good nick, rather than leaving it to settle self-adhesively in the bottom of a hot pan to be dealt with later. To ensure your pasta stays in good shape, you have two options depending on how you intend to use it:

Rinse immediately in cold water to stop the pasta from cooking further, then drain well. Seal in a plastic box or bag and keep in the fridge until you're ready to use it. This works best for pasta and noodles you want to add to soups, stews, sauces and frittata later.

Toss while still warm in your chosen dressing. Good oil, sea salt and black pepper will do. Alternatively, you could add some chopped herbs, even a little finely grated Parmesan; with oil as the carrier, the pasta will absorb these flavours and seasonings as it cools. This works well for pasta that you intend to use for salads.

ASIAN NOODLE SALADS

I'm a huge fan of these, using everything from translucent cellophane noodles to dark and earthy soba (buckwheat) noodles. Tossed in a tangy, Asian-inspired dressing, they wake up the tastebuds and are a great quick meal when I have lots of vegetables which I need to use up.

My Asian noodle salad formula is:

Make a dressing Bash a small peeled garlic clove and an equal-sized piece of peeled ginger together with a pinch of caster sugar. Combine with 1 tablespoon rice vinegar, 1 teaspoon tamari or soy sauce and the juice of ½ lime. Alternatively, use the dressing for spicy chicken and peanut butter salad (on page 76) or tamari greens with cashews and ginger (see page 162).
Cook the noodles Follow the packet directions, drain thoroughly (and in most cases, rinse well – check the packet), then toss with the dressing.
Assemble the salad Toss the noodles with your choice of leftover flavouring ingredients, depending on what you have to hand.

The following work well in Asian noodle salads:

Veg Shredded raw or cooked carrots, cabbage, peppers, mushrooms and spring onions.

Chicken or pork Shredded or torn and fried (with a good pinch of five-spice powder) to crispy shards.

Fish or shellfish Bits of cooked squid, flaked white crabmeat or mussels, or flakes of white or oily fish.

Toasted nuts and seeds Peanuts, cashew nuts, sesame seeds, pumpkin seeds and sunflower seeds, used alone or in combination.

Fresh herbs Use these generously, especially coriander, mint and Thai or ordinary basil. Toss well with the noodles and dressing, rather than simply scattering over the top, so that the aromatics really blend and mingle.

PASTA SALADS

The key to successful pasta salads – as with all salads – is generosity of spirit, a bold attitude to flavours and textures, and an easy hand with the herbs and spices. All of the following salads benefit from sitting for an hour or so for the flavours to develop, gently tumbling all together once or twice. Serve them at room temperature to enjoy them at their best.

Play around with the following assemblies:

Fish Flake cooked white or oily fish and combine with sliced flame-grilled red pepper, green beans, chopped spring onions, capers, lemon zest and juice. Toss through pasta shapes such as penne, orzo or tubetti with a good glug of olive oil.

Chicken Shred leftover chicken and combine with some cooked sweetcorn kernels, peas and/or broad beans with shredded herbs (tarragon, chervil and/or chives). Toss through pasta shapes, such as farfalle, rigatoni and fusilli, with a light dressing of half mayonnaise/half yoghurt, or a mustardy vinaigrette.

Ham and tomato Shred leftover ham and combine with cherry tomatoes, finely diced red onion and chopped cornichons. Toss through pasta shapes such as macaroni, cavatappi or cavatelli with a glug of good olive oil and a dab of Dijon mustard.

Salami and fennel Combine ribbons of salami and finely shaved fennel with chopped fennel fronds (if you have them) and/or chopped parsley. Toss through pasta shapes with a glug of good olive oil and a small splash of white wine (or cider) vinegar. Farfalle, rigatoni, fusilli and penne are all good candidates.

Tomato, olive and goat's cheese Toss fresh or roasted cherry tomatoes, crumbled soft goat's cheese, black or green olives, lots of shredded basil, a good pinch of dried chilli flakes and a small grating of lemon zest through pasta shapes with a glug of good olive oil. I like to use penne, tubetti or orzo pasta here.

PASTA BAKES

Like the poor pasta salad, the pasta bake has long been the object of derision. But that really is the most terrible snobbery. Assembled thoughtfully, it not only hoovers up all manner of leftovers, it makes an enormously satisfying family supper.

My pasta bake template is:

Combine cooked chunky pasta (medium shapes such as rigatoni, penne or farfalle work well) with some passata or tomato sauce or cheese sauce (see page 228).
Mix with an assembly of ingredients (see suggestions below).
Spoon into a buttered baking dish and finish with a topping of grated cheese and/or a scattering of breadcrumbs.
Bake at 200°C/Fan 180°C/Gas 6 for around 25 minutes until golden and bubbling.

Here are some ideas to get you started:

Meaty pasta bake Toss pasta with a little passata or tomato sauce, then add chestnut (or other) mushrooms sautéed with garlic, and cooked herby sausages chopped into chunks, or roughly chopped leftover roast pork, chicken or beef. For the topping, scatter over ripped mozzarella and breadcrumbs seasoned with thyme, black pepper and lemon zest.

Cheesy pasta bake Toss pasta with cheese sauce (for example, the one on page 228), seasoned with a dab of Dijon mustard, plus sautéed leeks and fried lardons or scraps of bacon and/or cooked chicken. Or leave out the meat and big up the veg, adding peas or sautéed mushrooms or both). Use grated Cheddar or Gruyère for the topping.

Veggie pasta bake Toss pasta with a little passata or tomato sauce. Add lightly cooked broccoli or purple sprouting broccoli, cherry tomatoes, green olives and crumbled ricotta or curd cheese (see page 216). For the topping, use grated Parmesan or other hard cheese and a sprinkling of breadcrumbs.

SAUCY TOMATO PASTA

A simple tomato sauce (home-made or from a jar) is a speedy way to a satisfying pasta supper. Just sling in anything that feels right. I often find it helpful to think in terms of cheaty versions of the classics, for example:

Roast dinner ragù Simmer finely chopped cooked meat and veg in your tomato sauce until merely a melting texture. Serve with spaghetti or linguine.

Catch of the (yester)day puttanesca To your tomato sauce, add leftover fish of any kind – white, oily or smoked, plus capers and halved black olives, and anchovies, if you like. Serve with penne, orecchiette or farfalle.

Arrabbiata Add any cooked leftover veg you like to your tomato sauce (but no meat) and a good dash of chilli sauce, freshly chopped chilli, or dried chilli flakes. Serve with spaghetti.

Bolognestew Chop all the meat and veg from your leftover stew fairly finely. Combine with the stew liquor, and a little tomato sauce or passata, and simmer until just right. This goes for lamb, pork, chicken and game stews as well as the obvious beef.

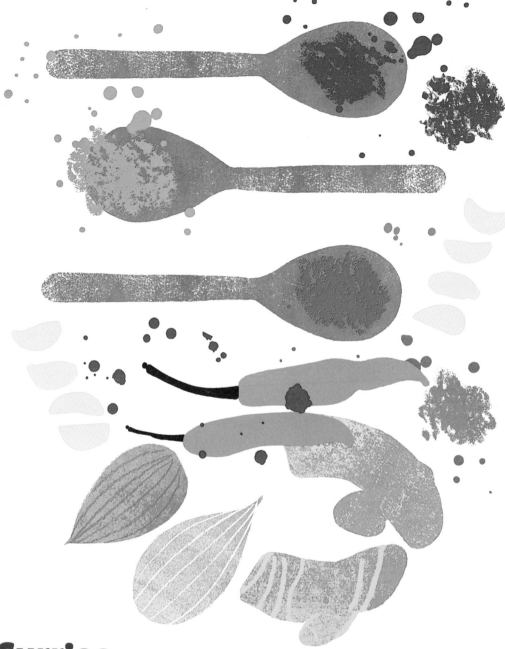

Curries

If you have good leftovers to play with, then it's rarely a stretch to turn them into a delicious curry. I make no promises here of authenticity or adherence to national and cultural boundaries. My only commitment is to marry together the disparate contents of my cupboards and fridge into a tempting spicy whole, as quickly and economically as possible. In that mission, I'm surely allowed a little international leeway.

For a hasty week-night supper, I see no shame in reaching for a bought jar of curry powder or paste to add zip to whatever assembly I have in front of me. If I have a little more time, I do like to make my own curry paste.

BASIC CURRY PASTE

This keeps well in a jar in the fridge for a couple of weeks or so. Alternatively, you can freeze it in ice-cube trays and decant the frozen curry cubes into a self-sealing bag – just take a few out every time you fancy a fiery feast.

My basic curry paste formula is:

In a small food processor, blitz 4 finely chopped shallots, 6–8 halved garlic cloves, 2 roughly chopped thumbs of ginger, 4–6 green chillies (membrane and seeds removed for less heat, if preferred), 2 teaspoons each of ground cumin and ground coriander and 1 teaspoon ground turmeric with just enough water to make a smooth paste. Either store in a jar in the fridge or freeze until needed.

Thai-style curry paste

For this, I leave out the ground spices and add 3 roughly chopped lemon grass stalks (tough outer layer removed) to the food processor, along with any fresh coriander stems and roots I have to hand.

SAUCY CURRY

Whether I'm brandishing a batch of my own freshly made curry paste or a jar of pre-mixed curry powder, my quick-curry enterprise tends to go something like this:

In a large frying pan or wide saucepan, sauté a couple of chopped onions in oil until softened. **Stir in** a generous dollop of (home-made) curry paste or 1–2 tablespoons of curry powder and cook for a few more minutes.
Add a few handfuls of fresh or leftover root veg and/or squash, aubergines, courgettes, cauliflower; stir until well combined with the spicy onions.
Tip in ½ x 400ml tin of coconut milk and a 400g tin of chopped tomatoes or a similar amount of tomato sauce or passata, or rooty tomato soup base (see page 33).
Add any leftover scraps of cooked chicken, lamb or beef; drained, rinsed chickpeas or kidney beans; softer veg such as green beans, peas, courgettes, spinach – either fresh or leftover. Simmer until everything is cooked through and hot.
Finish if you like with coriander or parsley, toasted cashew nuts or almonds.
Serve with basmati or other long-grain rice; raita (see page 88); naan breads or flatbreads and your favourite chutneys, of course.

BYRIANI STYLE CURRY

When I have some leftover rice to hand, and just a few choice morsels of leftover meat, or fish or veg, to perk it up with, this is the way I go. It's basically my kedgeree technique, expanded to encompass savoury nuggets other than smoked fish and eggs:

In a large frying pan or wide saucepan, sauté a couple of chopped onions in oil until softened. **Stir in** a generous dollop of home-made curry paste or 1–2 tablespoons curry powder and cook for a couple of minutes.
Add any leftover scraps of cooked fish or meat (especially chicken or lamb). Mix well and cook until the meat is hot and spicy.
Add a few handfuls of chopped leftover veg and/or defrosted frozen peas and/or cooked chickpeas or tinned beans, if you think it needs the extra heft. Quartered hard-boiled eggs, or strips of omelette, are always welcome. Plus a handful of raisins, if you like that idea.
Tip in the pre-cooked/leftover rice. Toss to combine with the other ingredients and stir until everything's cooked through, and the rice is well coloured by the spices.
Finish if you like with a scattering of coriander or parsley, toasted cashew nuts or almonds.
Serve with a dab of chutney and a cold beer.

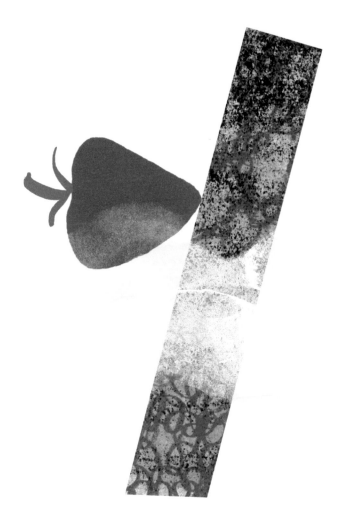

SWEET TRINITY

Many of the greatest puddings are constructed from a trinity of contrasting but complementary components: the creamy, the fruity and the crisp/crumbly/cakey. If you've got even one of these elements in your arsenal of leftovers, it's worth rooting around for the other two. And if you've got two it would certainly be rude not to seek out the third...

Let's take a look at some of my all-time favourite puddings: trifles, messes, crumbles, fumbles and sweet tarts: all trinity-based as it happens, highly versatile and obligingly receptive to leftovers.

Trifles

The classic trifle is lovingly constructed from sponge cake, a dash of booze, some seasonal fruit, real custard, jelly perhaps, lashings of cream, often topped with toasted almonds. Pure indulgence. But the concept is simple: the key elements are fruitiness, creaminess and cakey-ness.

So if I've got half a pot of yoghurt, a last slice of cake and a ripe banana, I could break up the cake into a glass, spoon over some yoghurt, slice half a banana over that. I might even top it off with a trickle of raspberry jam and toast the flaked almonds I spotted lurking in the larder to scatter on top. Purists might argue this isn't a real trifle. But does it matter? I doubt the trifle police will be knocking at the door...

So, let's look at ways in which we can play with our leftovers, and with the concept of trifle, to create infinitely variable, and invariably pleasing puds.

Just take one (or more) element(s) from each category – fruity, creamy and cakey – and knock yourself out a trifle. And, in case you want to top it off with a contrasting sprinkle, I've listed some suggestions for these too.

THE FRUITY ELEMENT

There are no end of possibilities here – and you can take your pick from the finest of the season – but here let's prioritise fruity leftovers in the widest sense:

Stewed fruit of any kind – especially plums, rhubarb, Bramley apples and blackcurrants. The last few spoonfuls often linger in the fridge, so polish them off on trifle duty.

Raspberries and/or strawberries that are less than perfect, a bit bruised perhaps. Lightly crush them with a little icing sugar and a squeeze of lemon, or even a splash of crème de cassis or framboise, if you have some handy.

Apples and/or pears lingering in the fruit bowl, perhaps because they are a bit bruised. Peel, chop and mix with lemon juice and a sprinkling of brown sugar or a teaspoonful of honey. Plus, if you like, a splash of calvados and/or some chopped crystallised stem ginger.

Overripe bananas are not everybody's cup of tea, but slicing and dousing with a good squeeze of lemon juice takes the queasy edge off them.

Dried fruit – especially apricots and prunes – but also raisins and sultanas. Bring the fruit to a simmer, ideally in apple juice, tea or cider, and leave to plump up as the hot liquid cools.

Jam pot ends make a good fruity sauce or topping. Scrape out the last spoonful or two and thin with a little warm water and a good squeeze of lemon.

Jelly cannot be ignored: a good old-fashioned trifle usually has a jelly layer, often made from a packet of jelly. Making a proper jelly from scratch with real fruit juice or purée is a great way to introduce the fruity element but it's a lot of trouble to go to for an improvised pud. If you happen to have some jelly in the fridge, leftover from a kids' party perhaps, then you could use that, even if it is made from jelly cubes...

THE CREAMY ELEMENT

There are more options here than you might at first think. And a crucial leap is the realisation that most creamy things can be successfully blended together. So the last of the yoghurt pot mixed with the final spoonfuls from the crème fraîche tub might be just what you need to rustle up two romantic wine glasses of improvised trifliness. Marriages have been saved by lesser gestures...

Vanilla custard features in a trifle more often than not. Luscious, home-made custard, flavoured with fresh vanilla, is clearly the best, but you could use shop-bought fresh custard. Even tinned custard or custard powder (the just-add-to-boiling milk kind) can be pressed into service.

Cream is the obvious creamy component. Use double or whipping cream, as these will thicken when whisked.

Crème fraîche keeps longer than regular cream, and is often still fine to use after its use-by date. The tangy edge goes particularly well against anything cakey.

Natural wholemilk yoghurt is perhaps my first choice dairy item for adorning fruit of all kinds. You could use sweetened or fruit-flavoured yoghurts too.

Ricotta is mainly thought of in a savoury context, but it is usually unsalted and its fresh dairy taste and wobbly texture is lovely with summer fruits like strawberries, raspberries, redcurrants and blueberries.

Mascarpone works wickedly well in the trifle context.

Cream-of-the-milk is a possibility if, like me, you buy unhomogenised whole milk rather than semi-skimmed. Sometimes this creamy treat sitting atop the milk is just enough, stirred into the last of any of the above creamy elements, to make the difference…

THE CAKEY ELEMENT

While I think it's probably fair to say that plain sponge is the trifle classic, there are many other cakey possibilities. The last slice, square, end or quarter of any of the following, even if a touch stale, can be assessed for trifle service. And sprinkling it with a dash of booze may just help it qualify. Sherry is classic, but sweet white wine, rum, brandy and whisky also work.

Madeira or sponge cake are the obvious choices, or a good old-fashioned Swiss roll.

Madeleines and muffins lurking in the cake tin, even teabread, gingerbread and brownies can be sliced and used.

Brioche and other enriched yeast-raised treats, like doughnuts or even hot cross buns, may also have sufficiently cakey qualities to be deployed here.

TOPPINGS AND SPRINKLES

You don't *need* to top off your creamy, cakey, fruity delight, but something crispy or nutty or nibblesome does make for a pleasing extra texture, and it's amazing what serviceable odds and ends the storecupboard can turn up:

Toasted almond flakes are the crowning glory of the classic trifle, though for some, hundreds and thousands would do the honours.

Crumbled biscuits are an easy win. And none better than the gingernut, with the digestive a close second. You only need one or two last biscuits in the pack or tin to provide a crisp crumby finish for two or more servings.

Chocolate – especially plain chocolate – grated or chopped over the top, gives a nice bitter-sweet contrast to creamy dairy and tart fruit.

Breadcrumbs tossed with a little caster or brown sugar and melted butter or sunflower oil, then baked in a hot oven for a few minutes until crispy, make a lovely topping. You can also mix in some chopped or flaked nuts and/or some oat flakes, if you like.

SUNDAES

Based on the same fruit/creamy/cakey concept as a trifle, the sundae is a great vehicle for leftovers. The fruity element is much the same (usually just a little saucier) and the cakey element is swapped out in favour of some kind of nutty topping. The creamy element is, of course, ice cream:

Spoon your chosen fruity element (see page 59) into tall glasses and top with a generous scoop of vanilla ice cream. You can pile on some whipped cream and chocolate (or other) sauce at this point, though I rarely do. Finish with a scattering of any of the trifly toppings or sprinkles (suggested above), or bashed up praline, peanut brittle or sesame snaps, or some crumble topping (see page 63). Even chopped leftover chocolate tiffin-type bars or your favourite branded chocolate bar (mine's a Crunchie), can be a crowning glory.

Messes

Eton Mess is another great pud that offers endless possibilities for leftovers. The original Eton Mess comprises sliced or crushed strawberries folded together with whipped cream and broken meringues. But chefs up and down the land have been tinkering with the fruity element, in particular, to ring the seasons in and out. As long as the meringue and cream remain, you are clearly not messing unduly with the Mess. These days I quite often mix through a little natural wholemilk yoghurt as well as the whipped cream – it nicely takes the edge off the richness. It's well worth making your own meringues, especially if you have some leftover egg whites to use up (see page 237).

The fruity element

Berries and currants that are just a little too soft or squidgy to serve on their own are ideal here, but there are other fruity potentials. Try the following folded through your creamy element, together with broken meringues:

Medley of summer berries such as sliced strawberries and lightly crushed raspberries, perhaps with a handful or two of added blueberries or redcurrants. Less-than-perfect fruits can be crushed with a little icing sugar, the best ones sliced or left whole.

Tart compote of lightly stewed gooseberries, rhubarb or blackcurrants, or Bramley apples and blackberries, sweetened subtly with just a little sugar or honey.

Boozy bottled fruits such as prunes, plums or cherries in brandy or kirsch, make a fine 'wintry' Mess, with a bit of the liquor mixed in.

Crumbles & Fumbles

There is nothing quite as comforting as a crumble: ripe seasonal fruit topped with a crunchy, buttery topping, served with custard, ice cream or thick cream.

A few years ago, I started to cook my crumble topping separately – for two reasons. Firstly, it would keep its crunch in the face of the juiciest of fruits. Secondly, it would keep in a sealed jar for a few weeks. To satisfy my crumble craving, all I had to do was scatter some topping over hot or cold fruit, slosh on some cream or custard, or scoop on some ice cream, *et voilà*

pudding. It's a classic example of deliberately creating leftovers, because you know how useful they will be.

Having the crumble topping on standby had a further benefit: it led to the birth of the fumble, which is essentially a fruity fool with a crumbly topping. It's yet another brilliant incarnation of the holy pudding trinity...

CRUMBLE TOPPING

In a large bowl, stir together 225g plain flour, 150g granulated, caster or demerara sugar and 100g medium oatmeal, ground almonds or porridge oats. Add 200g cold butter, cut into cubes, and rub together with your fingertips to make a crumbly dough. Squeeze some bits together to form clumps.

Scatter the crumble mixture on a baking tray. Bake in a preheated oven at 180°C/Fan 160°C/Gas 4 for about 25 minutes, stirring halfway through, until golden and crisp. Leave to cool completely, then store in an airtight container until you're ready to use it.

CRUMBLE

Spoon your fruity element into a pie dish, scatter over the crumble topping and bake in a preheated oven at 180°C/Fan 160°C/Gas 4 for about 20 minutes until the fruit juices are bubbling up around the topping. Serve with natural yoghurt, crème fraîche, whipped cream or custard.

Here are a few fruity options:

Stewed Bramley apples flavoured with a pinch of ground cinnamon.

Stewed rhubarb with strawberries.

Stewed gooseberries infused with elderflower (tie the heads in muslin and simmer with the fruit to impart fragrance).

Pears chopped and tossed with blackberries.

Plums or greengages – halved and stoned – with a trickle of honey.

FUMBLE

For this pud, I like to have all three elements at room temperature, but you might prefer a contrast; for example, warm stewed fruit topped with a chilled creamy element and a sprinkling of fumble at room temperature. For a rhubarb fumble, for example, in a glass I swirl together a couple of tablespoons of chilled rhubarb purée with a good tablespoon of slightly sweetened whipped cream and top with pre-made crumble.

To create your fumble, fold or swirl any of the fruity suggestions below with any of the creamy elements (more than one is fine) and top with a liberal scattering of crunchy crumble.

The fruity element:

Stewed fruit of any kind, especially plums, rhubarb, Bramley apples, blackcurrants – cooked until tender but retaining their shape.

Tangy fruit purée of apples, gooseberries, rhubarb, apricots or plums – cook the fruit until broken down to a purée.

Raspberries and/or strawberries crushed with a little icing sugar and a squeeze of lemon, or a splash of crème de cassis or framboise.

The creamy element (alone or in combination):

Vanilla custard with natural yoghurt or lightly whipped double cream folded through works particularly well. Use either home-made or a carton of shop-bought fresh custard.

Cream is lovely in a fumble, though I prefer it combined with yoghurt and/or custard. Double and whipping cream are the dependable choices, as they will thicken when whisked.

Crème fraîche does fine fumble service on its own, but is particularly pleasing swirled with custard.

Natural wholemilk yoghurt is always a good choice for a fumble – I like to mix it in with whipped cream.

Ricotta is delicious with summer fruits like strawberries, raspberries and blueberries.

For the crunchy element:

Crumble topping (see above).

Easy sweet tarts

This easy free-form tart (mentioned earlier in a savoury context on page 47) is wonderfully obliging when it comes to fruit, and is my final example of the sweet trinity at work. There's no blind baking, no pastry waste – just tender, crisp pastry and hot sweet fruit with cream, custard, ice cream or thick yoghurt. The creamy element is not intrinsic to the dish, but served over the top or on the side.

SWEET SHORTCRUST PASTRY

In a large bowl or food processor, mix together 200g plain flour, 1½ tablespoons icing sugar and a pinch of salt.

Add 120g chilled butter, cut into cubes, and rub in (or blitz in the processor, being careful not to overwork) until it resembles coarse breadcrumbs. Work in 1 egg yolk and a little cold milk or iced water – just enough to bind.

Turn out onto a lightly floured surface, knead gently to bring the dough together, wrap in cling film and rest in the fridge for 30 minutes.

FRUITY FILLINGS

Let the season dictate your choice of filling:

Summer berries Fruit that is a little too tired to serve raw will be fine. Use 400g berries (raspberries, blackberries, gooseberries, etc.) plus 2–3 tablespoons caster sugar.

Apple Peel and slice or cube a few apples and mix with 2–3 tablespoons caster sugar and a pinch of ground cinnamon, cloves, or even cardamom. You could add some blackberries if you have them.

Rhubarb Use about 300g rhubarb, cut into 3–4cm lengths and tossed with 75–100g caster sugar and the finely grated zest and juice of 1 small orange, scattering ground almonds over the base to absorb the juices (see right).

Apricot or plum Use about 12 ripe apricots or 6–8 ripe large plums. Halve, stone and sweeten with 2–3 tablespoons caster sugar or vanilla sugar (see page 242).

Dried fruit Plump about 200g unsulphured dried apricots or prunes by soaking in hot apple juice, cider or tea for about 30 minutes, and drain before using.

To make your free-form sweet tart:

Roll out the pastry to a circle, about 35–40cm in diameter, and place on a baking sheet lined with baking parchment. Brush with jam, and/or spread with a little cream cheese, and/or scatter with ground almonds, if you like.

Pile your chosen fruity filling into the middle of the circle and fold the edges of the pastry back over the filling so it partially covers it. You can either fold four sides almost to the middle, for a kind of pie-galette with a bit of fruit peeping in the middle. Or just roll the edges over to create a free-form open tart with hand-formed rim. The former is good for enclosing juicy fruits, like rhubarb and plums, and summer berries that will run in the oven; the latter is better for firm fruits, like apples and pears, that will caramelise nicely in the oven.

Brush the pastry edges with milk or beaten egg. Sprinkle a bit of extra sugar onto the pastry, and the fruit too, if you like. Bake in a preheated oven at 190°C/Fan 170°C/Gas 5 for 30 minutes, or until the filling is piping hot and the pastry is golden. Serve with something creamy, of course. *Anything* creamy.

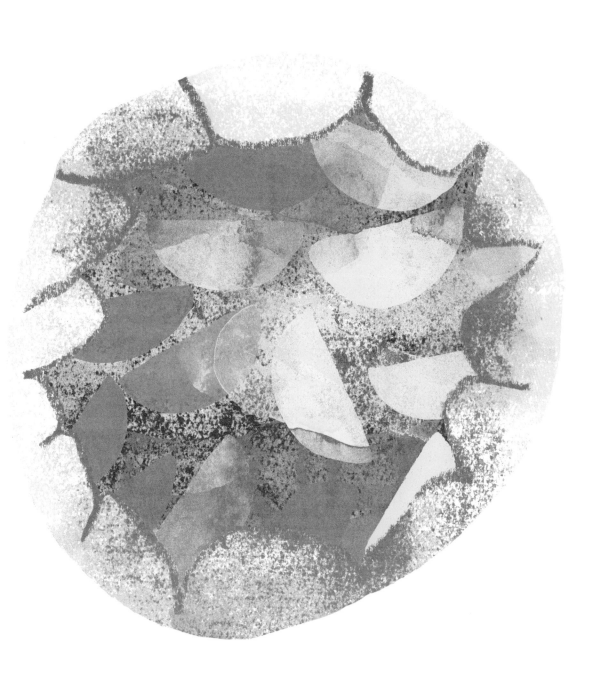

LEFTOVER MEAT

Meat is one of the richest and most flavourful foods we have at our disposal. It is a luxury in many senses, not least because a creature has died to provide it. I have long been an advocate of eating less meat, but better meat. Making that flesh go as far as it can is not only an act of thrift, but also of respect.

Thankfully, it's not difficult. Meat is one of the great engines of leftovers cooking and it almost always pays to prepare more than you need for a single meal. Not only do you benefit from economies of scale in terms of time spent, energy used and washing up generated but, after all the careful seasoning and marinating, chopping and stirring, simmering and basting, prodding and cosseting that often goes into getting meat onto the table, it's rather gleeful to be able to reap the benefits a second time around with barely a whisper of fuss or trouble.

This is when all that hard work really pays dividends: in a few shamefully easy steps, you can turn last night's beef stew into tomorrow's enchiladas (see page 72), Sunday's roast pork into a creamy casserole fragrant with rosemary (see page 98), or that leg or shoulder of lamb into a lovely shepherd's pie (see page 90).

Successful use of meat leftovers doesn't always depend on having lots to play with. Meat has bags of flavour and if you add even more in the shape of herbs, seasonings, condiments and spicy salad leaves, you can then use a considerable quantity of blander, bulkier carbs, veg and/ or pulses to really make the most of what you've got.

Scrape every last scrap and morsel from the bones. Even the tiniest meat shreds can deliver a real shot of savoury, 'umami' flavour, especially if fried until crisp, confidently seasoned and scattered on salads or soups. In a number of recipes you'll see I've referred to 'shards' of crispy meat, and indeed skin. Chicken skin especially can be roasted miraculously into delicious 'crackling' (see page 79). Deployed like this, meat almost becomes a 'spice' and a little can go a very long way.

Even when the meat is gone, never throw out any bones. These can be simmered into the stocks (see page 28) that are in themselves an absolute mainstay of leftovers cooking – meal-makers for the scraps and oddments of tomorrow. If you don't have quite enough bones to justify getting the stockpot out, or you simply don't have time right now, just toss them into a bag in the freezer until you do.

Chicken soup

There is a reason why this comforting classic is known as 'Jewish penicillin': studies suggest that its anti-inflammatory properties are scientific fact, not popular myth. Whatever the truth, it makes an easy and nutritious meal just as it is, or you can customise it with all manner of leftovers and even change its character by varying the garnish and seasoning.

The soup relies for its character on a really good chicken stock, simmered slowly for at least 3 hours with plenty of veg and then quite scrupulously skimmed to remove any scum and all but the lightest shimmer of fat. SERVES 4

1.5 litres chicken stock (see page 28)

2 carrots, thinly sliced

2 celery sticks, trimmed and thinly sliced, plus some leaves, finely shredded, if you have them

1 small leek, white part only (keep the green part for stock), very thinly sliced

120–200g cooked chicken, shredded

2–3 tablespoons finely chopped parsley (optional)

Salt and freshly ground black pepper

Pour the stock into a pan, add the vegetables and simmer for 20 minutes until they are tender. Add the shredded chicken and simmer for a further 5 minutes until heated through.

Add the chopped parsley and celery leaves, if using, and season well with salt and pepper.

Ladle the soup into bowls and serve straight away, with crusty bread if you like.

Tips and swaps

Chicken noodle soup Add about 50g vermicelli or angel's hair pasta. To preserve the clarity of the broth, cook the pasta separately and add it right at the end with the chicken, giving it just enough time to heat through.

Chicken and egg Cut leftover (or freshly made) omelette into thin strips and toss into the soup at the end.

Up the green veg (as shown) Add some fresh or leftover peas, green beans, mangetout and/ or broad beans, or some shredded lettuce (slightly limp leaves will do).

Swap the meat This is a good soupy base for other leftover roast meats, such as lamb, beef, pork, duck, goose or game. A handful of pearl barley is a good addition with lamb or beef.

Chicken and mushroom fricassée

My Mum used to make this classic regularly with our roast chicken leftovers. I've recently revived it for my family and it always goes down a treat. SERVES 4

2 tablespoons rapeseed or sunflower oil

1 onion, halved and finely sliced

1 carrot, diced

1 celery stick, diced

Sprig of thyme

1 bay leaf

100–200g chestnut or other mushrooms, thickly sliced, or left whole if button-small

1 garlic clove, finely chopped

1 tablespoon plain flour

150ml white wine

500ml chicken stock (see page 28), or a mix of chicken stock and leftover gravy, hot

200–400g cooked chicken

Handful of roast carrots, peas, broad beans or green beans (optional)

Few tablespoons of parsley and/or tarragon leaves, roughly chopped or torn (optional)

50g crème fraîche or double cream (optional)

Salt and freshly ground black pepper

Heat the oil in a heavy-based casserole over a medium-low heat. Add the onion, carrot, celery, thyme, bay leaf and a pinch of salt and sauté until softened, about 10 minutes.

Turn up the heat a little, add the mushrooms and fry until they take on a bit of colour and start to give up their moisture, about 5 minutes. Stir in the garlic and fry for a minute.

Add the flour, stir well and cook, stirring, for a couple of minutes. Add the wine along with the hot stock, or stock and gravy, and stir well – you want the liquid to combine with the floury residue in the pan.

Bring to a gentle simmer, stirring regularly, and cook gently until smooth and thickened, about 10 minutes. Remove the bay leaf and any woody thyme stems from the pot.

Add the chicken and any leftover vegetables you're using, and cook until heated through. Stir in the herbs, if using, season well with salt and pepper, and remove from the heat.

Stir in the crème fraîche or cream, return to the heat and warm through very gently. Serve with mash and roasted carrots or wilted greens.

Tips and swaps

Add dumplings Add more stock to make the fricassée a little more soupy then drop in some dumplings (see page 33) seasoned with chopped thyme or sage.

Chicken and mushroom pie This fricassée works well as a pie filling (see page 46), or you can top it with leftover roast potatoes and bake it as for Lancashire hot pot (see page 86).

Rabbit and mushroom fricassée Try replacing the chicken with leftover rabbit, or rabbit combined with a few chunks of ham or cooked bacon or pancetta.

Stew enchiladas

This is a terrific way to turn a few ladlefuls of leftover stew into a whole new meal. With apologies to purist Mexican chefs everywhere, almost any combination – based on almost any meat, or indeed veg – can take this treatment. Try it with the chicken fricassée (see page 70) or chicken, white bean and chorizo salad (see page 74), or even the Lancashire hot pot (see page 86). If you have only a small amount of stew, you can bulk it out with tinned borlotti, cannellini, kidney or black-eyed beans, drained and rinsed. SERVES 3–4

3–4 large (wrap-size) soft corn tortillas or 6–8 smaller ones

400–500g stew, or stew mixed with pulses (see above)

About 150g Cheddar, or other hard, strong cheese, grated

For the tomato sauce

1 tablespoon rapeseed or sunflower oil, plus extra to oil the dish

1 onion, diced

2 jalapeño or other medium-hot green chillies, halved, membrane and seeds removed (for a milder version if preferred), finely chopped

1 garlic clove, finely chopped

½ teaspoon ground cumin

½ teaspoon ground coriander

About 200g fresh or frozen sweetcorn, or tinned (drained and rinsed)

400g tin whole plum tomatoes in juice, chopped

Salt and freshly ground black pepper

To finish (optional)

2–3 tablespoons soured cream

2–3 spring onions, trimmed and roughly chopped

Handful of coriander leaves, roughly chopped

Preheat the oven to 180°C/Fan 160°C/Gas 4. Lightly oil an ovenproof frying pan or a medium baking dish, about 20 x 30cm.

To make the tomato sauce, heat the oil in a saucepan over a medium heat. Add the onion with a generous pinch of salt and sauté until softened, about 10 minutes. Add the chillies, garlic and ground spices and stir for a minute.

Tip in the sweetcorn and chopped tomatoes with their juice. Simmer gently for 10 minutes, stirring from time to time. Season well with salt and pepper.

Warm the tortillas in the oven or microwave, according to the packet instructions.

Pour half of the tomato sauce into the frying pan or baking dish and spread evenly.

Divide the stew-based filling between the tortillas, spooning it along the middle of each one. Roll up and place the stuffed tortillas seam side down in the pan or baking dish.

Pour over the remaining tomato sauce and sprinkle on the cheese. Bake until bubbling hot, about 25–30 minutes.

Serve each portion topped with a dollop of soured cream and a scattering of spring onions and coriander if you like, with plain rice and a crisp green salad on the side.

Tips and swaps

Non-meat version Try stuffing the warmed corn tortillas with leftover roast vegetables, moistened with a little of the tomato sauce and some of the grated cheese if you like. Roast potatoes are particularly good, folded in with some wilted spinach or any other wilted leaves you have to hand.

Not-so-Cornish pasties In place of the tortillas, roll out shortcrust pastry to a 3–4mm thickness and cut out 4 rounds. Spoon the cold stew onto one half of each circle, brush the edges with water, fold over the other half and crimp the edges to seal. Place the pasties on a lined baking sheet, brush with egg wash and bake at 190°C/Fan 170°C/Gas 5 for 35–40 minutes.

Chicken, white bean and chorizo salad

This is a great way to use up small amounts of chicken and sausage, and trusty pulses soak up all those meaty flavours beautifully. For added crunch, I sometimes sprinkle on some toasted seasoned breadcrumbs (see page 39). SERVES 3–4

1 teaspoon rapeseed or sunflower oil

100–200g cooking chorizo, or other spicy sausage, skin removed and broken into 2cm chunks

Any bits of roast chicken skin, cut into thin strips

1 red onion, halved and finely sliced

2 red, orange or yellow peppers, cored, deseeded and sliced

2 garlic cloves, halved and finely sliced

1 teaspoon ground cumin

150–200g cooked chicken, shredded

400g tin cannellini beans, drained and rinsed

Pinch of dried chilli flakes (optional)

Small handful of parsley or basil leaves, roughly chopped

Salt and freshly ground black pepper

Heat the oil in a large, non-stick pan over a medium heat. Add the chorizo to the pan, with any strips of chicken skin you have, and cook until the chorizo releases its fat.

Scoop the chorizo out of the pan with a slotted spoon and set aside. Leave the chicken skin in the pan and fry for a bit longer until it starts to crisp up. Scoop it out too and set aside with the chorizo.

Toss the onion and peppers into the pan and fry for about 5 minutes until softened, stirring from time to time. Add the garlic and cumin. Fry gently for a minute, until you have a fragrant mixture, but be careful not to scorch the spices.

Return the chorizo to the pan. Add the cooked chicken, beans and dried chilli flakes, if using, and heat through thoroughly. Season with salt and pepper to taste.

Spoon into bowls, top with any fried chicken skin and scatter over the chopped parsley or basil. Serve straight away.

You can also let this cool to room temperature before eating it – but don't leave it hanging around too long.

Tips and swaps

Chicken, bean and chorizo stew Add about 300ml chicken stock with the shredded chicken and beans and simmer for 15 minutes before seasoning. You could also add 3 tablespoons soured cream before finishing with the herbs.

Tortilla-topped pie Spoon the above hot stew into a flameproof dish, snip a couple of corn tortillas into rough triangles, scatter over the top and sprinkle on some grated Cheddar. Grill until the cheese is bubbling and finish with some finely chopped spring onions.

Swap the meat Use leftover cooked pork, beef, rabbit or duck to make the salad, or the stew or pie variations.

Spicy chicken and peanut butter salad

Peanut butter – and other nut butters – is one of my favourite ways to add depth and richness to spicy sauces and dressings. This particular dressing goes very well with chicken but it's good tossed through everything – from cooked green beans to griddled little gem lettuces. SERVES 4

250–300g roast or poached chicken

4–6 spring onions, trimmed and finely chopped

1 red pepper, cored, deseeded and finely sliced

Small handful of mint leaves, finely shredded

Small handful of coriander leaves, finely chopped

For the dressing

3 tablespoons crunchy peanut butter

1 tablespoon tamari or soy sauce

1 tablespoon mirin (rice wine)

2 garlic cloves, grated

1 teaspoon grated ginger

1 teaspoon clear honey

100ml hot chicken or veg stock (see page 28) or water

To serve

Lime wedges

Tear the chicken into shreds and place in a bowl with the spring onions, red pepper and herbs.

To make the dressing, in a small bowl whisk together all the ingredients, except the stock or water, until combined. Then gradually whisk in the stock or water.

Pour the dressing over the salad and toss until well combined. Serve with lime wedges.

Tips and swaps

Add peas or beans If you have any leftover green beans, broad beans or peas, toss them into the salad.

Pad out with noodles Serve the salad over rice noodles, cooked, rinsed in cold water and dressed with sesame oil and a squeeze of lime.

Swap the meat Replace the chicken with leftover roast duck, rabbit or pork.

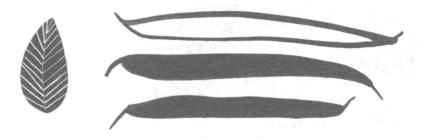

Turkish chicken with walnuts

This simple dish, based on a classic Ottoman recipe, creates something rather sophisticated from leftover chicken, a handful of walnuts and a bit of stale bread. It's traditionally made from poached chicken, with the broth used to moisten the creamy sauce, but roast chicken and a bit of stock or even a splash of gravy does the job very well. Serve it as it is, or with a crisp green salad, on crostini or rolled into wraps. SERVES 4

40–50g dry white bread, crusts removed, torn into pieces

80–100ml milk

About 50g shelled walnuts

1–2 garlic cloves, halved

50–100ml chicken stock (see page 28) or gravy

250–350g poached or roast chicken, skinned (skin saved for crackling, see right)

2 tablespoons coriander leaves, chopped, plus extra to finish

Knob of butter

½ teaspoon dried chilli flakes

½ teaspoon smoked paprika (optional)

Salt and freshly ground black pepper

Chicken crackling, to serve (optional)

Scatter the bread in a shallow dish, pour over the milk and leave for 15 minutes or so until it's fully absorbed.

Using a large pestle and mortar, bash the walnuts and garlic together to form a rough paste. (Or you can do this in a food processor.) Add the bread and pound (or whiz) it with the walnut mixture, adding enough broth, stock or gravy to make a creamy sauce.

Tear the chicken into shreds and place in a bowl. Add the walnut sauce and chopped coriander and fold through until well combined. Season with salt and pepper to taste.

You can serve the dish straight away but it's better if you cover and refrigerate it for an hour or so, to let the flavours mingle. It will keep well, covered and refrigerated for a couple of days. Bring to room temperature before serving.

Just before serving, melt the butter in a small pan over a low heat. Stir in the chilli flakes and warm gently for a minute, adding the paprika, if using, just before serving.

Divide the chicken and walnut sauce between plates and add the chicken cracking, if using. Scatter over the coriander leaves, trickle the spiced butter over the chicken, and serve.

Tips and swaps

Add a handful of green beans or some peas.

Use parsley rather than coriander.

Finish with a squeeze of lemon juice in place of the spiced butter.

Chicken crackling

Preheat the oven to 180°C/Fan 160°C/Gas 4. Lay some cooked or raw chicken skin in a roasting tin in a single layer and season with flaky sea salt and freshly ground black pepper. Roast for 10–15 minutes or until crisp; raw skin can take up to 15 minutes longer. Drain the rendered fat into a clean jar to use later. Serve the chicken crackling warm, either as it is or tossed with a little very finely chopped rosemary. Enjoy as a snack or use as a garnish where appropriate.

Lamb and mint couscous

What I love about this recipe is how easily it turns Sunday lunch into Monday's lunchbox. If you have some leftover gravy, heat it up and add it to the liquid or stock you use to cook the couscous. I've added carrots and peas, but you can be pretty inventive with what you throw in – if it tasted good with your roast dinner, it'll taste good in your couscous too. I season this with a dollop of mint sauce or jelly, and stir in some perky herbs too, to add freshness. SERVES 2 AS A MAIN COURSE, 4 AS A LIGHT LUNCH

150g couscous or barley couscous

300ml hot water or stock (see page 28) and/or gravy, if you have it (or the amount of liquid specified on the couscous packet)

1–2 tablespoons olive oil, plus an extra splash for the dressing

1–2 tablespoons mint sauce or jelly

Finely grated zest and juice of ½ lemon

½ teaspoon ground cumin

½ teaspoon ground coriander

¼ teaspoon ground cinnamon

100g roast lamb, diced

100g cooked peas

100g cooked carrots, diced

Small handful of mint, parsley and/or coriander leaves, roughly chopped or torn, plus extra leaves to finish

Salt and freshly ground black pepper

To prepare the couscous, put it into a bowl, add the hot water or stock and olive oil, then cover and leave to soak for a short time, according to the packet instructions.

When the couscous is swollen and tender, add the mint sauce or jelly, lemon zest and juice, and sprinkle on the ground spices. Fork the couscous gently to fluff it up and combine it with the seasonings.

Add the lamb, vegetables and herbs and toss gently to combine. Taste and season with salt and pepper, a little more lemon if you like, and a splash of olive oil.

Serve in bowls, scattered with extra herb leaves.

Tips and swaps

Fruity couscous and lamb Add a small handful of dried fruits such as raisins, barberries or chopped unsulphured apricots. First soak the fruit in hot water or tea for about 10 minutes to plump it up a bit, then drain before stirring it into the couscous.

Minted quinoa and lamb Use quinoa in place of the couscous.

Swap the meat This dish gives a good second life to roast meats other than lamb – try it with chicken, beef or pork.

Lamb and onion bhajjis

A straightforward onion bhajji, served blisteringly hot with a cooling raita on the side, is one of life's great treats. Add a bit of shredded roast lamb (or chicken, or beef) and it makes an even more substantial starter or snack. MAKES ABOUT 16

60g gram (chickpea) flour

30g rice flour

1 teaspoon baking powder

1 teaspoon ground cumin

1 teaspoon ground coriander

½ teaspoon ground turmeric

Pinch of salt

2 onions (about 200g), halved and thinly sliced

50–100g roast lamb, finely shredded

Small handful of coriander leaves, roughly chopped

1 green chilli, membrane and seeds removed (for a milder version if preferred), finely chopped

Vegetable oil, for deep-frying

3 tablespoons lemon juice

1 tablespoon ghee (see page 108) or butter, melted

100–130ml sparkling water

Raita (see page 88) and/or chutney, to serve (optional)

Sift the flours, baking powder, ground spices and salt together into a large bowl. Add the onions, lamb, chopped coriander and chilli and toss until everything is well combined. (You want to add the bhajjis to the hot oil as soon as you've mixed them with the fizzy water so it's important to heat the oil next.)

Heat about a 7cm depth of oil in a deep-fat fryer or large, deep pan (it shouldn't come more than a third of the way up the pan) to 170°C, or until a cube of dry white bread dropped in turns golden in a minute.

Trickle the lemon juice and ghee or butter over the bhajji mixture and toss again. Slowly pour in the water, stirring gently as you go, until everything is coated in the batter, which should be a little thicker than double cream – thick enough to hold the bhajjis together, but not so thick that it will make them heavy.

To avoid crowding the pan, you will need to cook the bhajjis a few at a time. Carefully drop heaped teaspoonfuls or small dessertspoonfuls of the mixture into the hot oil (don't make them any bigger or they won't cook through).

Fry for about 3 minutes until cooked through and golden brown, then carefully lift out the bhajjis with a skimmer or slotted spoon and drain on kitchen paper. Keep warm while you cook the rest – let the oil come back up to temperature before adding more batter.

Serve the bhajjis right away with raita and/or your favourite chutney if you like.

Tips and swaps

Parsnip bhajjis Use shredded parsnips instead of, or in combination with, the onions.

Swap the meat You can use almost any roast meat in place of the lamb, and also make veggie ones using leftover roast roots, peas and beans, chopped spinach and greens.

Lamb, potato and mint sauce salad

This is a wonderfully quick but substantial salad. Use leftover cooked potatoes with the lamb if you have them, or cook them from scratch and dress in the mint sauce while they're still warm, so they absorb as much flavour as possible. SERVES 4

About 500g fresh or cooked new potatoes

3 tablespoons mint sauce

200–300g roast lamb, cut or torn into strips

About 100g cooked green beans

About 100g cooked peas

4–5 spring onions, finely chopped

Plenty of herbs, such as chervil, parsley, mint and/or dill, roughly chopped or torn (2–3 tablespoons of each)

Salt and freshly ground black pepper

If you're cooking the potatoes from scratch, scrub them, halve any larger ones and bring a pan of salted water to the boil. Add the potatoes to the water, bring back to the boil and cook until tender, 10–15 minutes.

Drain the potatoes, tip them into a bowl and toss in the mint sauce while still warm.

If you're using cooked potatoes, just cut into bite-sized chunks and toss in the mint sauce.

Add the beans, peas, spring onions and herbs. Toss to combine and season with salt and pepper. Toss again before serving.

Tips and swaps

No mint sauce? Instead, use a handful of freshly chopped mint and 1 tablespoon each wine or cider vinegar and olive oil, plus salt, pepper and a good pinch of sugar.

No spring onion? Use a little finely sliced red onion or finely diced shallot instead.

Swap the meat and sauce Try roast pork, potato and apple sauce; roast beef, potato and horseradish; or roast chicken with the potatoes dressed in thinned gravy. (Even the broken-up jellified gravy can be whisked into a simple vinaigrette to dress the salad.) Freshen with chopped herbs if you have some: parsley goes with any meat; lemon thyme is good with most things; mint is great with pork; tarragon or chervil with chicken; dill with beef.

Lancashire hot pot

This quick version of the slow-simmered classic is a great way to use leftover lamb and potatoes from a roast dinner. I cram in lots of carrots and onions to boost the flavour and make the whole thing more substantial. Leftover roast spuds are a tasty topping for any casserole, but if you don't have enough simply use thinly sliced raw potatoes in the traditional way. SERVES 4–6

2 tablespoons rendered lamb fat, butter or sunflower oil, plus extra to finish

3 onions, halved and thinly sliced

3 carrots, sliced

1 bay leaf

Sprig of thyme

1 tablespoon plain flour

500ml hot lamb, chicken or veg stock (see page 28, or a stock cube is fine), or a mix of stock and gravy

250–400g roast lamb, torn into large chunks

1 tablespoon Worcestershire sauce

250–300g roast potatoes, or thinly sliced raw potatoes

Salt and freshly ground black pepper

Preheat the oven to 200°C/Fan 180°C/Gas 6.

In a heavy-based casserole, heat the lamb fat or oil over a medium heat. Add the onions and carrots, bay leaf and thyme, plus a good pinch of salt. Sauté, stirring from time to time, until softened and the onions are just beginning to take on some colour, about 15 minutes.

Add the flour, stir well to work it into the veg, then slowly add the hot stock, or stock and gravy, stirring to combine it with the flour. Stir in the lamb and Worcestershire sauce, season with salt and plenty of pepper and simmer for about 10 minutes.

If you're using roast potatoes, rough slice if they are large. Layer them over the top of the lamb and veg and brush with a little lamb fat, melted butter or oil. Place in the oven for about 20 minutes, until everything is piping hot and bubbling. If you like, put the hot pot under the grill for a final few minutes to crisp up the top.

If using raw, sliced potatoes, arrange them over the top of the lamb, brush with a little lamb fat or melted butter, cover with a lid or foil and cook for about 40 minutes. Remove the cover and return to the oven for a further 20 minutes or so until the potatoes have crisped up.

Tips and swaps

Mushroomy version Add some sautéed thickly sliced mushrooms, to give the hotpot another dimension of flavour and texture.

Bulk up with pulses If you're low on meat, bung in a tin of chickpeas, cannellini or other beans, or lentils, to add texture as well as substance; rinse and drain well before adding.

Spicy lamb and chickpeas

This is my leftovers riff on a lamb kebab, and you can certainly assemble it in kebab form, if you have some pittas handy (see tips and swaps, below). Chickpeas and other pulses take on spices beautifully. If you cook them like this – until they're a little crisp – they're good on their own as a snack, or tossed with roasted veg, or sprinkled over a salad. SERVES 4–5 AS A STARTER OR SNACK, 2–3 AS A MAIN COURSE

2 x 400g tins chickpeas, drained and rinsed

2 tablespoons rapeseed, olive or sunflower oil

2 teaspoons ground cumin

1 teaspoon flaky sea salt

½ teaspoon ground coriander

½ teaspoon cayenne pepper

150–250g roast lamb, torn into small strips

For the raita

140g natural wholemilk yoghurt

2 tablespoons coarsely grated cucumber

¼–½ garlic clove, grated

Pinch of salt

To finish (optional)

Handful of dill fronds or coriander leaves, roughly torn

Preheat the oven to 200°C/Fan 180°C/Gas 6.

Put the chickpeas into a large roasting tin. Trickle over the oil and sprinkle with the cumin, flaky salt, coriander and cayenne. Toss until well coated then spread the chickpeas out in an even layer. Bake for 20 minutes, until golden and slightly crisp.

Take out the roasting tin and toss the strips of lamb with the chickpeas. Return to the oven for a further 10–15 minutes, stirring halfway through, until the lamb and chickpeas look crispy and appetising.

Meanwhile, for the raita, mix the yoghurt with the grated cucumber, garlic and salt.

Divide the spicy chickpeas and lamb between serving bowls. Spoon the raita to one side and scatter over the dill fronds or coriander, if using.

Serve with warmed flatbreads, if you like, to scoop everything up. A simple salad of finely shredded raw cabbage – dressed with lemon juice, olive oil, salt and pepper – is a good crunchy complement.

Tips and swaps

Kebab version For a portable, in-the-garden or on-the-go kebab version, you'll need pittas and the cabbage salad. Warm up one pitta per person in the oven or under the grill and slice open. Pile in a good handful of the dressed cabbage and a generous amount of the spiced lamb and chickpeas, then spoon over the raita. Add a dash of chilli sauce or chilli oil, and/or torn coriander, if you like. You could also add hummus (made saucy by adding a little water and lemon juice).

Shepherd's pie

My Mum's shepherd's pie was the dish that really made me fall in love with leftovers. As everyone knows, it's best made with cold, cooked roast lamb rather than raw minced lamb. You can put the cooked lamb through a mincer, but it's easier, I think, to pulse it in a food processor until coarsely chopped. Frying before pie-ing is vital to bring out even more meaty, lamby flavours.

Ideally, you want about a kilo of leftover lamb. If you don't have that much, bump up the veg so the overall weight works out about the same – you can add some leftover roast carrots or spuds, cut into chunks, or a handful of peas or beans if you like too. SERVES 6

2 tablespoons rapeseed or sunflower oil

500g–1kg roast lamb, roughly chopped

2 onions, chopped

2 carrots, finely diced

1 celery stick, finely diced

2 garlic cloves, grated or finely chopped

Any extra roast vegetables (see above)

Any meat juices or gravy saved from the joint, and/or concentrated lamb stock (see page 28), or a stock cube

About 125ml red wine

2 tablespoons Worcestershire sauce

2 tablespoons tomato ketchup or tomato purée

Salt and freshly ground black pepper

For the mash

1.2kg floury potatoes, such as Desiree or King Edward, peeled and cut into even-sized chunks

150ml whole milk (approximately)

120g butter

Preheat the oven to 200°C/Fan 180°C/Gas 6.

Heat 1 tablespoon of the oil in a large, heavy-based frying pan or wide saucepan over a medium-high heat. Add half of the meat and brown it well all over, then transfer to another dish. Repeat with the rest. (If your pan is small, you might need to do this in 3 batches.)

Lower the heat a bit and add the remaining oil to the empty pan. Add the onions with a good pinch of salt and sweat until softened and turning golden, stirring occasionally, about

15 minutes. Add the carrots, celery and garlic, and sauté for a couple of minutes.

Tip the meat back into the pan, adding any extra veg (except peas and beans), the juices, gravy or stock, wine, Worcestershire sauce, ketchup and some salt and pepper. Simmer gently for a few minutes, adding a little water if the mixture looks too thick or dry.

Taste for seasoning and add more ketchup, Worcestershire sauce, salt and/or pepper, if you like. Simmer gently for 20–30 minutes, until the flavours are well blended.

Meanwhile, for the mash, add the potatoes to a pan of well-salted water, bring to the boil and cook until tender. Drain in a colander and leave to steam for several minutes.

Heat the milk and butter in the pan almost to simmering. Take off the heat, add the potatoes and mash, adding a little more warm milk if needed, but don't make the mash too soft. Season with salt and pepper.

If using peas and beans, add them to the meat now. Taste and adjust the seasoning again if necessary, and add a splash more liquid if it seems a bit thick. Pile into an ovenproof dish, with room for the mash to go on top.

Spoon and spread the mash over the meat, covering it completely. Use a fork to rough up the surface.

Stand the pie dish on an oven tray and bake for 30–40 minutes, until the mash is browned and the sauce is bubbling up around the edges.

Leave the shepherd's pie to stand for a few minutes before serving.

Tips and swaps

Cottage pie Use chopped-up roast beef in place of the lamb.

Cheesy topping Sprinkle some grated Cheddar or other hard cheese over the mash before the dish goes into the oven. You can stir a bit into the mash too if you like – this works particularly well with cottage pie.

Cheaty version Cut the leftover lamb into strips and season well. Fry until crispy at the edges, remove from the pan and keep warm. Deglaze the pan with a bit of red wine and stock, then add a splash of Worcestershire sauce. Serve the highly seasoned lamb on creamy mash, with the pan juices poured over, and a squirt of ketchup if you must.

Chinese-style spicy crispy beef

This take-away classic is very easy to make at home with a few handfuls of leftover roast beef – a little really does go a long way when you ramp up the seasoning and spices. SERVES 4

250–400g roast beef, the rarer the better

Vegetable or groundnut oil, for frying

3 tablespoons cornflour

1 teaspoon Chinese five-spice powder (optional)

A little very finely grated orange zest

Pinch of flaky sea salt

For the sauce

3 tablespoons sweet chilli sauce

2 tablespoons soy sauce

1 garlic clove, grated

¼ teaspoon finely grated ginger

Juice of ½ orange

For the salad

Few crisp lettuce leaves, such as romaine (or even the much-maligned iceberg), finely shredded

1 carrot, julienned or grated

½ small cucumber, seeds scooped out, then cut into thin batons

3 spring onions, trimmed and finely sliced, slightly on the bias

1 tablespoon rice wine vinegar

To finish

Handful of sesame seeds, lightly toasted if preferred

Sprigs of coriander (optional)

First make the sauce. Put all the ingredients into a small pan, simmer for a couple of minutes until thickened, then set aside.

Cut the beef into strips, 3–4mm thick. Heat a 2–3cm depth of oil in a wok or a deep saucepan – the fat will bubble up when you add the beef, so don't use a shallow pan. Heat the oil to 180°C, or until a cube of dry white bread dropped in turns golden in just under a minute.

Sift the cornflour and five-spice powder, if using, onto a plate. Toss the beef strips in the cornflour until well coated on all sides.

Fry the beef in a couple of batches to avoid crowding the pan. Lower into the hot oil and fry until golden and crisp, which should only take a couple of minutes. Scoop out with a slotted spoon and place on kitchen paper to drain. Let the oil come back up to temperature before adding the second batch of meat to the pan.

Mix the orange zest with the flaky sea salt and sprinkle over the beef.

For the salad, toss the vegetables together with the rice wine vinegar.

Pile the salad and crispy beef onto individual plates. Trickle on the sauce and add a scattering of sesame seeds. Garnish with coriander if you have some to hand.

Tips and swaps

Spicy beef and peppers Add a handful of finely sliced red or yellow peppers, if you have them.

Noodly version Serve the salad over noodles with the sauce trickled over and finished with the sesame seeds and coriander.

Spicy meat garnish You can use strips of roast beef – or pork, chicken or duck – fried like this in a spicy cornflour coating, to finish all manner of salads or soups.

Chilli beef noodles

I sometimes use black rice noodles in this dish as they look particularly dramatic against the bright red peppers and vibrant green vegetables, but you can use any noodles you like – egg, buckwheat, even instant rice vermicelli noodles work well. SERVES 2

80g noodles (see above)

30g peanuts or cashew nuts, roughly chopped

1 tablespoon rapeseed or sunflower oil

2 garlic cloves, halved and thinly sliced

Knob of ginger, about 3cm, peeled and cut into thin strips

1–2 red or green chilli(es), halved, membrane and seeds removed (for a milder version if preferred), thinly sliced

6–8 spring onions, trimmed and cut into 1cm slices on the diagonal

1 red pepper, cored, deseeded and thinly sliced

1 small courgette, thinly sliced or cut into batons

About 100g mangetout, fine green beans, peas, broad beans, or a mix

About 100g roast beef, cut or torn into thin strips

Handful of baby spinach leaves

1 tablespoon soy sauce, plus extra to serve

2 teaspoons fish sauce

Generous handful of coriander leaves, roughly chopped

8–10 mint leaves, shredded

Trickle of toasted sesame oil, to finish

Lime wedges, to serve

Cook the noodles according to the package instructions. Drain, rinse and set aside.

In a small pan, dry-fry the nuts over a medium heat until lightly toasted, then tip onto a plate to stop them cooking further.

Heat the oil in a wok or large frying pan over a medium-high heat. Add the garlic, ginger and chilli and fry for a minute, stirring.

Add the spring onions, red pepper, courgette, mangetout, beans, and/or peas and sauté for a minute.

Now add the beef, spinach and noodles. Toss to combine, then add the soy and fish sauces. Cook, tossing and turning everything, just until the beef is heated through. Stir in the coriander, mint and toasted nuts.

Finish with a little sesame oil. Serve straight away, with lime wedges and extra soy sauce on the table for everyone to help themselves.

Tips and swaps

Throw in salad leaves If you have some slightly limp lettuce leaves, shred them and add with, or instead of, the spinach. You can even use previously dressed leaves here – just blot off any excess dressing with kitchen paper first.

Swap the meat Leftover roast pork, chicken, duck or rabbit can be used with equal success.

Pea and ham soup

This is one of the simplest soups I know, and also one of the most delicious. It makes excellent use of the stock left over from boiling a ham and any remaining bits of the beast itself. The stock can be quite salty so check before adding it and dilute it with a bit of water if you need to. SERVES 4

25g butter

1 large onion, diced

1 bay leaf

100ml white wine (optional)

About 1 litre ham stock, left over from boiling a ham, or chicken or veg stock (see page 28)

About 400g fresh or frozen peas

100–200g cooked ham, torn into shards (100g is enough, 200g is a feast)

Salt and freshly ground black pepper

To finish

Crème fraîche and/or rapeseed oil (optional)

Chervil or flat-leaf parsley

Heat the butter in a medium saucepan over a medium-low heat. When it stops foaming, add the onion, bay leaf and a pinch of salt and sauté gently, stirring from time to time, until the onion is very soft, about 15 minutes.

If you're using the wine, add it now and let it simmer away until it has almost completely evaporated. (I don't always do this – it's good without – but I do if I have a glass to hand, or actually in my hand, as it adds a rather nice edge to the broth.)

Next, add the stock and bring it to a simmer. Add the peas and cook until tender; check after 4 minutes. Remove the bay leaf.

Allow the soup to cool slightly, then blitz in a food processor or with a stick blender until smooth. Return to the pan, add most of the ham and warm through. Taste and adjust the seasoning with more pepper and a little extra salt if necessary.

Serve in warmed bowls, with the extra bits of ham scattered over the top. Just before you bring the soup to the table, dot with the crème fraîche and/or rapeseed oil if you like and scatter over the chervil or parsley.

Tips and swaps

Ham, pea and pasta broth Instead of puréeing the soup, leave as a clear broth and add some small pasta, such as orzo or ditalini, with the peas. You could add a diced carrot and a diced celery stick when you sauté the onions too. Stir in a few tablespoons of chopped parsley and a couple of shredded mint leaves right at the end.

Pork in rosemary cream sauce

With its slightly old-fashioned but nonetheless delicious cream and mustard sauce, this is a rather elegant ending for leftover bits of roast pork. The rosemary is particularly good here – in fact, added with a light hand, it makes an excellent alternative to sage in many pork dishes. SERVES 4

25g butter

2 leeks, white and very pale green part only, thinly sliced (keep the rest for stock)

1 carrot, diced

1 celery stick, diced

1 bay leaf

2 small sprigs of rosemary (each about 4cm)

1 small garlic clove, finely chopped

About 150ml white wine, dry sherry or vermouth

500ml chicken stock (see page 28)

250–400g roast pork, cut or torn into chunks

150ml cream or crème fraîche (this can be quite mature)

1 tablespoon wholegrain mustard

Salt and freshly ground black pepper

Heat the butter in a medium, heavy-based casserole over a medium-low heat. When it stops foaming, add the leeks, carrot, celery, bay leaf, one of the rosemary sprigs and a pinch of salt. Sauté gently, stirring from time, until everything is softened, about 10 minutes. Add the garlic and sauté for another minute.

Pour in the wine, sherry or vermouth and simmer until it's almost completely evaporated, then pour in the stock. Bring to a simmer, add the pork and season with salt and pepper. Cook for about 15 minutes, then remove from the heat. Take out and discard the rosemary sprig and bay leaf.

Whisk the cream or crème fraîche and mustard together in a small bowl and then stir in a ladleful of the hot cooking liquid. Return the pan to a very gentle heat and slowly pour the cream mixture back in, stirring as you go. Don't let it boil or the sauce may curdle.

Strip the rosemary leaves from the other sprig and chop them finely – you don't need more than ½ teaspoon as the flavour is quite strong. Stir the chopped rosemary into the sauce and season with salt and pepper to taste.

Serve warm, with mash and perhaps some Savoy cabbage.

Tips and swaps

Creamy pork and pasta If you chop up the pork into smaller pieces, this makes a very good sauce for pasta.

Pork and rosemary pie Like many casseroles, this is a great pie filling (see page 46).

Swap the meat This recipe also works brilliantly with chicken and rabbit. Add a handful of peas towards the end of cooking too, if you like.

LEFTOVER FISH

In my hierarchy of leftovers, fish rides high; in fact, it's right at the top of the list. Given the preciousness of it as a resource, the perils of getting it to shore and the rightful expense of buying it, I don't want to waste even a morsel.

For that reason, I have over the years developed ways of using every scrap of fish at my disposal. I start with (or more often, end with) the skeleton: heads and bones can, of course, be used in stocks and soups (see page 116), but they can be stars of a dish too – see my spicy crispy skeletons on page 104.

Fish skin, meanwhile, carries so much flavour that I *never* toss it – I've even been known to collect it from people's plates, after a meal, without the merest blush of shame. Roasted or fried, it transforms into fish skin 'scratchings', which make a great little snack or garnish for salads as well as a kind of piscine crispy 'bacon' for sandwiches (see page 106).

Smoked fish has always been a favourite of mine. Its intensity of flavour is a highly desirable leftovers attribute: a small amount packs a lot of punch. That means you don't need much – and, let's face it, if you're dealing with fishy

leftovers, you probably won't have a lot. In fact, I think of leftover smoked fish almost as a seasoning – its smokiness adding depth and savour to the whole, without being the star event in itself. Dishes like the smoky fish gratin on page 118 illustrate just what I mean.

So keen am I on leftover fish and its myriad culinary uses, that it's one of those ingredients I quite often cook as a 'planned-over', not least because it's very much easier to part flesh from bone when it's still warm than wait until the next day. So, if you have some fresh raw fish that needs using but you're not sure what you want to do with it yet, get cracking and cook it.

Store properly after cooking (cool quickly, then keep in a sealed container in the fridge) to buy yourself an extra couple of days to decide upon some delicious use for it. Try flaking it onto salads, soups or blinis (see page 110), folding it into tasty, spicy tacos (see page 112), or creating some potted fish (see page 108). 'Cold fish' may not be the sexiest phrase in the book, but this stuff is leftovers gold – and you'll have no trouble transforming it into dishes that'll get a very warm reception indeed.

Freewheeling fishcakes

One of the things I love about this easy recipe is its adaptability. All manner of cooked fish can be used, including white fish such as pollack, coley or sustainably caught haddock (even the remnants of a fish supper from the chippie), mackerel and sardines (freshly cooked or tinned and drained).

I used to think that you should never have more potato than fish in a fishcake, but in these more freewheeling days, I'm not so worried about that. As long as I have fish equivalent to at least half the weight of the spud, then I'm good to go. SERVES 2, OR 4 AS A STARTER

250–400g mash or baked potato flesh (ideally mash should not be too smooth or creamy)

2–3 tablespoons finely chopped parsley or chives

1 tablespoon capers, roughly chopped if large, left whole if tiny

About 200g boned and skinned cooked fish (see above), broken into flakes

1 egg, lightly beaten

About 50g plain flour

Salt and freshly ground black pepper

For the crumb coating (optional)

1 egg, lightly beaten

Handful of breadcrumbs

For frying

Vegetable oil

Knob of butter

Put the mashed potato into a bowl and stir in the chopped parsley or chives and capers. Season well with salt and pepper and stir again.

Using a spatula, gently fold in the flaked fish and moisten with the egg. You may not need all of it – you don't want the mixture to be too wet. (Any unused beaten egg can go to the dipping egg for the coating.)

Divide the mixture into four and gently shape, with floured or wet hands, into flat round cakes, 3–4cm thick.

Place the fishcakes on a plate and refrigerate for 30 minutes; this helps firm them up before crumbing. If you're skipping that, just dust them lightly in seasoned flour and they're ready to fry, or they can be chilled for a few hours before using.

If you're crumbing the cakes, put the flour into a bowl and season well with salt and pepper. Put the beaten egg in a second bowl and the breadcrumbs in a third. Carefully dip each fishcake in flour, then in the egg and finally in the breadcrumbs. Press the eggy cake gently into the crumb, turn over, and repeat. Transfer carefully to a plate or board.

Pour about a 2mm layer of oil into a large non-stick frying pan. Add the butter and place over a medium-high heat. When hot, gently place the fishcakes in the pan and cook for 4–5 minutes on each side until golden brown and piping hot in the middle.

Serve immediately, with a leafy salad.

Tips and swaps

Spice them up A little curry paste or powder is a good alternative seasoning, especially if you're using smoked fish leftovers.

Add anchovy If you have a couple of anchovy fillets lurking in the fridge, chop them finely and stir into the fishcake mix to add piquancy.

Change the coating For a finer coating, swap the breadcrumbs for fine cornmeal, panko breadcrumbs or matzo meal, omitting the flour and egg. Simply season the coating well with salt and pepper and use it to coat the fishcakes evenly all over.

Spicy crispy fish skeletons

These are a great way to use up the backbones of fresh mackerel or sardines left over after filleting; they look pretty dramatic too! You can also use cooked skeletons retrieved from baked or barbecued whole mackerel or sardines (but not the hard skeletons from big fish like bass and pollack).

Though they're delicious and perfectly safe to eat, they are not something I would share with very small children.

3–4 mackerel skeletons, including the tail

For the seasoned flour

50g plain flour

2 teaspoons soft thyme leaves, roughly chopped

1 teaspoon dried chilli flakes

1 teaspoon cumin seeds, bashed a bit, or a generous pinch of ground cumin

Finely grated zest of 1 lemon

Freshly ground black pepper

For frying

Vegetable oil

To serve

Flaky sea salt

Lemon wedges

Chilli dipping sauce (optional)

Mix together all the ingredients for the seasoned flour in a bowl and tip onto a plate.

Bring a pan of water to the boil. Add the fish skeletons and blanch for 7–10 minutes to soften them slightly and strip them of any flesh still clinging to the bones. Drain in a colander then toss them in the seasoned flour to coat.

In a deep saucepan, wide enough to fit the length of the skeletons comfortably, heat a 4–5cm depth of oil to 180°C, or until a cube of dry white bread dropped into the oil turns golden in just under a minute.

Add the floured skeletons and fry until crisp and golden – this should only take a couple of minutes. Carefully remove them from the oil with tongs and lay on kitchen paper to drain.

Eat immediately, with a sprinkling of salt and a squeeze of lemon. They are also good with a hot and sweet chilli dipping sauce.

Crispy fish skin 'bacon' sandwich

This is a by-product of my enthusiasm for making sushi and sashimi from fresh catches of bream, pollack, trout and bass. The skin and flesh trimmings of these (or any) fish are simply too good to waste. Crisply fried and well seasoned, they become delectable morsels – the bacon of the fish world. Any fresh fish skin will work – you could even ask your fishmonger to save some for you (it can be frozen). The fish needs to be descaled, which is most easily done when it is still whole. Any flesh left on the inside of the skin is a good thing – don't scrape it off.

This mouth-watering sarny, topped with tartare sauce, gives crispy fish skin star billing. MAKES 2

At least 4 strips of fish skin, each about the size of a postcard, plus any boneless, fleshy fish trimmings

2 teaspoons rapeseed or sunflower oil

Salt and freshly ground black pepper

For the tartare sauce

3 tablespoons mayonnaise

1 tablespoon roughly chopped parsley

1 teaspoon chopped dill or chervil

2–3 gherkins, finely chopped

2 teaspoons capers, finely chopped

1–2 hard-boiled eggs, finely chopped

Good squeeze of lemon juice

To assemble

2 soft white or brown rolls, or 4 slices good fresh bread

Slick of butter, softened

First make the tartare sauce. Mix together all the ingredients and season with salt and pepper to taste. Set aside.

To cook the fish skin and trimmings, heat the oil in a non-stick frying pan over a medium-high heat. Season the fish bits generously with salt and pepper. Put them in the pan and press the skins down with a spatula straight away, so they don't curl up too much.

Fry, turning occasionally, until the skin and the bits of fish are golden and crisp: cook more than you normally would a piece of fish, to maximise the crispiness, but don't let them burn. Drain on kitchen paper and season with a bit more salt and pepper if necessary.

Lightly butter the rolls or bread slices. Pile up the crispy fish bits on the bases and spoon on a generous dollop of tartare sauce. Press the top on your sandwich and eat straight away.

Tips and swaps

BLT version Use plain mayo and add a few crisp lettuce leaves and some tomato slices.

Fish skin 'scratchings' Either season the fish skin and fry it as above or put it into a roasting tin and roast for 20–30 minutes at 180°C/Fan 160°C/Gas 4, until crisp, turning after about 15 minutes. Serve with a dollop of tartare sauce or mayo. A great snack with a cold beer or cider.

Potted smoked fish

This is a quick way to preserve bits and pieces of leftover cooked smoked fish for another dinner, another day. Try it with whatever smoked fish you have: mackerel, kippers, haddock, pollack or trout are all good. You can also use cooked leftovers of unsmoked but full-flavoured oily fish, like mackerel, sardines and trout. The recipe is easily scale-up-able, depending on how much fish you have, but you only need to increase the butter a little. SERVES 2–3

200–300g cooked smoked fish, broken into flakes

1 tablespoon chopped dill

1 tablespoon chopped parsley

Good squeeze of lemon juice

Pinch of cayenne pepper

Clarified butter or ghee, made from about 150g butter (see below), melted

Salt and freshly ground black pepper

To serve

Brown toast

Lemon wedges

Carefully pick over the fish for any small bones, then put the flakes into a bowl with the herbs, lemon juice and cayenne.

Trickle over about three-quarters of the clarified butter and fold everything together gently with a rubber spatula – don't mush it up too much. Taste and season with salt and pepper.

Spoon the mixture into a spotlessly clean bowl, large ramekin(s) or Le Parfait-type jar and press it down lightly with a fork.

Pour over the remaining clarified butter or ghee, giving the container(s) a sharp tap on the work surface to help eliminate any air pockets. Cover or seal and refrigerate.

The potted fish will keep for a couple of days in a bowl or ramekin, up to a week in a sealed jar. Bring it to room temperature about 30 minutes before serving, with warm brown toast and wedges of lemon.

Clarified butter/ghee

Great for extending the potential of butter that's slightly on the turn, these are also good solutions if you find you have more unsalted butter than you are likely to use. Sealed in a jar in the fridge, they can last for weeks, possibly months if you take care of them.

Clarified butter and ghee both have a higher smoke point than whole butter as the milk solids are removed, making them ideal for frying. They can also add buttery flavour to pasta, rice or other dishes, or be used as here to seal potted fish (or meat). About 1kg butter will yield 800g ghee or clarified butter.

To cook up a batch, warm the butter gently in a saucepan. The solids will drop to the bottom and foam will rise to the top. At this point, if you're making clarified butter, take it off the heat and let it sit for a minute. Skim off any foam and pour through a strainer lined with muslin into a clean jar. Seal and store in the fridge until needed.

To make ghee, simply proceed as above but let the butter cook for longer, until the clear butter is golden. Be careful not to let the solids at the bottom of the pan brown. Jar up as for clarified butter.

Tips and swaps

Spike with horseradish Add about 1 teaspoon creamed horseradish sauce to the mixture if you want to give it a bit of bite.

Speedy version For a near-instant un-potted take on this, for immediate consumption, simply mix the fish flakes up with a dollop of crème fraîche, some chopped herbs if you have them, and perhaps some chopped capers and/ or cornichons.

Fishy blinis with sauerkraut cream

This is a terrific way to give a little leftover fish a rather smart second outing, as a platter of delicious canapés. MAKES ABOUT 20

100–200g cooked white or oily fish, flaked

Salt and freshly ground black pepper

For the sauerkraut cream

30g prepared sauerkraut, drained and roughly chopped

4 tablespoons crème fraîche

1 teaspoon creamed horseradish

For the blinis

150g buckwheat flour

1 teaspoon baking powder

Pinch of salt

125ml beer, such as IPA

1 large egg, lightly beaten

1 tablespoon rapeseed or sunflower oil, plus extra for frying

To finish

Sprigs of dill or chopped flat-leaf parsley

For the sauerkraut cream, mix the ingredients together and season with a couple of grinds of black pepper. Set aside.

To make the blinis, put the flour, baking powder and salt into a bowl and whisk to combine. Make a well in the centre and slowly pour in the beer, egg and oil, whisking as you go. Keep whisking until you have a smooth batter. It should be quite thick, so it will hold its own shape and not spread out too much when you pour it into the pan – if it's too thick, just add a splash of water or milk.

Place a non-stick frying pan over a medium heat and brush with oil. When hot, drop in small ladlefuls of the batter, making each blini about 5cm across. Cook for 1–1½ minutes, until each one starts to rise and bubbles are showing on the surface. Flip over and cook for another 1–2 minutes until golden brown on both sides and cooked through. Remove to a warmed plate.

Repeat with the remaining batter, brushing the pan with a little more oil as you go. Keep the cooked ones warm as you complete the rest.

Put a spoonful of the sauerkraut cream on each blini, top with the flaked fish and add a grinding of black pepper. Finish with sprigs of dill or chopped parsley. Serve at once.

Tips and swaps

Using beer in the batter gives the blinis character, but you can use milk if you prefer.

Spicy fish tacos

This classic street food of Mexico's Baja peninsula is usually made with fried fish, but it's also a very tasty way to use up leftover cooked fish, whether it's fried, barbecued, poached or grilled. I've even made extremely tasty tacos with the remains of take-away fish and chips. **SERVES 2**

200–300g cooked fish, broken into large flakes, any bones removed

Generous pinch of ground cumin

Generous pinch of cayenne pepper

Squeeze of lime juice

Salt and freshly ground black pepper

For the salsa

1 small red onion, halved

1–2 ripe tomatoes, deseeded and diced

1 small garlic clove, finely chopped

1 jalapeño or other medium-hot green chilli, halved, membrane and seeds removed (for a milder salsa if preferred), finely chopped

3 tablespoons roughly chopped coriander leaves

Pinch of sugar

1–2 teaspoons rapeseed or olive oil

To serve

Soft flour tortillas

1 avocado, cut into slices

Small handful of coriander leaves (optional)

Lime wedges

Tabasco or other hot sauce (optional)

Put the fish flakes into a bowl, sprinkle with the cumin and cayenne, squeeze on a little lime juice and season with salt and pepper. Turn over gently with a rubber spatula.

For the salsa, dice one onion half finely (you only need 1–2 tablespoons).

Thinly slice the other onion half and soak in a bowl of iced water for about 10 minutes to mellow the flavour. Drain, pat dry on kitchen paper and set aside for serving.

Mix the diced onion with the tomatoes, garlic, chilli, coriander, sugar and just enough oil to moisten the salsa. Taste and season with salt and pepper.

Warm the tortillas according to the package instructions. Pile the fish on top of the tortillas, along with dollops of the salsa, the avocado, red onion slices and coriander.

Roll up your tortillas and serve at once, with lime wedges, and hot sauce on the side for heat freaks.

Tips and swaps

Add shellfish Toss some cooked mussels or bits of squid in with the fish if you have them.

Add crunch If you have some white cabbage knocking about, finely shred a few leaves and scatter over the tacos with the onion.

Tostadas (as shown) Heat the tortillas for longer, until slightly crispy at the edges, then pile everything on top and tuck in, rather than roll up.

Mackerel with Puy lentils and parsley

Rich, oily mackerel pairs particularly well with earthy lentils and the sharp bite of red onion in this simple, tasty salad. SERVES 2 AS A MAIN COURSE, 4 AS A STARTER

150–250g cooked mackerel, broken into flakes

1 small red onion, or ½ large one, halved and finely sliced

150–200g cooked Puy lentils

2 tablespoons roughly chopped flat-leaf parsley, plus extra to finish

Sprig of dill or tarragon, chopped, or a few basil leaves, roughly shredded (optional)

Salt and freshly ground black pepper

For the dressing

2 tablespoons rapeseed or olive oil

1 tablespoon cider vinegar or lemon juice

½ teaspoon mustard

To serve (optional)

Lemon wedges

In a bowl, gently combine the mackerel, onion, lentils and herbs, trying not to break up the fish too much – it's nicer if you keep it in flakes. Taste and season well with salt and pepper.

For the dressing, shake the oil, cider vinegar or lemon juice and mustard together in a screw-topped jar to combine and season to taste with salt and pepper. Trickle the dressing over the salad and toss gently.

Scatter some more chopped parsley over the salad and serve with lemon wedges on the side, if you like.

Tips and swaps

Party canapés Spoon the salad onto crostini.

Open sandwich If you don't have enough leftover mackerel for a full salad, use the assembly as a topping, especially on rye bread. Chop the onion quite finely and toss together with the fish, lentils and herbs, adding just enough mayonnaise to bind everything together. Season well with salt and pepper and serve with lemon wedges.

Fish head soup

This is essentially a good fish stock, made with the heads (and bones if you like), bulked up with some lovely veg, and finished with the best fleshy pickings of the fish. You can often get fish heads free from the harbourside or your fishmonger if you are a regular customer. You want the fish trimmings you use to be spanking fresh, but apart from that, this is simplicity itself and endlessly customisable.

I've made great versions of this with the heads of pollack, coley, haddock, gurnard, bass, grey mullet and even large trout. Very oily fish like mackerel and sardines are best avoided. SERVES 4

1½ tablespoons rapeseed or olive oil, or 20g butter

1 onion, chopped

1 celery stick, chopped

1 carrot, chopped

2 fennel bulbs, core and tough outer leaves removed, finely sliced (any fronds saved)

150g new potatoes, scrubbed and cut into 5mm dice

3–4 good size fish heads (see above), plus fish skeletons and trimmings if available

1 or 2 bay leaves, 2 or 3 thyme sprigs and a few parsley stalks, tied together with kitchen string

1 tablespoon lemon juice

2 tablespoons finely chopped parsley

Salt and freshly ground black pepper

To serve

2–3 tablespoons crème fraîche (optional)

Reserved fennel fronds or chopped parsley

Heat the oil or butter in a large heavy-based saucepan over a medium-low heat. Add the onion, celery and carrot with a pinch of salt and sauté very gently until softened, about 10 minutes. Add the fennel and potatoes and continue to cook gently, stirring, until they're slightly softened, about 5 minutes. Meanwhile, rinse all the fish trimmings.

Add the fish trimmings to the pan, along with the herb bundle. Add just enough cold water to cover – no more than 1.5 litres. Bring to a very gentle simmer and skim off any scum that rises to the surface. Let the soup simmer very gently for about 15 minutes, until the veg are tender. Don't let it boil hard as this can taint its flavour.

Remove from the heat. Scoop out and discard the bundle of herbs, then scoop out the fish heads and any skeletons or skin onto a board. Discard the skin and leave the heads and bones to cool a little.

Pick off the fish, discarding the bones and any shreds of skin as you go. You'll find some surprisingly generous little caches of fish flesh around the cheeks, lips and 'shoulders' (where the head was cut off) and a few morsels on the skeletons too. Set the fish bits aside.

Reheat the pan of vegetable-y fish soup, if necessary, and stir in the lemon juice and chopped parsley. Taste and season with salt and pepper.

Distribute the salvaged fish morsels between warmed bowls and ladle over the veg and soup. Finish with some crème fraîche if you like, and scatter the chopped fennel fronds or parsley over the soup.

Tips and swaps

If you don't have enough fish heads and skeletons to make the stock straight away, collect them in the freezer until you have assembled enough.

Veg options As well as, or instead of, the fennel, try adding finely chopped skinned, deseeded tomatoes, a handful of peas or sweetcorn, or some finely shredded, not-quite-good-enough-to-eat-raw lettuce. All of these are best added at the end of cooking.

Creamy smoky fish and spinach gratin

Surely one of the most gratifying of all comfort foods, the gratin is the quintessential 'bit of this, bit of that' dish that lends itself beautifully to leftovers. Just add a seasonal green salad and you'll have a delicious dinner. SERVES 4

1 teaspoon rapeseed or sunflower oil, plus extra to oil the dish

1 small onion, diced

Sprig of thyme (optional)

½ glass of wine (optional)

About 200g prepped spinach or chard leaves, roughly chopped

About 500g cooked potatoes, mashed, or in crumbled pieces (if roasted or boiled)

150ml cream or crème fraîche

Few gratings of nutmeg

200–300g smoked fish, such as mackerel, kippers, haddock or pollack, broken into large flakes

Salt and freshly ground black pepper

For the topping

40g breadcrumbs

40g Cheddar, Parmesan or Emmenthal cheese, grated

Preheat the oven to 200°C/Fan 180°C/Gas 6. Lightly oil an ovenproof dish, about 28cm in diameter.

Heat the oil in a medium-large, heavy-based saucepan over a medium-low heat. Add the onion, thyme, if using, and a good pinch of salt and sauté gently, until the onion is softened, about 15 minutes.

Pour in the wine (or half a glass of water) and bring to a simmer. Add the spinach or chard leaves, put the lid on and cook for a minute or two, until the greens are just wilted.

Remove from the heat and add the potatoes and cream or crème fraîche. Stir to combine and season with nutmeg, salt and pepper. Gently fold through the fish, then taste and adjust the seasoning.

Tip the fish mixture into the oven dish. Toss the breadcrumbs and cheese together and sprinkle over the top. Bake for 25 minutes until golden and bubbling.

Leave to stand for several minutes to cool slightly before serving, with a crisp green salad.

Tips and swaps

Veg options You can add other veg, as well as or instead of the spinach, such as halved cherry tomatoes, chopped spring onions, leftover roast roots and cooked peas.

Jansson's temptation version Sauté the onions in the oil from a small tin of anchovies until softened, then add sliced cooked potatoes (not mash) and stir in the chopped anchovies from the tin, plus your flaked smoked fish leftovers. Season with pepper. Tip into the prepared gratin dish, trickle over a few tablespoonfuls of cream or crème fraîche and bake as for the gratin, for about 20–25 minutes until crisp and golden on top. Irresistible.

LEFTOVER ROOTS

I don't think I can remember a day when I haven't cooked with one root vegetable or another, whether chopped up and tossed in with the onions at the beginning of a soup or stew, grated into a salad or roasted with bay and thyme and a slick of oil.

Inexpensive, good for you, always in season in one form or another, and so forgiving to cook, I am pretty much in thrall to this multifaceted gang of veg. Carrots, celeriac, beetroot, spuds (strictly tubers, but at home here) and parsnips – not to mention the odd turnip, Jerusalem artichoke and swede – often form the earthy heart of the things I like to eat. So, for me, a kitchen that harbours no root veg at all is a fairly unthinkable state of affairs.

The pleasure of creating a panful of creamy, buttery mashed potato, or filling a roasting tin with gloriously coloured roots and green herbs, is often increased by the knowledge that I have (accidentally on purpose) over-catered. There are so many things that can be done with leftover root veg that I think I'd be mad not to.

Mash has myriad uses: in potato cakes (see page 132), for instance, or as the topping for various pies, shepherd's and otherwise. And it's to roast roots that I turn most often when I really want to add both flavour and heft to my leftovers dishes.

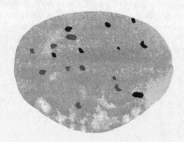

The charred edges of oven-cooked veg have such a sweet-savoury intensity that they can give an amazing jump-start to even the simplest of recipes, such as the roast root hummus on page 124 or the roast carrot pâté on page 122, and can hold their own in quick assemblies like the curried coconutty roots (see page 138).

I've even harnessed the natural sugars in some roots (notably carrots, beetroot and parsnips), so deliciously emphasised once they're roasted, to create a couple of sweet treats: beetroot and caraway seed cake on page 146 and carrot and ginger steamed pudding on page 144.

It's roots that have inspired some of the most engagingly thrifty recipes in this book too, tempting me to experiment and explore when previously I might have headed for the compost bin. Root vegetable peelings, it turns out, can be spun into surprisingly sophisticated soups (see page 126) or the sort of crisps (see page 130) that vie with the poshest of bar snacks.

And forgotten oddments of not-yet-cooked veg that are no longer in the first flush of youth can be treated with a quick pickling (see page 142) that transforms them into something very toothsome indeed.

So keep these earthy, subterranean stars on your radar, and you'll never find yourself rooting about for inspiration.

Roast carrot pâté

This is a very good, simple starter, snack or lunchbox treat that you can vary according to your own tastes and whims. If you are not keen on the taste of caraway, use cumin or coriander seeds instead. Toasting and grinding your own spice gives maximum depth of flavour, but it's fine to use ready-ground spices too. **SERVES 2–4 AS A STARTER OR SNACK**

¼ teaspoon caraway seeds

About 150g cream cheese

50–200g roast carrots

Finely grated zest of ½ lemon, plus a squeeze of juice

1–2 teaspoons finely chopped dill fronds

Salt and freshly ground black pepper

Put the caraway seeds in a small frying pan over a medium-high heat and lightly toast until fragrant, about 20–30 seconds. Using a pestle and mortar, bash the seeds to a coarse powder.

Put the cream cheese, roast carrots, ground caraway and the lemon zest and juice into a food processor and pulse until just combined – the pâté should still have some texture to it. Alternatively, you can do this in a bowl with a potato masher.

Fold in the chopped dill and season with salt and pepper to taste.

Serve with crusty bread, toasted sourdough or crudités.

Tips and swaps

Scandinavian twist (as shown) For a great open sandwich, spread on toasted sourdough, top with flaked cooked mackerel and finish with a grinding of pepper and some extra dill.

Fiery version Add some finely chopped green chilli or a sprinkling of dried chilli flakes or hot curry powder and/or trickle over some chilli oil just before serving.

Roast parsnip pâté Simply replace the carrots with parsnips. Or you can use a combination of root veg.

Roast root hummus

This is a great snack or starter, served with crudités or warm flatbreads, or spooned into toasted pittas with salad and/or some shredded cold meat. Use whatever leftover roast roots are to hand, and if you have some roast onions or garlic, chuck those in too. SERVES 2–4

400g tin chickpeas, drained and rinsed

100–300g roast roots, such as carrots, parsnips, celeriac and perhaps some roast onion

Juice of 1 small lemon

2 tablespoons tahini or thick natural wholemilk yoghurt

2 tablespoons olive or rapeseed oil, plus extra to finish

1–2 garlic cloves, finely chopped

½ teaspoon cumin seeds, bashed, or a good pinch of ground cumin, plus extra to finish (optional)

Good pinch of dried chilli flakes, plus extra to finish (optional)

Salt and freshly ground black pepper

In a food processor, whiz the chickpeas, roots, lemon juice, tahini or yoghurt, oil, garlic, cumin and chilli flakes together until fairly smooth. If it's too thick, thin with some hot water until you get the consistency you like.

Season to taste with salt and pepper. To serve, spoon the hummus into a bowl or onto a plate, sprinkle with a good pinch of crushed cumin seeds and chilli flakes, if you like, and trickle on some olive or rapeseed oil.

Sealed in a container, this hummus keeps well in the fridge for up to a week.

Tips and swaps

You can use leftover home-cooked chickpeas here if you like: 250g cooked peas is roughly equivalent to what you get in a 400g tin.

If you don't have any chickpeas, cannellini or butter beans work well too.

Potato peel soup

I understand that this might be a tough sell. But bear with me because it's miraculous. There's nothing humble about this soup's rich, creamy flavour – it tastes, remarkably, like mushrooms. And if it seems just a little too pared-back, it's very easy to jazz it up with some nice finishing touches (see below). Make sure the potatoes are well scrubbed before you peel them so the peels are very clean. SERVES 4

20g butter, or rapeseed or sunflower oil

1 large or 2 medium onions, diced

1 bay leaf

About 200g potato peelings (about as much as you'd get from preparing a decent-sized tray of roast potatoes)

500ml whole milk

500ml chicken or veg stock (see page 28)

2 tablespoons finely chopped parsley leaves (optional)

Salt and freshly ground black pepper

To finish (optional)

Fried sage leaves

Crisp-grilled bacon

Heat the butter or oil in a medium saucepan over a medium-low heat and add the onions, bay leaf and a good pinch of salt. Sauté gently, until the onions are soft but haven't taken on much colour, about 10 minutes.

Add the potato peelings and give everything a very good stir for a minute.

Pour in the milk and stock, season well with salt and pepper and bring to the boil. Reduce the heat and simmer gently until the peels are very tender – another 10 minutes or so.

Remove from the heat and cool slightly, then purée in a food processor, blender or using a stick blender until very smooth.

Return the soup to the pan and reheat gently. Season well with salt and pepper and stir in the chopped parsley, if using.

Serve in warmed bowls, topped with fried sage leaves and shards of crisp-grilled bacon, if you like. Finish with a generous grinding of pepper.

Tips and swaps

Top with an egg Float a poached egg on each portion and sprinkle the crispy bacon on top of it, if you like.

Chowder-y option Add a handful of cooked sweetcorn and some leftover smoked fish or cooked ham or bacon.

Parsnip or carroty version You can use other root peelings as well as potatoes – especially parsnips and carrots. But keep it 50 per cent spud or it can become too sweet. A good pinch of cumin goes well with a multi-root version.

Roast dinner soup

This is a favourite Monday evening supper in our house: substantial, flavoursome and a good way to use up all that remains of a roast lunch. It's a free-form feast so I haven't given even approximate quantities. Just use what you have, lightening it with a bit more stock or water if it becomes too thick.

Roast potatoes and other roots, roughly chopped

Roast meat, such as pork, beef, lamb or chicken, shredded or chopped

400g tin chickpeas or any white beans, drained and rinsed (optional)

Some well-flavoured chicken or veg stock (see page 28) or mushroom broth (see page 30)

Any greens, shredded

Some chopped herbs, such as parsley, thyme or rosemary (optional)

Pinch or two of curry powder or smoked paprika (optional)

Salt and freshly ground black pepper

Put the root vegetables into a pan, along with any meat and pulses you're using. Pour on enough stock to cover well. Bring to a simmer and cook for 5 minutes or so, to allow the flavours to blend.

Add any leftover greens and simmer for another couple of minutes to heat through.

Sprinkle in any herbs you're using and season very well with salt and pepper. If it is still coming up a little under-seasoned, add a pinch or two of curry powder or smoked paprika.

Serve in warmed bowls with crusty bread.

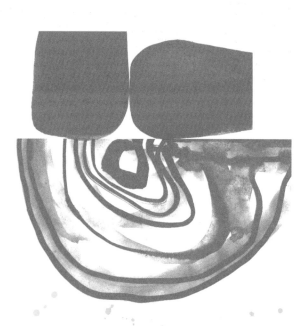

Tips and swaps

Finishing touches Add a trickle of well-flavoured oil, a dollop of crème fraîche or a scattering of grated cheese. (Also great with the following variations.)

Puréed version Hold back the meat. Let the simmered soup cool slightly, then blitz in a blender until smooth and thick. Fry any meat you wish to add until crisp and scatter over the soup as a garnish.

Roast dinner 'minestrone' Add a 400g tin plum tomatoes in juice, roughly chopped, or about the same amount of passata. If you have some cooked pasta, add it at the end.

Vegetable peel crisps

Step away from the compost bin! Those carrot, potato, parsnip and beetroot peels can be given another life as rather posh-tasting crisps. Just make sure they're really clean: the easiest way to do this is to give the veg a very conscientious scrub and a thorough rinse before you peel it, to remove any residual earth. These crisps make a great snack, and you can also sprinkle them on top of soups and salads as a tasty garnish.

Good handful or two of clean, dry vegetable peelings (carrot, potato, parsnip, beetroot)

Olive, rapeseed or sunflower oil, for frying

Flaky sea salt and freshly ground black pepper

Sweet or smoked paprika, to finish (optional)

Preheat the oven to 200°C/Fan 180°C/Gas 6. Place a large baking tray in the oven to heat up (or two if you're making lots of crisps).

Put a tablespoon or two of oil in a bowl and use your hands to toss the peels in the oil – you want them to be lightly and evenly coated all over. Sprinkle on some salt and pepper and toss again.

Take the hot tray(s) from the oven and carefully scatter over the peels, in an even layer. Quickly return to the oven and bake for 12–14 minutes, turning halfway through, until the peels are crisp and golden; don't let them burn or they will be bitter.

Toss the crisps in a little paprika, if using, and eat warm or cold.

Potato cakes

These crisp and fluffy beauties are terrific for a cooked breakfast or brunch, either served plain (but well seasoned) or with a traditional selection of fried, poached or scrambled eggs, bacon, black pudding, fried mushrooms, grilled tomatoes etc. Alternatively, you can use them as a vehicle for even more leftovers, stirring veg, herbs, cheese and/or extra seasonings into the basic mixture. SERVES ABOUT 4

300–500g mashed potato or well-crushed roast potatoes

1 large egg, lightly beaten

1–2 tablespoons plain flour, plus extra for dusting

1–2 tablespoons whole milk

Rapeseed or sunflower oil, for frying

Salt and freshly ground black pepper

In a bowl, mix together the potato, egg, flour and milk – the amount of flour and milk you should add will depend on the amount of mash. It needs to be a fairly thick dough, so you may not need any milk at all, especially if the mash is quite soft to start with.

Season the mixture well with salt and pepper and stir in any extra ingredients that you would like to add (see tips and swaps, below).

Using lightly floured hands, form the mixture into potato cakes, about 2cm thick and 7cm in diameter.

You'll need to cook the potato cakes in batches to avoid crowding the pan. Heat a thin film of oil in a large frying pan over a medium-high heat. Add 3 or 4 cakes and fry for 3–5 minutes each side, until crisp and golden brown.

Drain the potato cakes on kitchen paper and keep them warm in a low oven while you cook the rest.

Delicious with bacon and indeed any – or all – of your favourite breakfast components.

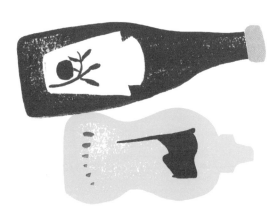

Tips and swaps

Add any of the following to the potato mix for extra flavour:

Herbs, such as chopped parsley, chives, soft thyme, lovage or chervil.

Sliced spring onions, finely diced shallots, or sautéed chopped onions and/or leeks.

A little finely chopped garlic.

Good pinch of English mustard powder.

Handful of grated cheese.

Some crumbled leftover cooked bacon, or even sausage, haggis or black pudding. Or try a few bits of shredded ham.

Cheesy potato gnocchi

These little dumplings, adapted from a recipe created by River Cottage Head Chef Gill Meller, are a firm favourite. They are so easy to put together with leftover mash or the inside of a baked potato.
SERVES 2–4

300–500g mashed potato

80–100g soft goat's cheese, crumbled

150–250g plain flour (half the weight of the potatoes), sifted, plus extra for dusting

1 large egg, lightly beaten

1 tablespoon finely chopped parsley, chives or sage (optional)

Salt and freshly ground black pepper

To serve

Butter

Generous chunk of hard goat's or sheep's cheese, or Parmesan, grated

Flaky sea salt

Tip the mash into a bowl and mix in the soft cheese, flour, egg and herbs, if using. Season generously with salt and pepper. You want a firm dough – add a bit more flour if necessary, but add it gradually so you don't overdo it.

Knead the dough gently for a minute – try not to overwork it or the gnocchi will become tough and gluey.

Next, roll the potato mixture into skinny sausages, about 1.5cm in diameter, and cut each into 3cm lengths. At this point, if you like, you can gently roll the gnocchi over the back of a fork to make grooves. This will help them hold on to any sauce you might want to add.

Bring a large pan of salted water to a gentle simmer. Drop in the gnocchi and cook for a minute or two, just until they rise to the surface.

Scoop the gnocchi out with a slotted spoon as they come to the surface and transfer them to a warmed, lightly buttered dish.

Toss the gnocchi with butter, grated cheese, some flaky sea salt and a grinding of pepper. Serve at once.

Tips and swaps

Other serving suggestions Instead of melted butter and hard cheese, try the following:

Crumbled gorgonzola or other soft blue cheese and finish with chopped, toasted walnuts.

Pesto and grated Parmesan or other hard cheese.

A simple tomato sauce with basil, finishing with grated cheese.

Browned butter, sage and grated Parmesan or other cheese.

Crème fraîche, chopped dill and a squeeze of lemon.

Other rooty gnocchi Use equal quantities of mashed potato and mashed carrots, sweet potatoes, parsnips or pumpkin – in all cases, either roast, plain steamed, or boiled.

Lentil and leftover veg curry

This makes a very satisfying midweek dinner and you can have it on the table in less than 30 minutes. It works particularly well with leftover roast parsnips from a Sunday lunch but roast spuds, carrots and onions can also be added at the beginning, along with any greens, peas, cauliflower, etc. at the end.

SERVES 4

1 tablespoon rapeseed or sunflower oil

1 onion, diced

2 garlic cloves, finely chopped

2 tablespoons home-made curry paste (see page 57), or a favourite ready-made curry paste

100g red lentils, well rinsed

200–300g roast parsnips (and/or spuds and carrots), cut into chunks

700ml chicken or veg stock (see page 28)

Any greens, peas, cauliflower florets, etc.

Small handful of coriander, stalks removed, coarsely chopped, plus extra to serve

60g cashew nuts, toasted and roughly chopped

Raita (see page 88), to serve (optional)

Heat the oil in a medium saucepan over a medium heat. Add the onion and sauté until golden, about 10 minutes.

Add the garlic and curry paste and stir for a minute or two. Toss in the lentils and roast parsnips and/or other roast roots and stir for a minute.

Now add the stock, bring to a simmer and cook until the lentils are starting to break down, about 15 minutes.

Add any greens, peas, cauliflower or other veg and bring back to a gentle simmer. Cook for another 2–3 minutes until everything is heated through thoroughly. Stir in the coriander.

Serve with the cashews and extra coriander scattered over the top, and a bowl of raita on the side, if you like. Accompany with rice and/or naan.

Tips and swaps

Up the green veg You can add fresh or frozen peas or greens such as spinach, as well as or instead of leftovers. Make sure peas have a least 5 minutes' simmering in the curry to cook right through. Greens only need to be wilted.

Eggy version Eggs, hard-boiled and peeled, can be added for the last 5 minutes of cooking, either whole or cut in half.

Turn into soup or dhal If you've any leftovers of your leftovers curry, give it a quick whiz in a food processor, with an extra dash of water or stock, to make a delicious dhal/soup.

Curried coconutty roots

Warming, satisfying and quick, you can make this curry good and hot by adding more chillies, or keep it comfortingly creamy with just a little kick, as it is here. It's a pretty saucy dish, bordering on a soup, and you could certainly eat it as such – in a bowl, with a spoon, rather than over rice. SERVES 4

2 tablespoons rapeseed or sunflower oil

2 onions, diced

2 tablespoons home-made Thai-style curry paste (see page 57), or a favourite ready-made Thai curry paste

2 garlic cloves, finely chopped

1 red or green chilli, deseeded and finely chopped

About 500g roast roots, such as carrots, parsnips, potatoes and/or celeriac, cut into large chunks

400ml coconut milk

200ml veg or chicken stock (see page 28)

Small handful of coriander leaves, roughly chopped, plus extra to serve

Few mint leaves, shredded

Juice of 1 lime

About 20g shaved coconut

Salt and freshly ground black pepper

Heat the oil in a medium saucepan over a medium-low heat. Add the onions and sauté until they just begin to take on some colour, about 10 minutes.

Add the curry paste, garlic and chilli and fry, stirring, for a further minute. Tip in the roast roots and stir until well coated with the spices.

Stir in the coconut milk and stock and simmer gently for about 10 minutes until the vegetables are heated through and the flavours are well blended. Season with salt and pepper to taste.

Just before serving, stir through the herbs, lime juice and coconut.

Serve scattered with extra coriander, with a bowl of jasmine or basmati rice on the side.

Tips and swaps

If you have any coriander roots, chop these finely and add them with the garlic and chilli.

Paneer curry Stir in cubes of mild Indian paneer cheese (see page 216 for my home-made version), with the coconut milk, to add some creamy protein to the dish.

Root gratin with blue cheese and nuts

*This is a flavoursome way to turn a few humble roasted roots into something more substantial.
I suggest carrots here as they're so good with the nuts and cheese, but the dish also works brilliantly
with cauliflower florets (see tips and swaps, below).* SERVES 4 AS A SIDE DISH

Knob of butter, to grease the dish

About 300g roast carrots, or other roast
veg, cut into thick slices

About 150ml veg stock (see page 28)

2–3 tablespoons crème fraîche or double
cream

Salt and freshly ground black pepper

For the topping

Handful of walnuts or hazelnuts,
coarsely chopped

About 30g breadcrumbs

½ teaspoon lemon thyme leaves, finely
chopped (optional)

50g blue cheese, such as Stilton,
Roquefort or Blue Vinney, or Cheddar
if you prefer

Preheat the oven to 200°C/Fan 180°C/Gas 6.

Lightly grease a small gratin dish with butter.
Lay the carrots (and/or other veg) in the dish
in a single layer – they should fit snugly.

Heat the stock to just below boiling. Whisk in
the crème fraîche or cream and then pour over
the veg. Season with salt and pepper to taste.

Cover tightly with foil, place on a baking sheet
and bake for 20 minutes. Remove the foil, turn
the veg over in the creamy sauce and return to
the oven for a further 10 minutes until almost
all of the liquid has evaporated.

Meanwhile, for the topping, mix together the
walnuts, breadcrumbs, thyme and a few grinds
of pepper in a bowl.

Remove the creamy veg from the oven, sprinkle
on the walnut mixture and crumble the cheese
over the top. Return to the oven and bake until
bubbling and golden, about 10 minutes.

Tips and swaps

Saucier coating Use a béchamel sauce, based
on milk or the stock and cream mix above
(prepare as for the sauce on page 228, omitting
the cheese), to coat the veg under the topping.

Cauliflower gratin This is particularly good.
Leftover or blanched cauliflower florets can
be added to a tray of roasting root veg, well

seasoned, for the last 10 minutes of the
roasting time (or roasted on their own).

Veg and chickpea gratin Toss a 400g tin of
chickpeas, drained and rinsed, with the veg
before you pour over the stock and cream mix
or béchamel sauce (see left) for a more
substantial dish.

Quick pickled roots

A light salting can refresh those slightly tired, yet-to-be-used roots found lurking at the bottom of the fridge. Finely slivered and lightly pickled, they make a great accompaniment to cold meats, salads and cheeses, especially in thickly filled baguettes, and they're also delicious with barbecued meat or oily fish. You may need more or less pickling liquid depending on the amount of vegetables you're using – just make sure you keep the proportions the same. MAKES 300–400g

For the pickling mixture

500ml rice vinegar

80g caster sugar

2 tablespoons flaky sea salt

1 teaspoon yellow mustard seeds

½ teaspoon black peppercorns

¼ teaspoon coriander seeds (optional)

¼ teaspoon celery seeds (optional)

Pinch of dried chilli flakes (optional)

For the vegetables

300–400g slightly soft, raw root vegetables, such as carrots, parsnips, radishes and beetroot

½–1 teaspoon flaky sea salt

Put all the ingredients for the pickling mixture into a stainless steel or cast-iron saucepan with 250ml water and place over a low heat, stirring until the sugar is fully dissolved. Remove from the heat and allow to cool, then chill.

Peel the vegetables, apart from radishes, if you're using them. Pare the veg very thinly with a mandoline or sharp vegetable peeler, or cut them into very fine julienne.

Place the veg in a colander in the sink or over a bowl. If using beetroot, place it in a separate colander, to stop it colouring the other veg. Sprinkle the veg with the sea salt, toss to mix then leave to stand for 30 minutes.

Rinse the vegetables under a running cold tap, drain and pat dry with kitchen paper or a clean tea towel.

Place the veg in a jar or plastic tub, pour over the pickling mixture and leave for at least a couple of hours before serving.

These pickled veg will keep sealed in the fridge for a week or so.

Tips and swaps

Scandi pickle mix You can vary your pickling mix and aromatics according to what's to hand. I particularly like a Scandi-style mix of cider vinegar, fennel or caraway seeds, crushed bay leaves, a little thinly sliced onion and fresh dill.

Pickled brassicas Small cauliflower and broccoli florets, and/or their finely shredded stems, pickle successfully. Shredded cabbage works well too. You could also try pickling finely sliced fennel or red onions.

Carrot and ginger steamed pudding

This is a great way to use up cooked carrots of any kind – steamed, boiled or roasted. You don't want any that are generously seasoned with garlic, but carrots roasted in oil with salt and pepper, and even a bit of thyme or a few bay leaves, work very well indeed. SERVES 4–6

5 balls of stem ginger in syrup, plus 4 tablespoons syrup from the jar

100g butter, softened, plus extra to grease the basin

50g light muscovado sugar, plus 2 tablespoons

50g caster sugar

2 large eggs, lightly beaten

140g self-raising flour

¼ teaspoon salt

About 100g cooked carrots, diced

Finely grated zest of ½ small orange

¼ teaspoon ground cardamom (optional)

2–3 tablespoons milk

Lightly butter a 900ml pudding basin. For the cover, lay a large square of foil on top of a square of baking parchment that's the same size. Fold a pleat of about 4cm, both layers together, down the middle.

Spoon the ginger syrup into the basin and pack the 2 tablespoons muscovado sugar on top of that. Thinly slice two of the ginger balls and layer them on top of the sugar. Dice the remaining stem ginger and set aside.

Using a hand-held electric whisk or mixer, cream the butter with the muscovado and caster sugars for several minutes until light and fluffy. Beat in the eggs, a little at a time.

Sift together the flour and salt then fold into the mixture. Fold in the diced carrots, reserved stem ginger, grated orange zest and ground cardamom, if using.

Stir in just enough milk to give the batter a light, dropping consistency. Spoon into the basin and smooth the top with the back of a spoon.

Cover the basin with the foil and parchment square, with the foil uppermost. Tie it securely with kitchen string under the rim of the basin.

Put a trivet or a heatproof saucer in the bottom of a large pan and sit the basin on top. Pour in enough boiling water from the kettle to come halfway up the side of the basin. Cover with a tight-fitting lid and simmer gently for 1½ hours, topping up with boiling water as necessary.

Carefully remove the basin from the pan and let it stand for 5 minutes. Remove the foil and parchment, gently run a palette knife around the inside to release the pudding, then invert the pudding onto a shallow serving dish. Serve immediately, with thick cream or custard.

Tips and swaps

Fruity option Soak a handful of chopped dried dates or raisins in tea or orange juice to plump them up a little, then drain and fold into the mixture with the carrots.

Parsnipy version Simply replace the carrots with roast parsnips. You can also swap the orange with lemon zest.

Beetroot and caraway seed cake

Based on a traditional seed cake, this is quick to make and has a light and tender crumb. It's a sweet way to use up leftover roasted (or boiled) roots, especially beetroot, which creates a particularly vibrant version! Roots roasted with salt and pepper, even with some bay and/or thyme, are great but don't use any roasted with garlic. This cake keeps well; if anything, it's better after a couple of days stored in an airtight tin. MAKES 1 LOAF CAKE

About 100g cooked beetroot

2–4 tablespoons milk

50g ground almonds

1½ teaspoons caraway seeds

150g butter, softened, plus extra
to grease the tin

150g caster sugar

3 large eggs, lightly beaten

150g self-raising flour, sifted

2 tablespoons pearl or demerara sugar,
to finish

Preheat the oven to 160°C/Fan 140°C/Gas 3. Lightly grease a 1.5 litre loaf tin and line with baking parchment, then butter the parchment.

In a bowl, mash the beetroot with some of the milk until smooth. You can do this in a food processor or with a stick blender if you like. Mix in the ground almonds and caraway seeds.

Using a hand-held electric whisk or a mixer, cream together the butter and sugar for several minutes until light and fluffy. Add the eggs a little at a time, beating well after each addition.

Gently fold in the flour, followed by the beetroot mixture, until just combined.

Spoon the mixture into the prepared loaf tin and gently smooth the surface. Sprinkle the pearl or demerara sugar over the top and bake for 55–60 minutes, until a skewer inserted into the centre of the cake comes out clean.

Leave in the tin for 10 minutes then turn out onto a wire rack to cool completely.

Tips and swaps

Carrot or parsnip seed cake Simply replace the beetroot with roast carrots or parsnips. You can use plain mashed or puréed veg too.

LEFTOVER GREENS & SALAD

I have suggested that it doesn't matter too much if the occasional cabbage leaf or cauli stem makes its way onto the compost heap but, in this chapter, I've rammed on my thrifty thinking cap and tried to find ways to avoid throwing out even the least promising looking scraps.

Tossing the odd limp lettuce leaf may not represent the same level of wastage as chucking out meat or fish, but it's a shame not to explore what longstanding tenants of the salad drawer have to offer. And, as it turns out, there are hidden glories here: layers of delicacy and sophistication, subtle and tempting flavours. Take a kindly and creative look at produce that's not pretty, or no longer in the first squeak of youth, and you will be rewarded.

Think, for example, of a nubbly, thuggish broccoli stem, often discarded while we flirt with its fine florets, despite it making up almost half the weight of the head. It can be put to excellent use: you can peel, pare and pamper it into a sophisticated little salad (see page 154). Or partner it up with other oft-rejected bits of cauliflower and cabbage to make a subtle stem soup (see page 152).

In fact, this is perhaps the most Cindarella-ish of all the chapters in this book, with trimmings and tired bits, sad salad, squishy tomatoes, and yesterday's uneaten cabbage

transformed. A splash of vinegar, a shake of spice, a bit
of fiery chopped chilli and it's quite possible to turn the
least prepossessing ingredients into dishes that will delight.

And then there are the gluts: the excess quantities of
vegetable matter that appear before you've even got to
the kitchen. If you grow any of your own veg, you'll be very
familiar with seasonal gluts. But even veg-box recipients
and farmers' market shoppers will know what I mean.
Vegetables do not grow with neat and tidy consistency
throughout their season: there is always a period of
exuberant uber-growth which results both in large
quantities and a corresponding accumulation of ageing
produce that you haven't been able to use yet.

So, in the summer, when courgettes are plentiful if you
grow them – and cheap if you buy them – try my Korean-
style pancake on page 166. In the colder months, when you
find yourself with too much kale in the garden or in the veg
box, make a batch of kale crisps (see page 150) or whip up
a dish of creamy greens with pasta (see page 160).

Finding delicious ways to cook plentiful, inexpensive
seasonal veg – and to ensure that every last leaf, stalk
and stem end is appreciated – will bring you satisfaction
off the scale.

Kale crisps

Kale crisps have become a rather fashionable snack in the past few years, and that's hardly surprising, given how easy they are to make and how delicious they are to eat. Making your own is a good way to use an excess of kale in the garden, even slightly-past-their-best leaves. They make a great nibble to go with drinks, or you can use them as you would crispy seaweed in salads, or sprinkled on soups.

Few handfuls of kale, thickest, woody stems removed

2–3 tablespoons rapeseed or olive oil

Flaky sea salt

Preheat the oven to 180°C/Fan 160°C/Gas 4.

Wash the kale and dry well: it will crisp up better if it is very dry. Tear the leaves into bite-sized pieces and place on a baking tray (or two if you're making a lot – you don't want to crowd the tray/s).

Trickle over the oil and massage it thoroughly into every nook and cranny of the leaves. Don't salt them yet – they roast better just with the oil. Spread the leaves out on the tray/s in an even, single layer.

Bake for 10 minutes, then take the tray from the oven and give the leaves a good stir. Return to the oven and bake for a further 5–10 minutes. The leaves should be crisp but don't let them get too dark or they will be bitter.

Sprinkle with flaky sea salt and serve.

Tips and swaps

Dust with a little paprika or some finely grated
lemon zest along with the salt.

Umami hit After massaging in the oil, shake
a few splashes of tamari or soy sauce over the
leaves; you won't need much as the flavour
intensifies as the leaves bake.

Stem soup

When you're slicing those tasty little florets from a head of cauliflower or broccoli, or shredding cabbage into the finest of strands, don't throw the stems or outer leaves into the compost. Either alone or in combination, they make a surprisingly delicate and delicious soup. SERVES 4

20g butter, or 20ml rapeseed or sunflower oil

1 onion, diced

1 bay leaf

1 small garlic clove, finely chopped

500–600g broccoli stems, cauliflower stems and outer leaves and/or cabbage stalks and outer leaves, roughly chopped

1.2 litres chicken or veg stock (see page 28) or water

50g crème fraîche, plus extra to serve (optional)

Salt and freshly ground black or white pepper

Extra virgin rapeseed or olive oil, to finish

Melt the butter or heat the oil in a saucepan over a medium-low heat, then add the onion, bay leaf and a pinch of salt. Sauté until the onion is softened, but don't let it take on any colour. This should take about 10 minutes.

Add the garlic and stir for a minute. Add the stems and fry them gently for a few minutes, stirring to coat in the onion and garlic.

Tip the stock or water into the pan and bring to the boil. Lower the heat and simmer until the vegetable stems are very tender, 10–15 minutes depending on their size.

Cool slightly, then add the crème fraîche. Blitz the soup in a blender or using a stick blender until smooth.

Return to the heat, season to taste with salt and pepper and heat through gently, being careful not to let it boil.

Serve the soup in warmed bowls, topped with a trickle of extra virgin oil and a little crème fraîche, if you like. Finish with a generous grinding of pepper.

Tips and swaps

Add crunch Omit the crème fraîche and scatter over some croûtons (see page 39), or toast some cheese-topped crostini and float one in each bowl just before serving.

Add cheese Stir ¼ teaspoon caraway seeds in with the sautéeing onions, then add 100g grated Cheddar or other strong cheese when you purée the soup at the end.

Broccoli stem 'carpaccio'

Ever-popular calabrese broccoli. Goodness knows how many millions of those thick, wrist-like stems must have been tossed, needlessly, in the bin. Once the tough green skin is peeled away, the crisp, pale interior is revealed. Of course, this can be cooked along with the florets, but left raw its fresh crunch lends itself brilliantly to this simple but rather sophisticated little salad. You can add a little richness with labneh or paneer, or keep it lean and green if you prefer. SERVES 2 AS A LIGHT STARTER

1–2 thick calabrese broccoli stem(s), depending on their thickness and length

Sprinkling of thyme leaves (lemon thyme is particularly good)

Pinch of dried chilli flakes, to taste

Few gratings of lemon zest and a squeeze of juice

2 tablespoons paneer (see page 216) or labneh (see page 218), optional

Trickle of extra virgin olive or rapeseed oil

Flaky sea salt and freshly ground black pepper

Using a vegetable peeler, peel the broccoli stem(s), then using a mandoline or the peeler, cut into the thinnest possible slices.

Arrange the broccoli slices in a single layer on a plate (or two) and scatter over the thyme, chilli flakes and lemon zest and juice.

Dot the paneer or labneh, if using, on top of the 'carpaccio'. Trickle on some extra virgin oil and season with salt and pepper to taste. Serve immediately.

Tips and swaps

Instead of thyme and chilli, try the following, in all cases adding a trickle of good oil at the end:

Chopped capers and/or anchovies.

Shaved Parmesan or hard goat's cheese.

Blue cheese or soft goat's cheese and a trickle of runny honey.

Cauliflower carpaccio This is particularly useful when you've trimmed off all the florets and find yourself left with the hearty bit in the middle of the cauliflower. Prep the cauli stem exactly as for broccoli.

Chilled cucumber and almond soup

Got a slightly bendy cucumber? Here's a refreshing way to put it to work. This pretty soup is loosely based on the Spanish ajo blanco and is perfect for a hot summer's day.

If your cucumber is a bit soft, just cut away any damaged flesh and peel away dimpled skin. Sometimes overripe specimens can be bitter, so simply scoop out the seeds with a spoon and discard. The cucumber's gone too far though if it's mushy and there are black spots. SERVES 4

150g blanched almonds

50g slightly stale white bread, crusts removed

300–400g cucumber

1 large garlic clove, peeled and halved

100ml extra virgin olive oil, plus extra to serve

1–2 tablespoons sherry vinegar or balsamic vinegar

Salt and freshly ground black pepper

Handful of flaked almonds, toasted, to finish (optional)

Preheat the oven to 180°C/Fan 160°C/Gas 4. Put the almonds on a baking tray and toast them in the oven for 5–8 minutes until fragrant and lightly golden brown – start checking on them after 5 minutes as they can scorch quickly. Spread them out on a cold plate to cool completely, then tip into a food processor and pulse them until quite fine but not oily.

Tear the bread into chunks and soak in cold water to cover for a couple of minutes. Squeeze out the excess water and add the bread to the almonds in the food processor.

Cut off a 10cm piece of cucumber and set aside. Peel the rest of the cucumber (use the peel to infuse a jug of water if you like, page 158). Halve the cucumber lengthways and scoop out the seeds with a teaspoon, then chop the flesh roughly. Add to the food processor.

Add the garlic, olive oil, 1 tablespoon vinegar, ¼ teaspoon salt and some pepper. Blend until smooth, adding a splash of cold water to thin a little if you like, but it's best kept pretty thick.

Transfer the soup to a bowl or jug, cover and refrigerate for several hours to chill thoroughly.

When ready to serve, taste the soup and add more salt or vinegar if it needs it. Cut the reserved cucumber into julienne strips.

Divide the soup between chilled bowls. Add a trickle of olive oil and finish with the cucumber julienne and toasted almonds, if using.

Tips and swaps

Add salad leaves If you have any slightly tired lettuce, rocket or watercress, you can toss the leaves into the soup before blitzing – simply tear off and discard the worst bits first.

Finish with grapes Float a handful of seedless green grapes on each portion instead of the toasted almonds.

Sautéed cucumbers

We seldom cook cucumbers in this country and I think it's a shame – they make a delicate and delicious accompaniment to fish. It's also a great way to use up a cucumber that isn't quite perky enough to chop up and toss into a raw salad. SERVES 2–4 AS A SIDE DISH

1 cucumber, slightly soft is fine

Generous knob of butter

Few tablespoons of chopped herbs (chives, dill, chervil are all good, either alone or in combination)

1–2 tablespoons crème fraîche (optional)

Salt and freshly ground black pepper

Peel the cucumber (save the peel, see below). Halve the cucumber lengthways and scoop out the seeds using a teaspoon, then cut the flesh into 3cm pieces.

Heat the butter in a frying pan over a medium-high heat. When it has stopped foaming, toss in the cucumber pieces with a pinch of salt and fry for 5–7 minutes, until they begin to turn slightly golden around the edges.

Add the herbs and crème fraîche, if using, stir and season very well with salt and pepper. Serve immediately.

Cucumber-infused water

You can use the peel of a cucumber – even a tougher, older one – to give a nice, refreshing flavour to a jug or glass of water.

Tips and swaps

Spicy version Sauté the cucumber in a little rapeseed oil with some chopped chilli or dried chilli flakes, sliced garlic and finely chopped ginger. Add a splash of soy sauce, a handful of coriander leaves and a few chopped spring onions at the end, and finish with a squeeze or two of lime.

Pasta and greens with goat's cheese

However much you love your leaves — and I bow to no one in my devotion — there are probably times when you find you have just a bit too much greenery in the fridge, at least some of which needs using up rather urgently. I make this quick pasta dish at precisely such moments. It works with almost-on-the-turn raw greens as well as leftover cooked greens; simply adjust the cooking time accordingly.

SERVES 4

300g pasta shapes, such as penne, fusilli or farfalle

1 tablespoon rapeseed or olive oil, or a knob of butter

2 shallots, finely diced

2 garlic cloves, halved and finely sliced

100–200ml chicken or veg stock (see page 28) or water

200–250g shredded cooked spring greens, Savoy cabbage, kale or Brussels sprouts, or a few handfuls of uncooked leaves, such as spinach or rocket, tough stems removed, trimmed and shredded

3 tablespoons crème fraîche

About 100g soft goat's cheese

½ teaspoon dried chilli flakes (optional)

Small handful of basil leaves, roughly chopped (optional)

2 tablespoons roughly chopped walnuts or pine nuts, lightly toasted (optional)

Salt and freshly ground black pepper

Bring a large pan of water to the boil and salt it well. Add the pasta and cook according to the packet guidelines, until *al dente*.

Meanwhile, heat the oil or butter in a frying pan over a low heat. Add the shallots and sauté gently for a few minutes until softened, then add the garlic and fry for a minute.

Now pour in the stock or water: if the greens are already cooked, add 100ml of liquid; if they're not, add 200ml.

Toss in the shredded greens and stir. If using uncooked greens, cover with a lid and simmer for a few minutes until just tender; for cooked greens, just heat through with the lid off.

Take off the heat, stir in the crème fraîche and season well with salt and pepper.

When the pasta is cooked, drain and add to the creamy greens. Crumble in the goat's cheese and add the chilli flakes, basil and/or toasted nuts, if using. Toss to combine.

Divide between warmed bowls and serve.

Tips and swaps

Punchier version Gently fry a diced onion in a little olive oil until soft. Add a few anchovies with some of their oil and a diced green or red chilli. Fry until the anchovies break up. Toss with the pasta, cooked greens and soft goat's cheese, or scatter over lots of grated hard goat's cheese or other well-flavoured hard cheese.

Tamari greens with cashews and ginger

Yesterday's boiled cabbage or greens are altogether more inviting when perked up with sesame, spices and soy. This dish is pretty and very simple – and it's good hot or cold too. **SERVES 4**

200–250g cooked green cabbage or Brussels sprouts, roughly shredded

2 tablespoons sesame seeds

Small handful of coriander, roughly chopped

½–1 teaspoon dried chilli flakes, or 1 finely chopped red chilli (optional)

50g cashew nuts, lightly toasted

For the dressing

1–2 tablespoons lime juice or lemon juice

1 tablespoon sesame oil

Dash of tamari or soy sauce

Dash of mirin

About 1 teaspoon finely grated ginger

½–1 garlic clove, grated

Pinch of brown sugar

Put the cabbage into a serving bowl.

To make the dressing, shake all the ingredients together in a screw-topped jar until thoroughly blended, or whisk together to combine.

Put a small frying pan over a medium heat, add the sesame seeds and gently toast until golden, shaking the pan to ensure they don't burn. This should only take a minute or two. Tip the toasted seeds into the bowl with the cabbage.

Add the coriander and chilli flakes if using, trickle over the dressing and toss to combine. Add the toasted cashews and toss the greens again before serving.

Vietnamese wilted greens salad

I can't bear to toss out a bowl of lovingly tended leaves from my garden and this is a great recipe if you've over-catered on the salad front. As long as the leaves are not too far gone, or drenched in vinaigrette, wilting them in a pan and perking them up with a tasty, garlicky dressing gives them a delicious new lease of life. Leaves with a bit of body and fire, such as rocket and mizuna, respond particularly well to this treatment, but you can use this recipe when you have an over-abundance of almost any greens. SERVES 1–2

2 teaspoons rapeseed or sunflower oil

1 garlic clove, halved and thinly sliced

Handful of salad leaves, such as Cos lettuce, rocket or mizuna

Small handful of cooked meat or white or oily fish, broken into shreds or flakes, and fried until crispy

Few torn mint and/or coriander leaves

For the dressing

1 garlic clove, finely chopped

½ red or green chilli, halved, membrane and seeds removed (for a milder version, if preferred), finely chopped

2 teaspoons rice vinegar

2 teaspoons fish sauce

Pinch of soft brown sugar

Juice of ½ small lime

First, whisk together all the ingredients for the dressing, or shake them in a screw-topped jar to combine. You probably won't need all the dressing, but it will keep well sealed in a jar in the fridge for a couple of days.

To prepare the salad, heat the oil in a wok or sauté pan over a medium heat. Add the garlic and fry for a minute, then toss in the leaves and cook until wilted – this should take no more than a minute.

Take off the heat and add the crispy shards of meat or fish, herbs and some of the dressing. Toss to combine and serve straight away, with the rest of the dressing in a dish on the side.

Tips and swaps

Extra veg Thinly sliced red, yellow or orange pepper, thinly sliced spring onions and beansprouts are lovely additions. Fry with the garlic for a minute before you add the greens.

Vegetarian option Instead of the fish or meat shards, top the salad with crisply fried, thinly sliced onion or shallot, and/or some cubes of fried or marinated tofu.

Noodly version For a more substantial salad, pile the wilted greens onto cooked noodles – rice noodles or glass noodles work best.

Korean veg pancakes with carrot salad

This recipe is based on the Korean 'pajeon' pancake, which is nicely chunky and substantial, and an ideal vehicle for all manner of vegetables and seafood. Thin spring onions are the mark of an authentic pajeon, but they are not compulsory here. As well as mopping up cooked leftover greens, beans and peas, the pancake is great with cooked courgettes and/or aubergines, or even leftover ratatouille if it isn't too wet. SERVES 2–4

For the salad

1–2 carrots, peeled and grated or cut into very thin matchsticks

1 teaspoon sesame seeds, lightly toasted in a dry frying pan

Small handful of tiny mint leaves

For the dressing

3 tablespoons soy sauce

1 tablespoon rice vinegar

¼ teaspoon sesame oil

1 garlic clove, finely chopped

Pinch of dried chilli flakes

Pinch of sugar

For the pancakes

100g plain flour, or a mix of 70g plain flour and 30g rice flour

150ml iced water

Sunflower oil, for frying

8 thin spring onions (including the green part), cut into 5cm pieces (optional)

50–100g chopped cooked greens, peas, courgettes, etc.

1 large egg, lightly beaten

Salt and freshly ground black pepper

For the salad, combine the carrot, toasted sesame seeds and mint leaves in a bowl.

For the dressing, whisk together all the ingredients in a small bowl.

For the pancake batter, whisk the flour(s) and water together until just combined (don't overwork) and season with salt and pepper.

Heat a thin film of oil in a 23cm non-stick frying pan over a medium heat. Add the spring onions, if using, with a good pinch of salt. Fry until wilted and just starting to colour, stirring from time to time, about 5 minutes.

Now add the green veg leftovers and stir-fry for a couple of minutes until heated through.

Pour the batter over the veg and swirl the frying pan to distribute it well. Fry for a couple of minutes until the bottom is cooked through and beginning to crisp up.

Now pour on the beaten egg, tipping the pan so it spreads out reasonably evenly over the pancake. When it looks almost set, use a wide spatula or a couple of smaller spatulas to carefully flip the pancake over.

Cook for a further minute or two until the pancake is completely set and beginning to crisp up around the edges.

Tip the pancake onto a plate, heap the carrot salad up in the middle and trickle on some of the dressing.

Serve warm, with more dressing on the side, as a dipping sauce. Try to scoop up a bit of pancake, some salad and dipping sauce in each bite.

Tips and swaps

Meaty/fishy versions If you have any leftover scraps of ham or chicken, or flakes of cooked fish, or squid or mussels, these are also very good scattered on top of the pancake just before you pour over the egg.

Fiery version Add a spoonful of kimchi (spicy Korean pickled cabbage) to the salad.

Slightly squashy tomato and egg toast

This deliciously savoury, speedy supper might seem a misfit in this chapter but is so good it had to go in somewhere. Tomatoes should really be stored at room temperature, which keeps them juicy and sweet, but also means that they ripen apace. If you find yourself with a couple of specimens that are heading into squishy territory – just a little too ripe to slice for a salad – this is the way to go. And if you feel greens are a must, serve the egg and tomato atop a layer of wilted spinach on the toast.
SERVES 1

2 large slightly overripe tomatoes

Splash of rapeseed or sunflower oil

1 garlic clove, finely sliced

1 large egg

1 good slice of robust bread

Butter

Salt and freshly ground black pepper

Slice the tomatoes in half around the 'equator'. Holding the skin side of one half in your hand, grate the tomato flesh on a box grater, into a bowl. Keep going until you have only the skin left in your hand and a nice juicy pile of tomato pulp beneath.

Heat the oil in a small, non-stick frying pan over a medium-low heat and add the garlic. Let it sizzle briefly until just starting to colour.

Add the tomato pulp and some salt and pepper. Increase the heat, bring to a brisk simmer and cook for about 5 minutes, to reduce the liquid down a little.

Meanwhile, break the egg into cup.

Carefully tip the egg gently into the middle of the simmering tomato mixture. Turn the heat down low and cook for 5 minutes or so until the white of the egg is set. You can also baste the egg with the tomato 'sauce' to help set the top, or you can flip it, to have it 'easy over'.

Meanwhile, toast and butter your bread.

Using a large spatula, scoop the egg carefully out of the pan and place it on the toast. Pour the remaining tomato sauce from the pan over the egg. Season again with salt and pepper and tuck in straight away.

Tips and swaps

You can use overripe cherry tomatoes here if you like – about 200g will do. There is no need to grate them. Just cut each one in half and give it a squish to get the juices flowing. Throw them into the hot frying pan when the garlic is nicely coloured.

Spice it up Doctor your tomato sauce with a pinch of spice – either ground cumin or curry powder. A spoon-tip of fiery harissa stirred into the tomatoes is also excellent.

Brunch option Add scraps of ham or cooked bacon or sausage to the sauce, or at the end.

Beetroot 'laces'

Beetroot stems make a fun snack when candied like this. Enjoy them as they are, use them as an unusual petit four at the end of dinner, or heap them in a sweet tangle on top of a chocolate and beetroot cake as an original garnish. How much sugar syrup you'll need depends on how many stems you have – just keep the proportions the same, using the same amount of sugar as water.

For the laces

Handful of large beetroot leaves with stems

Caster sugar, for coating

For the syrup

About 300g caster sugar

About 300ml water

Strip the leaves from the purple-red beetroot stems and set the stems aside (save the leaves to add to stir-fries, curries, frittatas, etc. as you would spinach).

For the syrup, put the sugar into a medium saucepan with the water and heat gently, stirring from time to time, until the sugar has dissolved. Bring to a rolling boil and boil for a couple of minutes until slightly syrupy.

Reduce the heat to low, add the beetroot stems and simmer very gently for 15 minutes or so, until the stems are very tender when pierced with the point of a small, sharp knife.

Place a wire rack over a baking tray (to catch the sugary drips). Carefully remove the stems from the sugar syrup with tongs and lay them on the rack. Leave to dry out for an hour or so.

Scatter some sugar on a large plate and toss the beetroot 'laces' in the sugar to coat. They will keep for a few days in an airtight container.

LEFTOVER BREAD, PASTA & PULSES

Carbs have taken a bit of a kicking in the last few years as we've turned away from their gentle comfort in favour of more assertive, micronutrient-rammed food groups. But they're standing by, patiently, waiting for us to remember their generous, soothing nature, and their accommodating capacity to turn a few random scraps into supper. Here I celebrate their ability to carry flavours and extend the possibilities of other ingredients, like nothing else (though be sure to check in with rice too, see page 194).

Even those of us, myself included, who try to eat less bread these days, are likely to have a few crusts and stale ends sitting about from time to time. These starchy staples are happy to soak up all manner of sweet and savoury flavours in the timeless, greater-than-the-sum-of-its-parts, classic eggy bread on page 174, or be transformed into breadcrumbs to sprinkle and coat and add pleasing crunch (see pages 54, 60 and 102), to thicken soups and sauces (see pages 32 and 78,) or give creamy character to my marmalade pudding on page 178.

And then there's pasta, that workhorse of so many hasty lunches and dinners, which can do double duty, both as a quick meal on its own and then, as a leftover second-time-around special, taking on board the best the fridge and cupboard have to offer. A well-sauced pasta dish can even make a good filling for an omelette (see page 180) or add substance to a frittata (see page 181).

Pulses and lentils have remained, even with the most ascetic of eaters, the more acceptable face of carbs due to their low glycaemic index. In my kitchen they prove their worth time and again – not just because they're such a handy standby, but also because they deliver so much, for so little effort.

Healthy, delicious and inexpensive, pulses and lentils are always ready to step up to the plate and pull together the disparate flavours of leftover roots and leafy veg, scraps of fish and roast meats, handfuls of fresh herbs and generous doses of spices. When it comes to adding texture they really shine too, whether it's adding body to soups like ribollita (see page 190), satisfying a creamy-yet-savoury craving in hummus or veg pâté (see page 184) or stepping up to the (dinner) plate to turn leftover roast meats into a rich and comforting cassoulet (see page 192).

So embrace the staunchly starchy and the deliciously dense for what they are: brilliant, belly-filling building blocks that have an unmatched ability to make meals comforting, satisfying and sustaining.

Eggy bread

French toast, eggy bread, pain perdu, whatever you like to call it, is one of my family's favourite ways to kick-start the morning and it's a good way to use up slightly stale bread, Flavoured with vanilla, this sweet version is particularly delicious made with brioche, panettone and challah-style loaves. And if you have any extra egg yolks left over from making meringues, seize the chance to make a richer, more luxurious custard here. For a savoury option, see tips and swaps, below. SERVES 2-4

4 thick slices of white bread, slightly stale is ideal

4 large eggs, plus 1 or 2 extra egg yolks if you have them

2 tablespoons milk

1–2 teaspoons caster sugar

½ teaspoon vanilla extract

Generous knob of butter

1 teaspoon rapeseed or sunflower oil

To serve

Sugar, honey or jam

Lay the bread slices in a large shallow dish.

In a jug, whisk the eggs and any extra egg yolks together with the milk, sugar and vanilla extract.

Pour the custard over the bread and leave it to soak for at least 10 minutes and up to half an hour, carefully turning the slices over halfway through the soaking time.

Heat the butter and oil in a large non-stick frying pan over a medium heat and lay the bread slices in the pan. (You may need to fry the bread in 2 batches; if you do, keep the first batch warm in a low oven while you fry the rest.) Fry for 2–3 minutes on each side until golden.

Serve the eggy bread straight away, sprinkled with some sugar, or with a trickle of honey or a dollop of jam.

Tips and swaps

Spice it up Season the batter with a pinch of cinnamon or a few gratings of nutmeg. A small amount of very finely grated lemon or orange zest is also very good.

Fruity version Instead of jam, scatter with strawberries, blueberries and/or raspberries and a dollop of thick yoghurt. Or top with a compote of apples, plums or dried fruit, plus a generous spoonful of yoghurt, if you like.

Savoury eggy bread Leave out the sugar and vanilla, and instead season the egg with salt, pepper and ½ teaspoon English mustard powder. You can also add a bit of finely grated cheese, if you like. Serve as part of a traditional breakfast or easy supper with any combination of bacon, black pudding, roasted tomatoes, fried mushrooms and baked beans.

Bread and butter pudding

This is a simple – and almost endlessly customisable – version of the comforting, classic pud. Here, I've soaked the fruit in some brandy to give it a little more zip, but soaking it in brewed tea will also make it plump and delicious and less likely to scorch in the oven. SERVES 6–8

Large handful of raisins

Good splash of brandy or Calvados, or brewed black tea

About 600g white bread, 1 or 2 days old, crusts removed and cut into thickish slices

About 80g butter, softened, plus extra to grease the dish

300ml double cream

300ml whole milk

1 vanilla pod

6 large egg yolks

200g caster sugar

Put the raisins in a small bowl with just enough brandy or brewed black tea to cover, and leave to macerate for an hour, until plumped up.

Lightly butter a shallow baking dish, about 24cm square. Butter the bread and cut the slices in half on the diagonal to form triangles.

Pour the cream and milk into a saucepan. Split the vanilla pod lengthways, scrape out the seeds with the point of a small, sharp knife, and add them to the pan with the pod. Place over a medium heat until bubbles appear around the edges.

Take the pan off the heat and leave to infuse for 10 minutes.

In a large bowl, briefly whisk together the egg yolks and 150g of the sugar to combine. Pour in the hot milk and cream, including the vanilla, whisking all the time. Drain the raisins.

Arrange the triangles of bread in the baking dish in rows, propped up and leaning on each other so they come just proud of the dish, sprinkling the raisins in between. Try to conceal the raisins beneath the bread as they may scorch if exposed to the direct heat.

Strain the custard through a sieve over the bread (save the vanilla pod for vanilla sugar, see page 242).

Let the pudding stand for 30 minutes or so, to allow the custard to soak in. Heat the oven to 180°C/Fan 160°C/Gas 4 and boil the kettle.

Sprinkle the rest of the sugar over the surface of the pudding. Sit the dish in a roasting tin and pour in enough boiling water to come halfway up the sides of the dish. Bake for 25–30 minutes, until the custard is just set in the middle – it should have a slight wobble to it.

Serve the pudding hot or warm, with cream or a scoop of ice cream.

Tips and swaps

Add jam or marmalade If you have a few spoonfuls of either left in a jar, spread on the sliced bread before assembling and pouring over the custard.

Apricot or date version Substitute toffee-ish dried Hunza apricots or pitted dates for the raisins. These are better soaked in tea rather than brandy. Chop the dried fruit into small pieces after soaking.

Banana and chocolate version Tuck a sliced banana or two and some coarsely chopped chocolate beneath the bread slices.

Marmalade pudding

For centuries, humble breadcrumbs have been used to stretch the possibilities of other, more glamorous ingredients. Here, they form part of a simple and satisfying pudding, which makes use of that other storecupboard stalwart, a jar of marmalade. SERVES 6-8

Knob of soft butter, to grease the dish

About 300g marmalade

2 large eggs, separated, plus 2 extra egg yolks

200ml double cream

100g caster sugar

1 teaspoon orange flower water, whisky or Drambuie (optional)

150g white breadcrumbs, slightly stale is fine

Icing sugar, for dusting

Preheat the oven to 180°C/Fan 160°C/Gas 4. Butter a 1.5 litre ovenproof dish.

You want the marmalade to have a loose consistency, like a thick compote. If it is very thick, 'let it down' a bit by mixing with a little boiling water, then leave it to cool completely.

Mix the marmalade with the 4 egg yolks, the cream, caster sugar and orange flower water or alcohol, if using, until creamy and thoroughly blended. Set aside a heaped tablespoonful of the breadcrumbs and stir the rest thoroughly into the mix.

In a separate, scrupulously clean bowl, whisk the egg whites to soft peaks. Gently fold them into the batter with a metal spoon. Carefully pour into the prepared dish and sprinkle the reserved breadcrumbs over the top.

Stand the dish in a roasting tin. Pour boiling water from the kettle into the tin so it comes halfway up the sides of the dish, then carefully transfer to the oven. Bake for 50–60 minutes until set – it should have a little quiver about it, and not be too solid.

Remove the dish from the roasting tin. Dust the pudding with icing sugar and serve with cream, yoghurt or ice cream.

Tips and swaps

Dried fruity version Plump up a handful of raisins, sultanas, dried apricots or pitted prunes by soaking in some tea for 10 minutes, then drain and place in the bottom of the ovenproof dish before adding the batter.

Fresh fruity version You can also replace the marmalade with a fruit compote – of apple,

rhubarb or plum, for example. You might need to add an extra dash of sugar.

Jammy version This pud works very well if you replace the marmalade with any favourite jam – especially tart jams like raspberry, gooseberry and blackcurrant. As with the marmalade, loosen with a dash of hot water if needed.

Spaghetti bolognese omelette

Spaghetti bolognese is given a second life here as a tasty – if unlikely – filling for an omelette. And in my house it's become a whole new favourite family supper in itself! It also works well as a quick lunch with a crisp green salad, or as a late-night snack. SERVES 1–2

Few spoonfuls of leftover spaghetti bolognese (the pasta and the sauce)

Knob of butter

3 large eggs, lightly beaten

Few gratings of Parmesan or other hard cheese

Salt and freshly ground black pepper

Put the spaghetti bolognese into a small pan with a small splash of water over a low heat until the pasta and sauce are just heated through (or you can heat it up in a microwave).

Heat the butter in a 23cm frying pan over a medium-high heat until bubbling. Tip some of the melted butter into the bowl of beaten eggs. Stir and season with salt and pepper, then pour the eggs into the pan.

Let the base of the omelette set a bit, then push the set parts of the omelette into the middle of the pan, tilting the pan to swirl the uncooked egg around the edges of the pan.

When the omelette is almost set, spoon the hot spaghetti bolognese into the middle of it and grate over some cheese. Fold the omelette in half and tip onto a plate. Eat immediately.

Tips and swaps

This is also a great way to use up the last spoonfuls of all sorts of pasta suppers, from macaroni cheese to any kind of pasta in pesto.

Frittata version Follow the method on page 44, adding as much spaghetti bolognese as the eggs will hold – a good couple of ladlefuls. Use a vegetable peeler to pare Parmesan or other hard cheese over the top before putting it in the oven or under the grill to finish cooking.

Many bean salad

This is the sort of thing I can rustle up quickly in the middle of the working day, as long as I have some leftover pulses or tinned beans. Softer pulses fare best: cannellini, borlotti, pinto, kidney or black beans, and chickpeas. At its simplest, this salad may be just a tin of cannellini beans drained and tossed in a mustardy vinaigrette with some chopped spring onions and flaked tinned fish. At its most exuberant, it has many more ingredients. Indeed, it can be a great clear-the-fridge assembly. SERVES 2–4

400–500g cooked pulses, either alone or in combination (see above), drained and rinsed if tinned

160g tin sustainably fished tuna (such as Fish4Ever)

5–6 spring onions, trimmed and sliced

Small bunch of parsley, leaves picked and roughly chopped

3–4 tablespoons mustardy vinaigrette (see page 38)

Salt and freshly ground black pepper

Additional flavouring ingredients:

Preserved artichoke hearts, thickly sliced

—

Chunky cubes of avocado

—

Capers

—

Celery, very finely diced (use the leaves too, if you have them, instead of or as well as the parsley)

—

Cornichons, chopped

—

Hard-boiled eggs, halved or quartered

—

Soft goat's cheese or feta, crumbled

—

Red onion, halved and thinly sliced, instead of or with the spring onions

—

Sweetcorn, cooked, or raw if very fresh

—

Cherry tomatoes or sun-blush tomatoes

—

Olives, pitted (whole or halved)

Toss everything together with the dressing, adding any ingredients you fancy from the suggestions listed.

Toss the salad again, taste and add a little more salt and pepper if needed. Give it a final mix and serve.

Tips and swaps

Dressing thrift If you're using ingredients preserved in oil, such as artichoke hearts, olives or sun-blush tomatoes, taste the oil; if it has a good flavour, use it to make your vinaigrette. Also taste the vinegar from your caper or cornichon jar. If it tastes alright and you fancy a sharp, punchy dressing, use this too.

Lemony version Instead of the vinaigrette, dress the salad with a little finely grated lemon zest, a squeeze of lemon juice, a splash of well-flavoured extra virgin olive oil and some black pepper and flaky sea salt. You could also add some chopped salted lemon peels (see page 268) to the salad.

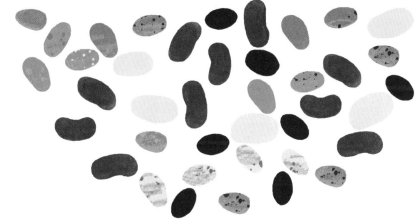

Spicy bean pâté

This spicy pâté is incredibly tasty and gives you the chance to use up any leftover pulses you might have hanging around – you can use them alone or in combination. It will keep in a sealed tub in the fridge for a couple of days and it also freezes quite well, so you could use half and freeze half for later.

SERVES 3–4 AS A SNACK OR DIP

1 teaspoon rapeseed or sunflower oil, or a knob of butter

2 shallots or 1 small onion, finely chopped

1 garlic clove, finely chopped

1 small red or green chilli, finely chopped (membrane and seeds retained if you like a bit of heat)

½ teaspoon ground coriander

½ teaspoon ground cumin

About 250g cooked chickpeas, kidney beans, borlotti beans, or other favourite pulse, drained and rinsed if tinned

50g sun-blush tomatoes, roughly chopped, plus 1 tablespoon of their oil (or use quartered cherry tomatoes, and an extra dash of olive oil)

Grating or two of lemon zest and a good squeeze of juice

3–4 tablespoons roughly chopped coriander leaves, plus extra to serve if you like

1–2 spring onions, trimmed and sliced

Salt and freshly ground black pepper

Heat the oil or butter in a small frying pan over a medium-low heat and sauté the shallots or onion with a pinch of salt until softened, about 5 minutes. Add the garlic, chilli and spices and sauté for a further minute – be careful not to burn the spices.

Scrape the onion mixture into a food processor, add the pulses, sun-blush tomato oil, lemon zest and juice, and the coriander. Pulse to a coarse paste – you really don't want it to be smooth. Taste and season with salt and pepper.

Scrape the pâté into a bowl and stir in the chopped sun-blush tomatoes. Cover with cling film and chill for at least an hour to allow the flavours to blend and the pâté to firm up.

Let the pâté come to room temperature before serving, with the spring onions and extra coriander, if using, sprinkled over the top.

Tips and swaps

Pâté patties A tasty way to use any leftover bean pâté. You need quite a dry consistency for this, so if the mix is too soft to hold together when you try to form the patties, add some ground almonds or breadcrumbs to get it to a workable stiff consistency. Form the pâté into little cakes about 6cm in diameter and 2cm thick and roll them in flour, gently shaking off any excess. Heat a film of sunflower oil in a large frying pan over a medium-high heat and fry the patties, turning them over 2 or 3 times, for about 8 minutes until crisp on the outside and hot on the inside. Serve with guacamole and/or thick wholemilk yoghurt seasoned with salt and pepper and some freshly chopped dill or parsley.

Crispy Puy lentil salad

This is a great way of using up some leftover cooked lentils. In fact, you can simply fry the lentils on their own until crisp, season them well and eat them as a snack if you like. The secret to getting them to crisp up is to make sure they're as dry as possible before frying them, so pat them on some kitchen paper or a clean tea towel before tipping them into the hot pan. SERVES 2

1 small red onion, halved and thinly sliced

1 tablespoon rapeseed or sunflower oil, plus extra rapeseed oil or well-flavoured olive oil for dressing

About 150g cooked Puy lentils

Sprinkling of paprika (optional)

1–2 avocados, halved, peeled, stoned and cut into thick slices

Handful or two of parsley or coriander leaves, roughly chopped, or some peppery rocket leaves, roughly torn

Good squeeze of lemon juice

Salt and freshly ground black pepper

Place the sliced onion in a bowl of iced water for 10 minutes – you don't have to do this, but it will maximise the crunch and take away some of the raw heat. Drain and pat dry on kitchen paper.

Heat the oil in a medium frying pan over a high heat. Add the lentils – they should sizzle as they hit the oil. You don't want to crowd the pan too much, so you may need to fry them in batches. Sauté for about 3–4 minutes, shaking the lentils around in the pan quite a bit, until they start to crisp up.

Remove from the heat, tip the lentils onto kitchen paper to drain and immediately season them with salt, pepper and a bit of paprika if you like.

Transfer the lentils to a large plate or bowl. Toss gently with the onion, avocado, herbs, lemon juice and a generous trickle of rapeseed or olive oil. Season with salt and pepper and serve.

Tips and swaps

Punchier dressing Toss the lentil salad with a mustardy vinaigrette (see page 38) rather than the simple lemon and oil dressing.

Tahini dressing Mix 2 tablespoons tahini with 4 tablespoons yoghurt then thin to a creamy consistency with a splash of hot water if necessary. Season with a grated garlic clove and a pinch of salt. Trickle over the salad just before serving.

Sprouting pulses

For years, sprouting pulses, seeds and grains has been seen as a left-field and somewhat worthy branch of meat-free cookery. But the tide has turned as we look more widely for tasty, easy, sustainable, inexpensive and nutritious things to eat. I'm happy to declare myself a sprouter, loud and proud – and you can be too. I'd wager that, in your cupboards right now, are packets and jars of glossy, dried mung beans, chickpeas, lentils or aduki beans waiting to be summoned from their dormancy into exciting, shooting life. No special equipment is needed, just check you have some large glass jars, muslin and string or a few rubber bands.

Some dried pulses (a handful or so for each jar): aduki beans, chickpeas, whole lentils (not the split variety) and mung beans work well

Make sure the jars are scrupulously clean, rinsed and dry. Put the pulses or lentils into each jar (one variety per jar). You don't want them to be more than two deep when the jar is later tilted on its side, so don't cram them in too tightly. Pour on cold water to cover; larger pulses like chickpeas need to be covered by about 10cm water as they soak up a lot of liquid.

Cover the top of the jar with a layer of muslin and secure it tightly with string or an elastic band. Leave to soak for 4 hours or overnight; older pulses may need longer.

Drain off as much water as you can, through the muslin. Prop the jar up on a tray at an angle, so that the water can continue to drain and the pulses spread out along the length of the jar. Place out of direct sunlight.

Every 12 hours, with the muslin cover still in place, rinse and drain your crop and return the jar to its tilted position. That's it. Some pulses will take longer than others, but after 5–7 days, they should all be up and perky and ready to rinse and add to your salads, sandwiches, wraps and stir-fries.

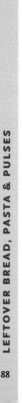

Tips and swaps

Don't use Butter beans, flageolets, haricots, cannellini and kidney beans are not suitable for sprouting.

Storing your sprouts If you're not going to eat them as soon as they're ready, rinse the sprouts in cold water, drain well and lay on kitchen paper. When dried a bit more, store the sprouts in self-sealing plastic bags or plastic containers in the fridge – they'll keep for 2–4 days.

Rough-and-ready hummus Mash sprouted chickpeas with a squeeze of lemon and some tahini, salt and pepper.

Ribollita

This thrifty Italian classic is a triumph of forgiveness when it comes to making the most of leftovers. Its name means reboiled – the intention being that it could be made in vast amounts, then reheated on subsequent days. It's not only a great vehicle for leftover cannellini beans, but also all manner of cooked and raw veg, and even a scrap of Parmesan rind. SERVES 4–6

2 tablespoons olive oil, plus extra to finish

1 onion, finely chopped

1 carrot, finely chopped

1 celery stick, finely chopped

1 garlic clove, finely chopped

Small sprig of rosemary

Any roast roots, such as carrots, parsnips, celeriac, even potatoes, chopped fairly small

1–1.5 litres veg or chicken stock (see page 28), depending on the amount of veg and pulses you're using

400g tin whole plum tomatoes, roughly chopped

200–400g cooked cannellini beans, drained and rinsed if tinned

100–150g cooked chickpeas, drained and rinsed if tinned

Piece of Parmesan rind (optional)

Few handfuls of shredded greens, fresh or leftover (see tips and swaps)

Salt and freshly ground black pepper

To serve

4–6 slices of slightly stale sourdough bread

1 garlic clove, halved

Some well-flavoured extra virgin olive oil

Heat the olive oil in a large saucepan over a medium-low heat. Add the onion, carrot and celery with a pinch of salt and sauté until softened, about 10 minutes. Add the garlic, rosemary and any leftover roots, and give everything a stir for a minute.

Tip in the stock, tomatoes and pulses. Add the Parmesan rind, if you have one, and season with a few grinds of black pepper. Bring to a simmer and lower the heat.

Cook gently for 30 minutes, adding any raw greens 5–10 minutes before the end to become tender. Add cooked leaves at the end, just to heat through.

Fish out the rosemary sprig and Parmesan rind and season with salt and pepper to taste.

Lightly toast the bread. Rub with the cut surface of the garlic, then place a slice of toast in each warmed bowl. Ladle the ribollita over the top and trickle over a little extra virgin olive oil before serving.

Tips and swaps

Leftover greens These can be the odd raw and less-than-perky leaves of cabbage or cavolo nero, or leftover cooked vegetables. You can also add salad leaves, such as radicchio, rocket and lettuce.

Quick cassoulet

I publish this recipe with a sense of mild terror, lest any of the honourable people from Toulouse, Carcassonne or Castelnaudary, who take cassoulet very seriously indeed, ever come across my rough-and-ready version. But I make no apology: it may not be authentic but it pays homage to the original while taking less than an hour (rather than a couple of days) to make – and it tastes great. It's the perfect solution to a coincidence of leftover meat and leftover pulses, but also worth cracking open a couple of tins of beans for. SERVES 4–6

3–6 cooked Toulouse sausages or other well-seasoned butcher's bangers

200–400g cooked pork, ham, lamb or poultry, or a combination

4 slices of smoked or unsmoked bacon (optional)

1 teaspoon rapeseed or sunflower oil

1 onion, finely chopped

1 bay leaf and 1 sprig of thyme, tied together with kitchen string

3–4 garlic cloves, finely chopped

1 tablespoon tomato purée

1 tablespoon red wine vinegar

400g tin whole plum tomatoes, roughly chopped (or 400ml passata)

300–500g cooked haricot or cannellini beans, or a mix of haricots, cannellini and chickpeas, drained and rinsed if tinned

Salt and freshly ground black pepper

For the topping

About 50g seasoned breadcrumbs (see page 39)

Knob of butter

Cut the cooked sausages into largish bite-sized pieces and the other meat (including the bacon, if using) into strips or bite-sized chunks.

Heat the oil in a medium-large heavy-based casserole over a medium heat. Add the onion, along with the bacon if using, and sauté until the onion is soft and golden.

Add the herb bundle, garlic, chopped sausages and other meat, along with a pinch of salt. Sauté for a couple of minutes, then stir in the tomato purée and wine vinegar and let it simmer for a couple of minutes.

Tip in the tomatoes and pulses, and season with salt and pepper. Add a splash of water if it looks a bit dry, bring to a simmer and cook for 20 minutes. Remove the herb bundle.

Heat up the grill (or oven to 220°C/Fan 200°C/Gas 7 if your pan won't fit under the grill).

Sprinkle the breadcrumbs on top of the cassoulet and dot with the butter. Place under the grill (or in the oven) until the top is golden and crisp; this will take just a few minutes under the grill, 5–10 minutes in the oven.

Serve with crusty bread and a crisp green salad.

Tips and swaps

Add tomatoes If you have some slightly soft
tomatoes, chop them up and add to the mix.

Swap the meats Feel free to add other leftover
cooked meat to the cassoulet, such as confit
duck leg.

LEFTOVER RICE

Cooked rice is one of the most thrown-away staples there is. A WRAP (Waste and Resources Action Programme) report in 2012 noted that in the UK we chucked away an alarming 40,000 tonnes of the stuff every year. I imagine the reasons are twofold.

The first is that it's always a challenge to believe that so little dried rice can, when cooked, feed so many and we're often tempted to cook too much. The second is a very real fear of food poisoning, which cooked rice is particularly adept at passing on (see page 19). But as long as you cool it quickly, store it properly and use it within a day, two tops, revisited rice is perfectly safe to eat.

Wasted rice is a terrible shame, both for the planet and for our dinner plates, where it can most certainly find a happy second life. If you inadvertently cook too much rice (and who doesn't?) from time to time, remember that whether it's fluffy or nutty, creamy or crispy, it carries flavour in a near-spectacular way, making it an excellent vehicle for other leftovers.

Rice's mild starchiness enables it to take on other flavours beautifully. Try adding all manner of chopped herbs: experiment with enough to make it almost completely green, it can take it. Or pep it up with spices like cumin and coriander, or warming blends such as curry powder and garam masala. Or fork through toasted nuts and seeds, dried fruits such as raisins, barberries and chopped apricots, and/or fine gratings of citrus zest.

You can combine rice with other grains too, such as spelt, quinoa or pearl barley to add texture and flavour, or extend its potential with lentils, chickpeas or other pulses. Given this generous and imaginative treatment, rice can swell meagre scraps of meat, fish and veg into a sustaining meal.

One final suggestion, honed from years of hastily assembled leftover inspirations: whatever else you have to fling into your rice, an egg never goes amiss...

Please refer and adhere to the instructions on how to chill cooked rice safely on page 19.

Egg fried rice

Surely one of the great leftover opportunities, this can be taken in so many different directions, the only given being eggs and rice. The rest is a cornucopia of other ingredients – leftovers you may have lurking in the fridge and fresh items you fancy adding. Once you've fried the rice you can just chuck the egg in and start stirring it around, but to get those nice little niblets of cooked egg distributed through the rice, follow the technique I use here. SERVES 2

1–2 eggs, lightly beaten

Pinch of dried chilli flakes (optional)

1 tablespoon rapeseed or sunflower oil

150–200g cold cooked rice

Some chopped herbs – parsley, chervil, thyme, oregano, chives all work well (optional)

Salt and freshly ground black pepper

Additional flavouring ingredients:

Shards of cooked pork, chicken and beef

Flakes of cooked fish, chopped cooked squid and cooked mussels

Cooked veg, such as thinly sliced courgette; finely chopped pepper, mushrooms and spring onions; peas and broad beans

Shredded greens, such as spinach, chard or lettuce leaves

Sprinkling of spices, such as ground cumin, five-spice powder or cayenne

Lots of chopped leafy herbs, such as parsley, coriander, mint and Thai basil

In a small bowl, whisk the egg(s) with some salt and pepper. Add some chilli, if you like. Have to hand anything else you might want to add, so you can work very quickly once you start cooking.

Heat the oil in a wok or deep non-stick frying pan over a medium-high heat. Throw in the rice and stir it well until coated in the oil and thoroughly heated through – it should be sizzling nicely in the pan.

Push the rice to one side so you have a half-empty pan then tip the beaten egg into the empty side. Cook it for 30 seconds or so, like an omelette – pushing it around so the runny bit goes back into the gaps and sets firm.

Now break the egg up a bit and start bringing back the rice. This is also the right time to toss in any other pre-cooked items, fresh leaves and spices you wish to add. Keep stirring and tossing everything together until well mixed, thoroughly hot and any leaves are just wilted. Toss in chopped herbs right at the end.

Eat at once, with a splash of soy sauce or chilli sauce, even brown sauce is pretty good!

Ricey pancake

This is a useful reworking of the egg-rice partnership, for when you have less rice but plenty of eggs. It's a kind of omelettey, ricey pancake, and can be pleasingly topped with other goodies or even rolled up around them like a wrap. SERVES 1–2

2 large eggs, lightly beaten

About 70g cold cooked rice

Some chopped herbs – parsley, chervil, thyme, oregano, chives all work well (optional)

Generous knob of butter

Salt and freshly ground black pepper

Stir together the eggs and cooked rice. Season generously with salt and pepper and add some chopped herbs, if you like.

Warm the butter in a small, non-stick frying pan over a medium-high heat. Tip half of the butter into the rice and egg mixture and stir, then pour the mixture into the pan. Smooth it out with a spatula and let it set. Don't be too quick to flip it – you want it to develop nice crispy bits around the edges. Turn it over and let it cook through.

Turn the pancake onto a plate and finish off with one of the combinations suggested below.

Tips and swaps

Top or wrap your ricey pancake with any of the following combinations:

Mushrooms sautéed with garlic, plus crème fraîche and chopped dill.

Leftover ratatouille or sautéed sliced pepper, courgette, aubergine and garlic with some chopped basil.

Leftover curry and seasoned yoghurt.

Leftover flaked fish, thinly sliced red onion, capers and crème fraîche.

'Arancini' patties

If you have some leftover risotto, one of the most delicious things you can do with it is transform it into these Italian-style fried rice balls. They're good quite plain with just some cheese worked into them, or with other scraps of leftover meet or veg mixed in. Authentic arancini are deep-fried and have a molten centre of mozzarella, but these simple patties are much less fuss to assemble and easy to shallow-fry. MAKES ABOUT 6

250–350g cold cooked risotto

50–70g Parmesan or other hard cheese, grated

Any scraps of cooked meat or fish, torn or chopped into small pieces

Any cooked veg, such as mushrooms or courgettes, chopped small, and/or peas

Some soft herbs, such as parsley, dill, lovage, chervil and/or chives, chopped (optional)

1 egg, beaten, to bind (if needed)

Salt and freshly ground black pepper

For the coating

Some plain flour

1–2 eggs, lightly beaten (optional)

Couple of handfuls of fine breadcrumbs (optional)

For frying

Sunflower oil

Tip the cold risotto into a bowl and stir in the cheese. Add any extra scraps of cooked meat, fish or veg that you think will work well. Add some chopped herbs if you like, taste, then season with more salt and pepper if necessary.

Mix everything together well. It should be sticky enough to hold together, but add a little beaten egg to bind if needed.

Roll the mixture into walnut- to golf-ball-sized balls, then flatten lightly to form plump patties.

Dust the patties with flour, and, if you want to go the whole crispy-coating hog, dip them in beaten egg, then into fine breadcrumbs – but just flouring them is fine, too.

Heat about a 1cm depth of oil in a large, non-stick frying pan over a medium-high heat. Shallow-fry the arancini patties, in batches if necessary, fairly gently until golden brown on the outside and piping hot in the centre. Serve immediately.

Tips and swaps

To make large arancini with a surprise centre, take 2 patties (*before* flouring them), make a dimple in the middle of each and spoon a tasty filling into one of them (see right). Place the non-filled patty, dimple side down, on top then squish the 2 patties together to seal in the filling and make a single, fat patty. Repeat with the rest. Fry as above and serve piping hot.

Filling options

Cubes of mozzarella or blue cheese (as shown).

Fried mushrooms, with cooked peas, if you like.

Scraps of ham or chunks of cooked sausage.

Cooked spinach and pine nuts, mixed with some soft goat's cheese.

Stuffed vegetables

If you have leftover risotto, pilaf or even kedgeree, it makes a great stuffing for baked tomatoes. Try it with other veg too – peppers, the round varieties of courgettes, and small, acorn- or butternut-type squashes all work well. With squashes, you may need to part-bake them for 15 minutes or so to get them started before adding the filling. SERVES 4

4 extra-large tomatoes

120–150g cooked risotto, pilaf or kedgeree

150ml white wine

2–3 tablespoons olive oil

Salt and freshly ground black pepper

Preheat the oven to 180°C/Fan 160°C/Gas 4.

Slice the lids off the tomatoes, scoop out the centres and chop the fleshy bits, discarding the seeds, then tip into a bowl. Season the insides of the tomato shells with salt and pepper; reserve the 'lids'.

If you're using leftover kedgeree, chop any eggs in the mix quite small.

Add the ricey leftovers to the chopped tomatoes and mix well, seasoning with salt and pepper to taste.

Spoon the rice filling into the tomato shells, then replace the tomato lids. Arrange the tomatoes fairly snugly in an oiled baking tin or ceramic dish and pour the wine and olive oil around (but not over) them.

Bake for 45–60 minutes until the tomatoes are slightly charred and the filling is piping hot.

You may need to adjust the cooking time with other vegetables – courgettes and peppers will take 30–45 minutes, squash rather longer (see introduction). You want the stuffed vegetables to be charred slightly and the skins should be easy to pierce with a small, sharp knife.

Tips and swaps

Stuffing variations Season plain leftover rice generously with salt and pepper to taste and combine with any of the following:

Cooked spinach or chard, crumbled ricotta, grated nutmeg, toasted pine nuts and grated Parmesan or other hard cheese.

Pesto, chopped green or black olives and cubes of mozzarella.

Sautéed onion, garlic and courgettes, chunks of cooked sausage and chopped sage.

Few spoonfuls of leftover bolognese or stew and Parmesan or other hard cheese.

Risottover

I know for some of you this might be a rice resurrection too far – pure leftover folly – but on a chilly evening, it's comforting and tasty and fast! If you have leftover rice, cook the veg; if you have leftover veg, cook the rice; if you've got both, there is little to do other than combine the two. SERVES 4

1 tablespoon olive oil

Knob of butter

1 onion, chopped

1 bay leaf

Cooked veg, such as roast root veg, boiled or steamed carrots, Brussels sprouts, greens, peas, broad beans or green beans

Any bits of roast meat or crumbled cooked sausages (optional)

2 garlic cloves, finely chopped

About 300g cold cooked rice

About 100ml gravy, diluted with boiling water, or hot stock

Handful of grated Parmesan or hard goat's cheese, plus extra to serve

Some finely chopped parsley leaves or torn basil leaves (optional, but adds vitality)

Salt and freshly ground black pepper

Pan grattato (see below), to serve (optional)

Heat the olive oil and butter in a large saucepan over a medium-low heat. Add the onion and bay leaf with a pinch of salt and sweat gently, stirring from time to time, until the onion is softened and translucent, about 10 minutes.

Meanwhile, cut whole or chunky veg and any larger pieces of meat into smaller pieces.

Add the garlic to the onion and cook for about a minute, then stir in any cooked root veg and meat. Heat through, stirring well.

Scatter over the rice and add any green beans, peas, broad beans or greens. Stir, then pour on enough hot diluted gravy or stock to moisten the rice – you don't want to drown it or the rice will become mushy.

Cover the pan, lower the heat and cook for 3–5 minutes, removing the lid for an occasional stir, until thoroughly hot.

Sprinkle on the grated cheese and chopped herbs, if using, and fork through gently.

Serve immediately, with pan grattato sprinkled over the top if you like, and more cheese to pass around the table.

Pan grattato

Make a batch of these Italian-style dried breadcrumbs and keep on hand to sprinkle over gratins and to thicken soups, and sauces such as salsa verde. Break up pieces of slightly stale, crustless white bread into big chunks, scatter on a baking tray and dry out in the oven at 160°C/Fan 140°C/Gas 3; about 15 minutes should do it. Leave to dry out completely on the oven tray, then pulse to coarse crumbs in a food processor. They'll keep, sealed in a jar in a cool place, for a couple of months.

Leftovers laksa

A dab of spice paste, some tasty stock, a handful of veg and some leftover rice make for a quick and tasty meal with this laksa-inspired soup. Basmati is great here, but brown rice can be very good too. Make it as thick or as thin as your hunger and leftovers dictate – fairly thin for a light meal, or, if you are really hungry, bulk up the carbs with extra rice or thin rice noodles, making it almost a risotto-ish consistency. SERVES 4

1–2 tablespoons home-made curry paste (see page 57), or ready-made laksa paste

750ml chicken or veg stock (see page 28)

400ml tin coconut milk

1 tablespoon fish sauce

½ teaspoon light muscovado sugar

100 –200g cooked rice, or half cooked thin rice noodles and half cooked rice

Salt and freshly ground black pepper

Additional flavouring ingredients:

Fresh or cooked green beans or peas

Shredded cooked chicken, beef or pork

Flaked cooked fish

Cubed tofu

Sliced raw mushrooms

Shredded lettuce, or a handful of baby spinach

To serve

Coriander, mint and/or Thai basil leaves, shredded

Lime wedges

Heat a wok or saucepan over a medium-high heat and fry the curry paste for a couple of minutes, stirring to make sure it doesn't burn – it should smell wonderful.

Add the stock, coconut milk, fish sauce and sugar and bring to the boil. Simmer for 5 minutes, then add the rice and noodles, if using, along with any of the other ingredients you fancy, and cook until heated though.

Serve in warmed bowls with the herbs scattered over the top and lime wedges on the side.

Rice veggie burgers

These are very tasty and easy to make. Customise them as you like, adding pretty much whatever chopped veg and pulses you have hanging around. MAKES 2 LARGE OR 4 SMALL BURGERS

50g cooked pulses, such as borlotti beans or chickpeas and/or lentils, well drained

200–250g cold cooked rice

1 shallot, finely diced, or 2–3 spring onions, trimmed and finely sliced

1 small garlic clove, finely chopped

2 tablespoons finely chopped parsley

¼–½ teaspoon cayenne pepper

Any leftover roasted, steamed or boiled root veg, including potatoes, diced quite small

Handful or two of cooked peas

2 eggs, lightly beaten

Vegetable oil or rapeseed oil, for frying

Salt and freshly ground black pepper

To serve (optional)

Burger buns

Slices of cheese

Slices of tomato

Lettuce and/or cucumber slices

Mayonnaise, mustard and/or ketchup

Pickle

Put the pulses into a bowl and mash lightly with a fork. Add the rice, shallot, garlic, parsley and cayenne and fork everything together. Stir in the vegetables, season very well with salt and pepper, and then stir in the beaten eggs.

Put to one side for 15 minutes or so, to allow the flavours to blend.

Heat a 1–2mm layer of oil in a large non-stick frying pan over a medium-high heat. Drop 2 ladlefuls of the ricey batter into the pan for large 'burgers', or 4 large spoonfuls for smaller ones and coax them into neatish circular shapes with a spatula.

Turn the heat down slightly and fry for about 5 minutes (they're ready to flip when they hold together easily when you try to turn them). Flip them and fry the other side for 5–6 minutes until they are piping hot all the way through and tasty crispy bits have developed around the outside.

Fix your burgers as you like them, in buns with cheese and/or salad and condiments, or bunless with condiments and a simple green salad on the side.

Tips and swaps

Curried burgers Add ½–1 teaspoon curry powder or garam masala to the basic mixture.

Chilli burgers For some pleasing heat and freshness without the whole spectrum of curry flavours, add a finely chopped, small green or red chilli, leaving the seeds and membrane in if you like it hot.

Cheesy burgers Stir a few tablespoonfuls of finely grated Cheddar or other hard cheese, or some chopped mozzarella, into the basic mix.

Ricey pudding

This sweetened, ricey custard makes a cosy pudding. Most rice works well – basmati, jasmine, long-grain – but avoid anything that's heavily seasoned, and wholegrain rice, which will never take on the required creamy texture. SERVES 6

1 tablespoon melted butter, plus extra to grease the dish

200ml whole milk

1 large egg, lightly beaten

2 tablespoons cream (optional)

1½ tablespoons vanilla sugar or caster sugar

½ teaspoon vanilla extract

Pinch of salt

150g cooked rice

Few handfuls of blueberries (optional)

Preheat the oven to 180°C/Fan 160°C/Gas 4. Lightly butter an ovenproof dish, about 1 litre capacity.

Whisk the melted butter, milk, egg, cream, if using, sugar, vanilla extract and salt together in a jug.

Put the rice into the ovenproof dish, pour over the custard mixture and give it a stir. Scatter the blueberries over the top, if using.

Stand the dish in a roasting tin and pour in boiling water from the kettle to come about halfway up the sides of the dish.

Carefully place in the oven and bake for about 40 minutes, until set but still a bit wobbly. Carefully remove from the oven.

Serve warm or cold, with an extra splash of thick cream or crème fraîche and some jam or fruit compote, if you like.

Tips and swaps

You can vary and adapt this recipe by adding one or more of the following to the rice before pouring on the custard:

Pinch of ground cinnamon and/or some freshly grated nutmeg.

Some finely grated lemon or orange zest.

Handful of raisins or sultanas.

Some dried cranberries and chopped walnuts.

Some chopped, unsulphured dried apricots.

Ricey pudding slices Once cold, the pudding can be cut into slices and fried in a little butter. Dust with icing sugar just before serving.

Coconut ricey pudding Stir the rice together with a 400ml tin coconut milk, 1 tablespoon light muscovado sugar, a little finely grated orange zest, a good pinch of ground cinnamon and a few gratings of nutmeg. Bake as above, in a dish lightly greased with sunflower or coconut oil.

LEFTOVER DAIRY

When I do my weekly trawl through the fridge to work
out what needs using up, it's very often the dairy section
that calls to me most. Milk, yoghurt, butter and cheese
are ingredients I regularly keep in stock, but their relative
delicacy means that a constant check must be kept on their
fresh-and-lovely status.

   Often, I need to use up bottles of milk before separation
anxiety sets in, scrape up the last scraps of cream or crème
fraîche, dig out some dry ends of cheese or rescue tubs
of yoghurt that have become a bit too acidic to spoon onto
my breakfast fruit.

   Luckily, transforming end-of-the-day dairy into dinner
is a simple proposition. It's also often creative: most
dairy products fall naturally on a spectrum of separation,
fermentation and maturation – that's how we make butter,
yoghurt and cheese in the first place. Dealing with leftovers
is sometimes just a matter of moving that process along.

   Milk that is inclining towards sourness can be turned
into paneer or curd cheese (see page 216). Wholemilk
yoghurt is easily strained to make creamy labneh (see page
218), which adds a luxurious note to salads. Gently ageing
cream, meanwhile, is the best starting point for making
your own butter.

The liquid by-products of these simple manipulations – buttermilk from butter and whey from cheese – can be used too. They're great as a substitute for water or milk in pancakes, waffles, breads and cornbread, or in marinades for meat (they will help tenderise it). Finally butter itself can, when close to the turn, be stabilised by clarifying into ghee (see page 108).

Cheese is perhaps the most amenable leftover of all. It rarely goes off, it just dries out and matures, which only intensifies its delicious cheesiness. And, because it melts so obligingly, it's ripe for scattering over other leftovers as well as turning into wafers (see page 294) or rarebits (see page 232). It's only marginally more effort to turn it into potted cheese (see page 230) or a big pan of cheese sauce (see page 228), which you can freeze in batches to set you up for easy meals in the weeks and months to come.

So whether your leftover dairy forms the main event, as in macaroni cheese (see page 229) or fried spiced paneer (see page 217), or is used in small scraped-from-the-carton quantities to round out and enrich sauces, casseroles or soups at the last minute, it's one of your best allies when it comes to elevating simple ingredients into rich and delicious dinners.

Home-made butter

The first time you make butter, you'll wonder why you've never done it before, because it's really not hard – and it's fun! Mature cream 'breaks down' more easily into butterfat and buttermilk than very fresh cream does – so seize the chance to give it a go if you have some double cream which is just on the turn, or you see some very close to its sell-by date in a shop. MAKE ABOUT 220g

500ml double or whipping cream,
at room temperature

Iced water

Flaky sea salt (optional)

Put the cream into the bowl of an electric mixer and beat on a low speed for several minutes. It will start to form buttery clumps and liquid (i.e. buttermilk) will appear at the bottom of the bowl. Strain off this buttermilk into a container and reserve for another use (see below).

Now you need to remove the excess buttermilk within the butter itself; if you don't, it will turn rancid more quickly. Put the clumps of butter into a bowl and pour over some iced water. Use a couple of spatulas or wooden spoons to press and work the butter – the water will become cloudy as the buttermilk comes out. Do this 3 or 4 times with fresh water until the water remains pretty clear.

Return the butter to a clean, dry bowl and continue to knead it with a wooden spoon until it comes together smoothly, pouring off any liquid as it accumulates in the bowl. This is the point to knead a little salt into the butter if you wish – to add flavour and improve its keeping qualities.

Either work the butter into a block and wrap it in waxed paper, or press it into ramekins and wrap in cling film. It will keep in the fridge for a week or, well wrapped in waxed paper and cling film, in the freezer for a couple of months.

Cultured buttermilk

Add a tablespoon or two of live yoghurt to the buttermilk (created as a by-product of your butter-making) and leave it overnight at room temperature so the lactic bacteria can get going. It will then be more acidic and can be used in the same way as commercial buttermilk, for soda bread, scones and fluffy pancakes, or to tenderise chicken for fried chicken dishes.

Tips and swaps

Jam jar butter If you only have a small amount of cream, try making this. Tip the cream into a scrupulously clean jam jar – it should be more than a third full. Seal tightly and shake the jar until the liquid separates and you have a ball of butter and some buttermilk. Pour off the buttermilk (to use later) then pour enough iced water into the jar to just cover the butter. Shake for about 10 seconds and pour off the cloudy liquid. Repeat a few times until the water is clear. Knead lightly with clean hands to remove excess liquid, adding a pinch of salt if you like. Cover and refrigerate.

Cultured butter For a great, tangy flavour to your butter, add 1–2 tablespoons live yoghurt to the cream then leave at room temperature for an hour or so, before processing into butter.

Paneer

This mild, pressed Indian cheese is so easy to make, and one of the best ways of using up slightly on-the-turn milk. It's great to have a tub in the fridge, ready to add cubes to curries or soups, or to crumble onto baked potatoes. And you can make a soft curd cheese using the same technique (see tips and swaps, below). As with all simple cheeses, use unhomogenised milk and make sure everything, including your hands, is scrupulously clean before you start. MAKES ABOUT 300g

About 1 litre unhomogenised whole milk, ideally 'just on the turn'

2 tablespoons lemon juice

1 teaspoon rennet

Salt (optional)

Pour the milk into a large saucepan and heat very gently, stirring from time to time so it doesn't catch on the bottom, until it reaches 85°C, or until it just starts to steam and tiny bubbles appear around the edges. Remove from the heat and slowly stir in the lemon juice and rennet.

Cover the pan and leave it for an hour for the curds to separate from the whey.

Line a sieve with a double layer of muslin or cheesecloth and suspend it over a pan. Pour the separated milk through the muslin; keep the whey for another use (see page 214).

Rinse the curds briefly under the cold tap and drain. Pull the edges of the muslin together around the curds and tie into a fairly tight bundle with string. Tie the string to a wooden spoon and suspend over a deep bowl or pan for 20–30 minutes to let the excess liquid drain away. Unwrap the curd cheese and season with salt, if you like.

Shape into a block and re-wrap in the muslin. Place a board or other weight on top to press out more moisture. It should take no longer than 30 minutes to form a firm block.

The paneer can be sliced or fried to add to salads or enjoyed as a snack. You can also stir cubes of paneer into curries or soups.

Any unused paneer can be kept covered with water in a sealed plastic container, in the fridge for up to a week. It also freezes well, for a month or so.

Tips and swaps

Soft curd cheese Follow the above recipe, but don't rinse the soft curds before straining. Tie (but not tightly) in the muslin and suspend over a bowl for a few hours – just until enough whey has drained off to give you the texture you like. The cheese is then ready to use, but can be kept in a tub in the fridge for up to a week. Eat it trickled with a splash of extra virgin oil, and a sprinkling of chopped chives or parsley, flaky sea salt and/or dried chilli flakes. Or crumble into pasta dishes or salads. Or serve it with berries or sliced ripe peaches, a trickle of honey and chopped, toasted hazelnuts.

Add richness If you have a carton of cream, crème fraîche or natural wholemilk yoghurt with just a spoonful or two left that needs using up, you can stir it into the milk before warming for added richness.

Omit the rennet I've taken a rather belt-and-braces approach here by using rennet, but it is possible to use lemon juice on its own to encourage the curds to separate from the whey. Allow approximately the juice of 1 lemon to 1 litre milk.

Fried spiced paneer

Roll paneer cubes (or coat a larger slab) in a mix
of crushed coriander seeds and black pepper, grated
lemon zest and a pinch of dried chilli flakes, then
fry in a little rapeseed oil. Serve topped with dried
rose petals or chopped herbs (thyme, parsley and/
or coriander), a pinch of flaky sea salt and a trickle
of rapeseed oil (as shown).

Labneh

If you have a tub of plain yoghurt that's getting a little too sour, transform it into labneh – or yoghurt 'cheese' – a fabulously useful ingredient for savoury dishes. You may even want to emphasise that acidity by adding some lemon juice. The yoghurt will lose about 25 per cent of its weight in the process, so I like to start out with at least 250g. MAKES ABOUT 180g

250g natural wholemilk or thick, Greek-style live yoghurt (i.e. not low-fat)

Good pinch of salt

Lemon juice and zest (optional)

Whisk the yoghurt together with the salt, adding a squeeze of lemon juice and a few fine gratings of lemon zest if you want a lemony labneh.

Line a bowl with a double layer of muslin. Spoon the yoghurt onto the muslin, pull up the edges around the yoghurt and tie it together tightly with a long piece of string. Tie the string to a wooden spoon and suspend the muslin ball over a deep bowl or jug.

Place in the fridge or in a very cool place and let it drip for about 24 hours. You will be left with a ball of soft, creamy, yoghurty 'cheese'.

Transfer to a plastic container or clean glass jar, seal with a lid and it will keep in the fridge for 10 days.

Serve the labneh sprinkled with za'atar, with a trickle of good olive oil over the top and flatbreads to scoop everything up. Or enjoy it for breakfast trickled with honey, with fresh or poached dried fruit and toasted nuts and/or seeds. It's also good alongside leftover meats in salads, with a spicy dressing that includes a little thinned-down harissa paste.

Tips and swaps

Labneh balls (as shown) Form the labneh into little balls, about the size of large walnuts, then roll in any combination of white and black sesame seeds, chopped chives, parsley or other soft herbs, and chopped almonds, hazelnuts or pistachios. Serve as a canapé with drinks.

Labneh dip Thin the labneh with a little milk if needed and stir in any of the extras suggested for the labneh balls (above), in any combination. Serve as a dip with crudités or bread.

Spiced yoghurt chicken

The acidity of yoghurt, especially more mature yoghurt, makes it a terrific marinade for tenderising meat, helping to carry flavours deep into the flesh. This dish is simple to make, but it has a pleasing complexity of flavour. I use skinless chicken thighs here, as they have such great texture and taste, but you can use any parts of a jointed bird – don't forget to use the skin you remove to make 'chicken crackling' (see page 79). SERVES 4

8 chicken thighs, bone in, skin removed (see above)

1 tablespoon rapeseed or sunflower oil

1 small onion, halved and thinly sliced

For the marinade

1 shallot, finely chopped

1 thumb-sized piece of ginger, peeled and grated

3 garlic cloves, chopped

1 tablespoon garam masala

1 teaspoon ground turmeric

300g natural wholemilk yoghurt (less than fresh is fine)

Juice of 1 lemon

Salt and freshly ground black pepper

To finish

Flaked almonds, lightly toasted

Coriander leaves (optional)

First make the marinade. Either pound the shallot, ginger, garlic and spices together with a good pinch of salt using a pestle and mortar or whiz them to a rough paste in a mini food processor.

Scrape the paste into a bowl (large enough to hold all the chicken) and whisk in the yoghurt, lemon juice and some black pepper. Add the chicken thighs and turn them over to coat in the marinade.

Cover the bowl with cling film and leave to marinate in the fridge for at least 4 hours or overnight if you can.

Remove the chicken from the fridge 30 minutes before you bake it. Preheat the oven to 200°C/Fan 180°C/Gas 6.

Heat the oil in a small frying pan over a medium heat and sauté the onion until soft and just starting to turn golden, about 8 minutes.

Arrange the chicken in an ovenproof dish in a single layer and spoon the yoghurt marinade over the top. Scatter over the onion. Bake for 30–35 minutes, until the chicken is cooked through and the juices run clear (not pink) when the thickest part of the thigh is pierced with a small, sharp knife.

Scatter with toasted almonds and coriander leaves, if you have some to hand. Serve with basmati rice.

Tips and swaps

Swap the meat This works very well with lamb, pork or rabbit too.

Barbecue option Barbecue the thighs for 16–20 minutes, flipping a couple of times, and basting with the marinade from time to time, until the juices run clear when the thickest part of the thigh is pierced with a small, sharp knife.

Lemon and yoghurt pudding cake

This is a version of that cosy favourite, lemon delicious pudding. On cooking, the batter separates, leaving a pool of lemon curd-y sauce at the base of the dish and a tender, light sponge on top. The recipe makes great use of slightly mature yoghurt. If you don't have quite enough, simply combine the yoghurt with some whole milk to bring it up to 250g. SERVES 6

40g butter, melted and cooled, plus extra to grease the dish

160g caster sugar

3 large eggs, separated

Finely grated zest and juice of 2 unwaxed lemons

3 tablespoons self-raising flour

½ teaspoon baking powder

250g thick Greek-style or other natural wholemilk yoghurt (less than fresh is fine)

Icing sugar, to finish

Preheat the oven to 180°C/Fan 160°C/Gas 4. Lightly butter a 1.5 litre ovenproof dish.

Using an electric hand mixer, or free-standing mixer, beat together the butter and sugar until light, pale and fluffy, about 5 minutes, scraping the bowl down with a spatula a couple of times.

Beat in the egg yolks and lemon zest, then sift the flour and baking powder together over the batter and lightly fold in.

Whisk together the yoghurt and lemon juice, then gently stir this mixture into the batter until just combined.

Whisk the egg whites in a scrupulously clean bowl until they form soft peaks then gently fold into the lemon mixture, using a metal spoon.

Spoon the mixture into the prepared dish. Stand the dish in a roasting tin and carefully pour in boiling water from the kettle to come halfway up the sides of the dish. Bake for about 50 minutes until the pudding is puffed up and lightly golden on the top – it should still have a slightly tender wobble to it.

Carefully remove from the oven, then lift the pudding out of the roasting tin. Leave to stand for 5 minutes before serving.

Dust with icing sugar to serve. Hand round a jug of double cream or a bowl of thick fresh yoghurt for everyone to help themselves.

Granny's jam ice cream

This recipe, for possibly the world's easiest ice cream, comes from River Cottage head chef Gill Meller – or, more accurately, from his Granny. You don't need an ice-cream maker, you don't even have to take the mix out of the freezer to stir it, you just whip it all together and freeze. It's a good way of using up double cream that's about to turn because the condensed milk is sweet enough to mask any slightly sour flavours. **MAKES ABOUT 1.3 LITRES**

800ml double cream (less than fresh is fine)

400ml tin condensed milk

1 teaspoon vanilla extract

About 150g jam, whatever flavour you like

Using an electric hand mixer, or free-standing mixer, whisk the cream, condensed milk and vanilla extract together until the mixture holds soft peaks.

Use a spatula to scrape the creamy mixture into a plastic container. At this point, you could put the ice cream base into two containers and make two different flavours (see tips and swaps below).

Beat your jam a little if necessary, to soften it, then dollop it over the surface of the ice cream mixture and use a knife to ripple it through – don't overmix it. Seal and freeze for at least 6 hours.

Remove the ice cream from the freezer around 20 minutes before you want to serve it, to allow it to soften slightly.

Tips and swaps

Any kind of fruit curd makes a good alternative to jam.

Peanut butter and jam ice cream Replace half the jam with peanut butter before you ripple it through. Thin the peanut butter with a little hot water first to make it easier to spread through the ice cream.

Salted caramel ice cream Ripples of bought *dulce de leche* are fabulous in place of the jam – or you can use up leftover homemade butterscotch or salted caramel sauce.

Ultimate cheese straws

These moreish cheese straws are great served with drinks, or as a snack. Dried-out, past-its-prime cheese is ideal to use here as it packs an intensely cheesy punch, well above its weight. MAKES ABOUT 20

100g plain flour, plus extra for dusting

Good pinch of cayenne pepper

100g butter, chilled and cut into cubes, plus extra for greasing

150g grated cheese mix (see right), or dryish, crumbled blue cheese

1 egg yolk, lightly beaten with 1 teaspoon chilled water

Freshly ground black pepper

Preheat the oven to 200°C/Fan 180°C/Gas 6. Line a large baking sheet with a sheet of baking parchment and lightly butter the paper.

Sift the flour and cayenne pepper together into a large bowl and mix in a few grinds of black pepper. Now rub in the butter cubes, using your fingertips, until the mixture resembles coarse crumbs.

Mix in the grated cheese, then make a well in the middle. Add the egg and water mix and 'cut it in' with a butter knife until it comes together to form a rough dough.

Transfer to a lightly floured surface and gently form the dough into a ball with your hands.

Roll out the dough into a square, about 5mm thick, and neaten the edges with the side of your hand. With a sharp knife, cut the square into strips, then cut each strip into fingers.

Gently lift the strips onto the prepared baking sheet, leaving a little space between each one. Bake until they are very pale golden brown, about 8 minutes, but check after 6 minutes.

Leave the cheese straws on the baking sheet for 5 minutes to firm up a bit, then carefully lift them, using a fish slice or palette knife, onto a wire rack to cool.

Tips and swaps

Try adding any of the following to the basic mixture:

¼–½ teaspoon English mustard powder.

A few gratings of nutmeg.

A good pinch of caraway seeds or cumin seeds.

A sprinkling of chopped thyme or oregano, or a pinch of dried herbs, or herbes de Provence.

Quick puff pastry straws Unroll a packet of ready-to-roll puff pastry, scatter over some cheese, then fold in half. Lightly roll out on a floured surface to a rectangle, 6–7mm thick. Brush with a light coating of egg wash then scatter over a bit more cheese. Gently run the rolling pin over it just enough to encourage the cheese to stick. Cut into 1cm strips. Lay on a prepared baking sheet and twist each one 3 times. Bake at 220°C/Fan 200°C/Gas 7 for 12 minutes or until golden. Cool on a wire rack.

Grated cheese medley

When you have an array of cheese odds and ends a little past their prime, cut off
the rinds (saving flavoursome ones from Parmesan to add to soups), then grate
all the remaining bits and mix them together, except blue cheese which is best
crumbled and kept separate. If they're really dried out, you'll find it easier to use
the grating disc of a food processor. Keep your grated cheese medley in a jar
in the fridge or bag it up and freeze it, for future use in recipes such as cheese
straws (see left), cheesy biscuits (see page 49), cheese sauce (see page 228),
pasta bakes (see page 54) and frittatas (see page 44).

Big cheese sauce

If I have a bit of time on my hands and a groaning fridge, I sometimes make a mammoth batch of cheese sauce, using up much of the butter, milk and cheese that's close to its final countdown. It then keeps in the fridge for a week, or it can be frozen in batches, and gives me a good head start on all kinds of easy family meals to come. If you find you have a huge surfeit of milk and cheese, as often happens around Christmas, simply scale up the quantities. MAKES ABOUT 1.2 LITRES

1 litre whole milk

1 bay leaf (optional)

½ small onion (optional)

1 celery stick (optional)

Blade of mace, or pinch of powdered mace (optional)

50g butter

35–50g plain flour (depending how thick you want the sauce to be)

¼–½ teaspoon English mustard powder or cayenne pepper

Few gratings of nutmeg (optional)

150–300g grated hard cheese (see page 227)

Salt and freshly ground black pepper

Heat up the milk in a pan, adding the bay leaf, onion, celery and mace to flavour it if you like. Bring it close to boiling then take it off the heat.

Melt the butter in a medium saucepan over a medium-low heat. When it stops foaming, stir in the flour. Increase the heat to medium and stir the mixture with a wooden spoon for about a minute, until the roux bubbles.

Strain the hot milk if you've added flavouring ingredients.

Slowly add the hot milk to the roux, a splash at a time at first, beating with a wooden spoon to keep it smooth. When you've added half the milk, pour in the rest and keep stirring until the sauce is thickened and smooth.

Simmer very gently for 2 minutes to thicken and 'cook out' any raw floury taste, then season with salt and pepper, the mustard or cayenne, and nutmeg if using.

Take the pan off the heat and stir in the cheese, then return it to a very low heat, just until the cheese is fully melted – don't overheat the sauce at this stage or it will become grainy.

Let the sauce cool completely and then decant it into self-seal bags or plastic pots. Freezing it in 300–500ml batches works best for most of the things I want to do with it, though I do freeze smaller batches to make rarebits (see page 232). It freezes well for 2 or 3 months.

You need to defrost the sauce before using – either for a few hours at room temperature, or overnight in the fridge. Then reheat, gently but thoroughly, until piping hot but not boiling.

Use for macaroni cheese (see right) or other pasta bakes, cauliflower cheese, all manner of vegetable gratins, cheesy eggs Florentine, rarebits or for a croque monsieur or madame.

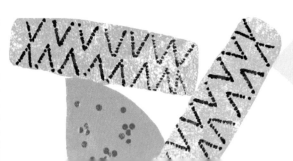

The ultimate macaroni cheese

Cook 300g macaroni in boiling salted water until *al dente*. Drain thoroughly, then add to 600ml (½ quantity) of hot cheese sauce. Toss to coat the macaroni well then transfer to a lightly greased ovenproof dish. Scatter generously with breadcrumbs and a handful or two of grated cheese. Add a sprinkling of paprika or cayenne and bake in a preheated oven at 190°C/Fan 170°C/Gas 5 for about 20 minutes until golden and bubbling. Serves 4.

Potted cheese

This is a great way to use up leftover bits of cheese. Though I recommend English cheeses here, you can use pretty much anything you have – the exception being strong blue cheeses, as their flavour tends to dominate. Sealing the cheese with clarified butter means it keeps brilliantly in the fridge for several weeks, though once you break the seal you should use it within a few days. MAKES ABOUT 300g

200g Wensleydale, Cheshire or Cheddar, or a mixture, grated or crumbled

80g butter, softened

Slosh of dry sherry

Few gratings of nutmeg

Salt and freshly ground black pepper

A little clarified butter, cooled but still liquid, for sealing (page 108)

Using a free-standing mixer, food processor, or a large bowl and a wooden spoon, beat or pulse together the cheeses, butter, sherry and nutmeg until fairly smooth – you still want some texture to the mix.

Taste, add salt and pepper if necessary, then spoon into a bowl or jar, and pour over some clarified butter to seal.

Serve with bread, crackers, oatcakes or crostini, with your favourite chutney and/or fruit cheese.

Tips and swaps

Try adding a pinch of paprika, ground mace, mustard powder or cayenne, in place of, or as well, as the nutmeg.

Swap the sherry for a slosh of port, wine or brandy.

Potted cheese and the French version, fromage fort (see right) makes lovely cheese on toast. Or try spooning onto split baked potatoes then flash under a hot grill until golden and bubbling.

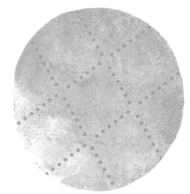

Fromage fort

De-rind about 200g of cheese and chop, crumble or grate. Using a fork or
knife blade, mash a crushed garlic clove with a pinch of salt to a paste. Put
the cheese and garlic into a food processor and pulse until combined but still
fairly coarse. Instead of adding butter to bind the mix, throw in some cream
cheese – you may not need much if you've used soft goat's cheese or creamy
brie in the mix. Add a splash of white wine, a few grinds of pepper and a good
pinch of cayenne pepper. Pulse again until you have a rough paste. Add some
chopped chives and/or parsley if you like. Spoon into a bowl, cover with cling
film and refrigerate; use within a couple of days.

Rarebits

A rarebit is the world's most comforting and substantial form of cheese on toast. A good one is so tempting when it emerges, charred and bubbling, from the grill that it's hard to resist eating it in its scorch-the-roof-of-your-mouth piping hot state. It's worth freezing some cheese sauce in small quantities so you can magically pull a rarebit out of a hat as often as you like. Some people – I admit I'm one of them – like to replace some of the milk in the cheese sauce with warmed ale to add an extra hit of flavour. SERVES 1

1 thick slice of bread (a bit stale is fine)

Ladleful of cheese sauce (see page 228)

Dab of English mustard

Splash of Worcestershire sauce

Small handful of grated Cheddar or cheese medley (see page 227)

For a buck rarebit (optional)

Knob of butter

1 egg

Toast the bread on both sides and leave the grill on.

In a small bowl, mix together the cheese sauce, mustard, Worcestershire sauce and extra grated cheese. Spoon the cheesy mix over the toast and flash under the grill until bubbling hot.

If you're making a buck rarebit, fry the egg in the butter and place it on top of the cheesy toast just before serving.

Tips and swaps

Here are some extra bits you may like to add to your rarebit:

Few anchovies.

Couple of chopped spring onions.

Some cooked cauliflower or broccoli florets.

Handful of lightly wilted spinach.

A sautéed sliced leek and a sprinkling of thyme, if you have some to hand.

A little leftover crumbled sausage or haggis.

Spoonful of chutney or chilli jelly – beneath the cheese, rather than mixed in.

Some sliced tomatoes under the cheese.

Scattering of snipped chives on top.

Hammy eggy cheesy For moments when only molten cheese will do, I recommend this variation on the buck rarebit. Just toast a thick slice of white bread then butter it generously. Place a slice of ham on top then pile on some grated cheese – Cheddar is good, but really, just use whatever good melter you like or have to hand. Place under a hot grill and cook until golden and bubbling. While it's grilling, fry an egg. Put the toasted ham and cheese on a plate and top with the fried egg. Devour immediately.

LEFTOVER EGGS

'Go to work on an egg', one of the most successful ad
slogans of all time from a 1950s campaign for the Egg
Marketing Board, still resonates today, perhaps because
so many of us still do. Whether it's a weekday boiled egg
and soldiers or a weekend fry-up, an egg in some form or
another is for many of us the favourite way to start the day.
This compact protein food punches well above its modest
weight when it comes to creating a satisfying, sustaining
breakfast, lunch or dinner.

It's true that these perfect little ingredients don't fall
neatly into any leftovers category because they keep so
well and we normally eat just one or two at a time. In fact,
eggs are often the things I reach for in order to carry other
leftovers towards greatness, to magically transform,
enhance or complete my odds-and-ends concoctions.
That's why they have their own space in 'launchpads for
leftovers', focusing on omelettes, frittatas, even crustless
tarts (see pages 43–5). These can take on almost any
foraged-out fridge findings you care to throw at them.

And there are few savoury dishes not made better and
more nourishing by a yellow-yolked, plumply poached egg.

I rarely cook more eggs than I'll use except, on occasion, hard-boiled eggs, but these find their way into salads, sandwiches, kedgeree, curries and tartare sauce.

However, there's a whole cache of classic recipes that call for eggs to be separated – and the extraneous yolks or whites can present a challenge. Worry not: turn the page and you'll find a host of ideas for using them. I've given you lots because, of course, just one would not be *un oeuf*...

When cooking with whole eggs, yolks or whites, I have a piece of advice: egg dishes soar or sink on their seasoning. With savoury dishes, take extra care with getting the right balance of salt and pepper, spices and herbs. With sweet ones, pay attention to the sugar, nutmeg and vanilla. An extra bit of vigilance here makes all of the difference.

So whether it's the creaminess of the yolks or the airiness of the whites you have to play with, I hope in this chapter I'll give you some inspiration to go to work with – and on – an egg, or two, or ten. Don't let them languish in the fridge, gradually creeping further and further to the back of the shelf. Bring them up front and centre, eagerly waiting to be transformed into all manner of sweet and savoury delights.

THINGS TO DO WITH EGG YOLKS

Make some mayonnaise Follow the method for aïoli (see page 238), using just ½ small garlic clove (no need to blanch it).

Make a creamy dressing Add an egg yolk to a batch of vinaigrette (see page 38) to make it more creamy.

Glaze and seal pastry Mix an egg yolk with a little splash of water and use to glaze a pie or to 'seal' a blind-baked tart shell before the wet filling goes in. (Actually, very lightly beaten egg white makes a decent glaze too, especially on sweet pies, if sprinkled with a little coarse sugar, and will also seal a pastry case.)

Enrich a sauce Beat an egg yolk with a little cream or crème fraîche and slowly whisk in some of the hot sauce or stock. Slowly stir it back into the completed dish and warm very gently, as in the fricassée on page 70.

Bind burgers Add some beaten egg yolk to the minced meat mix to help bind it together so your burgers won't fall apart on cooking.

Enrich pastry Beat an egg yolk with a splash of iced water and use to replace some of the water in shortcrust pastry for an extra rich result.

Make a quick carbonara Lightly beat an egg yolk or two with some grated Parmesan, salt and pepper. Fry some pancetta until crisp, then toss in the cooked, drained pasta. Take off the heat and stir through the egg yolk mix.

For luxurious mash If you go easy with the butter, 1.5kg cooked potatoes will take 2 egg yolks and a splash of cream. Mash thoroughly, then pipe or simply fork the potato onto fish pie or shepherd's pie (see page 90), then glaze the top with a bit more egg yolk mixed with a splash of water before baking. Or you can use the mash to make freewheeling fishcakes (see page 102).

For silkier eggy bread or richer omelettes Add an extra egg yolk for every 2 whole eggs (see pages 174 and 43).

Lemon curd This has no end of uses. Make a batch and keep it in the fridge, ready to spread on bread or scones, ripple through yoghurt or fill tartlets.

Make a classic custard Pour 250ml double cream and 250ml whole milk into a saucepan. Split a vanilla pod lengthways and scrape the seeds into the pan; add the split pod too. Bring to just below the boil, take off the heat and leave to infuse for a few minutes. Meanwhile, in a bowl, whisk 4 egg yolks with 100g caster sugar and 1 teaspoon cornflour. Gradually whisk in the hot, creamy mixture. Pour through a sieve into a clean pan and heat very gently, stirring constantly, until it is thick enough to coat the back of a spoon. Serve immediately, or cool and then refrigerate in a sealed container for up to 2 days. Serve hot with pies, tarts or crumbles, or use cold in trifles and fumbles.

Home-made ice cream Churn a batch of classic custard in an ice-cream maker to make delicious ice cream that you can then flavour with all manner of leftovers: finely chopped chocolate, preserved stem ginger, dried fruit soaked in brandy etc.

For advice on storing and freezing leftover egg yolks, see page 21.

THINGS TO DO WITH EGG WHITES

Make a batch of meringues In a scrupulously clean bowl (free of any traces of grease), whisk 2 large egg whites (at room temperature), with an electric hand whisk, until they hold soft peaks. Add 100g caster sugar, a tablespoonful at a time, whisking after each addition, until the mixture forms thick peaks and is thick and glossy. Drop tablespoonfuls onto a parchment-lined baking sheet. Bake at 120°C/Fan 100°C/Gas ½ for 2½ –3 hours until the meringues are crisp on the bottom and can be removed from the paper easily. Cool on a wire rack. Serve with fruit and cream or yoghurt, or turn into a Mess (see page 61).

Make a soufflé omelette Allow 1 or 2 extra egg whites per whole egg. Whisk until light and foamy and then fold gently into the basic omelette mixture.

Make a glaze Whisk an egg white with a little cold water and brush onto breads, buns and bagels to add a glossy shine. It helps any poppy or sesame seeds stick too.

Spice up nuts Whisk an egg white with some garam masala or other mix of powdered spices, a bit of sugar and some flaky sea salt. Toss in some blanched almonds, cashews, pecans or other nuts to coat. Using a slotted spoon, lift them from the mixture and scatter on an oiled baking sheet. Bake at 160°C/Fan 140°C/Gas 3 until golden and crisp, about 20 minutes – the egg white ensures the seasonings will stick.

Rustle up a cocktail Several classics use egg whites, including whisky sour and pisco sour.

For advice on storing and leftover freezing egg whites, see page 21.

Aïoli

In spring and summer, I can think of few more delicious ways to start a meal than with a plate of beautiful vegetables straight from the garden – either raw in the case of radishes or tiny carrots, or very lightly steamed in the case of asparagus, spring onions or baby leeks – and a bowl of aïoli. In fact, I find this addictive, Provençal garlicky mayonnaise so delicious that I often make it into a meal if I have plenty of veg to serve it with. SERVES 2–4 AS A STARTER, WITH VEGETABLES

2 garlic cloves, peeled

Pinch of flaky sea salt

2 large egg yolks

1 teaspoon Dijon mustard

200ml mild olive oil (not extra virgin) or rapeseed oil

2 tablespoons lemon juice

If the garlic is quite mature and strong, bring a small pan of water to the boil and blanch the garlic cloves for 10 seconds, then drain.

Put the garlic and salt on a board and chop together to form a paste. Scrape into a bowl and whisk in the egg yolks and mustard until well combined.

Begin to add the oil a drop at a time, whisking vigorously as you go. When you've used about 30ml of the oil, start to drip in a little more at a time. After you've used 100ml of oil, whisk in half the lemon juice – this will turn the aïoli much paler. You can now begin to add the oil a little more quickly, whisking as you go.

When all of the oil is incorporated, add the rest of the lemon juice. Taste the aïoli, and add a bit more salt if you think it needs it.

Serve with crudités, crisp leaves such as treviso or chicory, or lightly steamed vegetables. The aïoli will keep in the fridge, sealed in an airtight container, for a day or two.

Tips and swaps

Uses for aïoli This garlicky mayonnaise will lift so many dishes. Try the following suggestions:

Blob generously over just-cooked new potatoes and add a sprinkling of chives.

Use to dress a warm green bean and chickpea salad.

Dollop aïoli on top of fish soups or stews just before serving.

Serve as a dip for fried goujons of fish, prawns or scampi.

Egg white version Finding myself with spare egg whites rather than yolks I tried making this aïoli with 2 egg whites. It certainly works and I'd recommend it if you would like a lighter, more subtle result.

Cheesy egg custards

Given the timeless love affair that exists between eggs and cheese, it's surprising how seldom we bake them together in savoury custards. This is a great way to turn some leftover yolks into lunch or dinner, served simply with hot toast or crusty bread and a green salad. SERVES 6–8

250ml double cream

250ml whole milk

Sprig of thyme or rosemary

Pinch of caraway seeds (optional)

3 large eggs, plus 3 extra egg yolks

100–120g finely grated hard cheese –
Cheddar, Gruyère, Parmesan, goat's
cheese, either alone or in combination
work well

Salt and freshly ground black pepper

Preheat the oven to 150°C/Fan 130°C/Gas 2.

Pour the cream and milk into a small saucepan and add the thyme or rosemary, and caraway seeds if using. Heat just until bubbles appear around the edge of the pan – don't let it bubble up furiously.

Remove the pan from the heat and leave the creamy mixture to infuse for 5 minutes.

Put the eggs and egg yolks into a bowl and whisk until just blended. Stir in the cheese. Slowly pour the hot, infused creamy mixture through a sieve into the bowl, whisking as you go. Season with salt and pepper – it may not need very much salt, depending on the cheese you use.

Stand 6–8 ramekins, about 125ml capacity, in a roasting tin. Pour the custard into the ramekins then carefully pour enough hot water from the kettle into the tin to come halfway up the sides of the ramekins. Bake for 25–30 minutes until the egg custards are just set – they should still have a slight wobble in the centre.

Serve warm, with toast or crusty bread and a green salad.

Tips and swaps

Add ham or fish If you have some leftover ham or flakes of smoked fish, tear into shards and spoon into the bottom of the ramekins before pouring the cheesy custard over the top.

Add spinach A spoonful of creamed spinach in the bottom of the ramekins works very well.

Crème brûlée

This is my carefully honed, foolproof crème brûlée recipe – the perfect way to use up an abundance of egg yolks. Sometimes I like to create a sweet little surprise by spooning some ripe fruit into the bottom of the ramekin under the custard. SERVES 6–8

500ml double cream

1 or 2 vanilla pods

100g caster sugar

6 large egg yolks

3 tablespoons light muscovado sugar, to finish

Preheat the oven to 150°C/Fan 130°C/Gas 2.

Pour the cream into a small saucepan. Cut a slit along the length of the vanilla pod(s) and scrape out the seeds into the cream, with the tip of a small, sharp knife, then chuck the pod(s) into the pan too.

Heat the cream over a medium heat to just below boiling – you want bubbles to appear around the edge of the pan but you don't want it to bubble up in the pan. Take the pan off the heat and leave for 5 minutes to infuse the cream with the vanilla.

Whisk the caster sugar and egg yolks together in a bowl, then slowly whisk in the hot cream.

Strain through a fine sieve into a jug. (Save the vanilla pod(s) for vanilla sugar, see below.)

Stand 6–8 ramekins, about 125ml capacity, in a roasting tin. Pour the custard into the ramekins then carefully pour enough hot water from the kettle into the tin to come halfway up the sides of the ramekins. Bake for 25–30 minutes until the custards are just set – they should still have a bit of wobble in the centre.

Remove from the oven and carefully lift the ramekins out of the roasting dish. Leave to cool, then chill thoroughly.

About 30 minutes or so before serving, sprinkle a very thin, even layer of muscovado sugar over each custard. Put them under a very hot grill until the sugar melts and bubbles, or use a cook's blowtorch, if you have one, waving it slowly over the surface of each custard.

Leave to cool, then refrigerate until the sugar is hard – 15 minutes or so should do it.

Vanilla sugar
Don't discard vanilla pods once they've been used to infuse milk or cream. Wash and dry them well, then submerge in a jar of caster sugar. The vanilla fragrance will permeate through. Sprinkle vanilla sugar onto pancakes and use in puds and cakes.

Tips and swaps

Add a fruity layer Spoon some fruity jam or marmalade, ripe berries, fruity compote or roasted rhubarb into the ramekins before you pour in the custard. This is a good way to use up these fruity treats, and adds an extra special dimension to crème brûlée.

Pavlova

There are few simpler show-stopping puds than the pavlova. The sum really is greater than its parts – simple meringue, whipped cream, ripe fruit. Its key to greatness is in its scale. A great, rough wheel of meringue, with dollops of whipped cream (mixed with some thick yoghurt, for me), piled high with delicious seasonal fruit – what could be better? SERVES 6–8

For the meringue

4 large egg whites, at room temperature

220g caster sugar

2 teaspoons cornflour, sifted

2 teaspoons white wine vinegar or cider vinegar

1 teaspoon vanilla extract (optional)

For the topping

300ml double cream or whipping cream

200ml natural wholemilk yoghurt

400–500g ripe, seasonal fruit (see tips and swaps, below)

Preheat the oven to 130°C/Fan 110°C/Gas ½. Line a baking sheet with baking parchment and draw on a circle, about 25cm in diameter. Turn the paper over.

Use either a freestanding mixer or a bowl and electric hand mixer with a whisk attachment, making sure they are scrupulously clean and free of any grease. Whisk the egg whites to firm peaks, but do not over-beat or they'll turn grainy.

Add the sugar a tablespoonful or two at a time, beating well between each addition. Keep whisking until the meringue is very stiff and glossy. Using a spatula, gently fold in the cornflour, vinegar and vanilla, if using.

Heap the meringue within the marked circle on the parchment and swirl it out into a round, gently pushing it up a bit towards the sides. Use the spatula to create some soft peaks in the surface.

Bake for 1¼–1½ hours until the meringue is firm and crisp around the edges but still slightly soft inside.

Turn off the heat and leave the pavlova to cool and dry out a little in the oven.

Whip the cream until it forms very soft peaks – be careful not to over-beat it until stiff. Fold together with the yoghurt.

Carefully transfer the meringue to a serving plate. Spoon on the cream and yoghurt mixture, spreading it almost to the edges, then pile the fruit on top.

Tips and swaps

Vary the fruit Ring the changes according to the seasons. Try the following:

Strawberries (larger ones halved or quartered), raspberries, blackcurrants, blackberries – either alone or in combination. About an hour before assembling the pavlova, tip them into a bowl and let them macerate with a sprinkling of icing sugar and/or a small trickle of framboise, kirsch or crème de cassis.

Ripe peaches or nectarines, peeled and sliced, with a handful of redcurrants if you have some. Leave to macerate for about an hour with a sprinkling of icing sugar and a splash of orange flower water.

During the winter, slices of ripe mango and passion fruit pulp is a really good mix to heap on top of a pavlova (as shown). Finish with a scattering of shredded mint leaves.

Hazelnut meringue roulade with raspberries

Once you've mastered basic meringue (see page 237) and seen how easy it is, I've no doubt you'll be keen to whip up your egg white repertoire to even greater heights. Adding toasted, ground hazelnuts to a meringue mixture gives it a praline-like flavour and an irresistibly gooey texture. A roulade always looks impressive but is surprisingly simple to pull off. SERVES 8–10

For the roulade

100g hazelnuts

250g caster sugar

A little sunflower oil, for greasing

5 large egg whites, at room temperature

For the filling

100ml natural wholemilk yoghurt

400ml double cream

2 tablespoons caster sugar

Finely grated zest of 1 small orange

250g raspberries, plus extra to serve

Heat the oven to 180°C/Fan 160°C/Gas 4. Spread the hazelnuts out on a baking sheet and toast for 5–8 minutes, until golden. Leave to cool, then tip into a food processor with 1 tablespoon of the sugar and pulse to chop finely. Do not over-process so the nuts become oily – it's fine if there are a few chunkier bits in the mix.

Turn the oven up to 200°C/Fan 180°C/Gas 6. Line a 23 x 33cm Swiss roll tin with baking parchment and grease lightly with oil.

Use either a freestanding mixer or a bowl and electric hand mixer with a whisk attachment, making sure they are scrupulously clean and free of any grease. Whisk the egg whites for several minutes until thick, white and holding firm peaks.

Continuing to whisk, gradually add the caster sugar a tablespoonful at a time. Once it is all incorporated, you should have a very thick, glossy meringue that holds firm peaks. Use a spatula or large metal spoon to fold in the chopped hazelnuts as lightly as you can.

Spread the mixture in the prepared tin. Bake for 8 minutes, then lower the oven setting to 160°C/Fan 140°C/Gas 2½ and cook for another 15 minutes, until golden and crisp.

Leave the meringue to cool completely in the tin, then carefully turn out, upside down, onto a sheet of baking parchment.

For the filling, whip the yoghurt, cream, caster sugar and orange zest together in a bowl to soft peaks.

Spread the filling evenly over the meringue, leaving a 2cm clear margin along the edges. Sprinkle the raspberries on top, then roll up the roulade from a long edge, using the paper to help you. The surface will crack but don't worry.

Serve the roulade cut into thick slices, with extra raspberries on the side.

Chocolate macarons

These meltingly delicious treats are best made with slightly mature egg whites, so they're just the thing for using up a cache which has been languishing in the fridge for a few days. MAKES 12

For the macarons

A little flour for marking the templates

125g icing sugar

3 tablespoons cocoa powder

170g ground almonds

3 large egg whites

60g caster sugar

¼ teaspoon vanilla extract

For the ganache

100g plain chocolate (about 70% cocoa solids), chopped into small pieces

100ml double cream

Heat the oven to 150°C/Fan 130°C/Gas 2. Line 2 baking sheets with baking parchment.

Dip a 4.5cm plain biscuit cutter or a small glass (with the same diameter rim) in flour and use it to mark out 24 circles on the parchment, set about 3cm apart to allow them to expand a bit. This will make it easier to make evenly sized macarons.

Sift the icing sugar and cocoa into a bowl and whisk in the ground almonds.

In a separate bowl, whisk the egg whites, using an electric hand whisk, until foamy, then whisk in the sugar, a little at a time, until the mixture is stiff and glossy.

Stir half the almond mixture into the egg whites, then add the rest, along with the vanilla extract, and fold until just combined.

Transfer the mixture to a sturdy plastic bag and cut a 1cm hole in the bottom. Pipe into rounds on the baking sheets, using the flour circles as your guide. Tap the sheets hard against the kitchen worktop to eliminate any air bubbles.

Bake until the macarons feel slightly firm, about 18 minutes. Remove and allow to cool slightly, then carefully lift the parchment with the macarons onto a wire rack to cool completely.

Next, make the ganache. Put the chocolate into a smallish bowl. Heat the cream in a small saucepan until barely simmering, then pour this over the chocolate. Leave to stand for a couple of minutes and then stir until the mixture is smooth and cool.

Spread some of the ganache onto half of the macarons and sandwich together with the rest of them. Any that are not eaten immediately can be stored in an airtight container in the fridge for up to 4 days.

LEFTOVER FRUIT

Gorgeous, juicy, lovely fruit. It so often book-ends my days: the first thing I eat in the morning – banana sliced onto my yoghurt, or apple grated into my muesli – and frequently the last thing I eat at night, when I sink my teeth into a plum, peach or pear before I go to bed.

Few of us eat enough fruit, though, and I wonder if this might be because it is a tad temperamental. We've all had unfortunate fruit-buying experiences – gorgeous red strawberries that turned out to be disappointing, bananas so green that they weren't edible for a week, or perfidious pears – rock hard one moment and overly soft the next. Onions, potatoes, even greens and salads, can be bought in a reliably tasty state and stored easily. But fruit is on a constant journey from under-ripeness to over-the-topness and it's not going to wait around for you. If you don't have the right recipe – and the right time to eat it – it's easy to miss the fruit boat, as it were.

But don't let fruit's contrary nature put you off. It is both delicious and enormously good for you and, as this chapter shows, there are many ways to tackle its fickleness. I'd be the first to agree that perfect, blushingly ripe specimens are best enjoyed *au naturel*, just as they come, but slightly under- or overripe fruit can be turned into many delectable

things. Cooking can work wonders – and, conversely, freezing too. And the addition of a little spice, vinegar, sugar, honey or cream can be quite transformative.

Smoothies, frozen yoghurts, granitas and lollies (see pages 252–9), can be very forgiving of slightly blowsy specimens. Cordials and vinegars (see pages 272–5), meanwhile, will preserve summer ripeness well into the winter, adding sunshine-y zip to drinks, dressings and marinades on the gloomiest of days.

I've had a lot of fun experimenting with things I would normally have thrown on the compost. Not every one was a success but when the experiments paid off, they paid off big. I can recommend salted lemon peels (see page 268), pickled watermelon peel (see page 276) and pickled pineapple core (see page 278) wholeheartedly. Apple peel and orange salad (see page 260) and brown-banana drop scones (see page 264) will never quite displace a whole crisp Cox, or perfectly yellow bananas in my family's affections, but it's great to have them up our sleeve.

I hope this chapter will inspire you to seek out your own sweet successes, and not to lose faith in the slightly past-it, the bruised, battered or faded: there's still plenty of fruity potential in there, just waiting to be released.

Smoothies

I love smoothies – so much goodness, so quickly – and I love the fact that, between fridge, fruit bowl and garden, I almost always have the makings of a good one kicking around. In fact, these fruity drinks are one of the best ways I know of hoovering up all manner of slightly softened apples and pears, less-than-perfect berries or browning bananas. They're also a good vehicle for slightly limp greens, softening cucumber and avocados that are past their jade-green prime. Just chop away any bad bits and get whizzing. EACH SERVES 2

Pear, spinach and ginger

2 very ripe pears, peeled and cored

Couple of handfuls of baby spinach

3cm piece of ginger, peeled and grated

Juice of ½ lime

About 400ml coconut water

2–3 mint leaves

3–4 ice cubes

Mango

2 ripe mangoes, peeled, stoned and roughly chopped

350ml ice-cold milk

100g natural wholemilk yoghurt

50ml coconut milk (optional)

Pinch of ground cinnamon or cardamom (optional)

Berry and banana

200g berries (blueberries, raspberries, strawberries, blackberries)

2 ripe bananas, peeled and cut into chunks

About 200ml orange juice

1 tablespoon rolled oats

3–4 ice cubes

Banana and nut butter

2 ripe bananas, peeled and cut into chunks

2 tablespoons peanut butter, or other nut butter

400ml milk or almond milk

Few gratings of nutmeg

3–4 ice cubes

When you've assembled the ingredients for your smoothie, tip them all into a blender and process until very smooth. If the smoothie is too thick, add a splash of milk or water; if it's not sweet enough, trickle in some honey. Then blitz again, and drink immediately.

Tips and swaps

Freezing leftover fruit Smoothies always taste best cold. I often add ice to the mix, but you don't need to if you freeze at least some of the fruit first. And freezing is a great way to fix very ripe fruit before it goes over. Before freezing, pick over berries and discard any that are mouldy or rotten. Halve large strawberries.

Peel bananas (overripe, browning ones are ideal for this treatment) and cut into 2cm slices. You can even freeze cubes of very ripe peeled pear. Scatter the fruit on a baking sheet in one layer and freeze for a couple of hours until hard. Bag up and return to the freezer, so you can just grab a handful when you need one.

Berry good frozen yoghurt

This is so quick and easy. Start with frozen fruit (see page 253) and you don't need to churn it – it's ready to eat straight away. You can also use this recipe as a blueprint for other combinations (see tips and swaps, below). SERVES 3–4

300–400g frozen ripe berries, either alone or in combination (raspberries, blackberries, blueberries and strawberries are all good)

125g natural wholemilk yoghurt or thick Greek-style yoghurt

2–3 tablespoons clear honey, depending on the sweetness of the berries

1 tablespoon lemon or lime juice

Put all the ingredients into a food processor and whiz until very smooth.

Eat immediately or scrape into a plastic tub with a spatula, cover and freeze.

Banana ice cream

Bananas make a good and amazingly creamy 'ice cream' on their own. Use bananas from the fruit bowl that are ripe and speckled with brown – don't wait until they're really overripe, as the flavour can be overwhelming. Peel, thickly slice and 'open-freeze' on a tray, then bag up and return to the freezer. When you fancy a near-instant banana ice cream, grab a couple of handfuls of the frozen banana pieces and blend them in a food processor, scraping down the sides a couple of times, until very smooth and creamy. This healthy ice is great just as it is but you can add a couple of tablespoons of nut butter, some cocoa powder or chocolate chips, a sprinkling of cinnamon or a little vanilla extract if you like.

Tips and swaps

Using 3 parts very ripe frozen fruit to 1 part yoghurt, try these delicious combinations:

Mango and raspberry Peeled mango flesh, a handful of raspberries, a squeeze of lime and yoghurt.

Peach and strawberry Peeled and stoned peaches, strawberries, ¼ teaspoon vanilla extract and yoghurt.

Frozen yoghurt lollies To freeze any of these frozen yoghurts as lollies, see page 258.

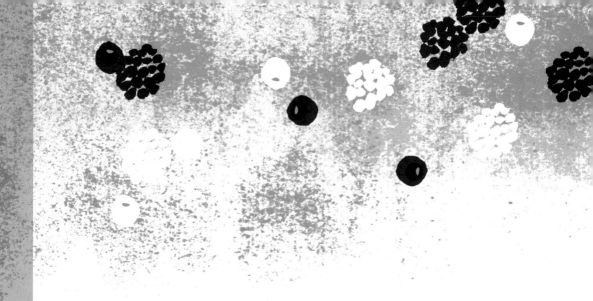

Granita

No ice-cream machine? No problem. If you have an abundance of soft fruits getting softer by the hour and in need of using up, a mouthwatering granita is a simple and refreshing way to ensure they don't go to waste. SERVES 3–4

About 400g soft fruit, such as strawberries, raspberries, blackberries and blackcurrants

80–100g icing sugar, depending on how tart the fruit is

Juice of 1 lemon

Crush the fruit in a bowl with a potato masher, then pass it through a fine-meshed sieve to remove any seeds.

In a small bowl, whisk 80g icing sugar with the lemon juice, then mix it with the fruit purée – you're aiming for a strong combination of sweet and tart, as both tastes will be muted when frozen. Taste and add more lemon juice or icing sugar if necessary until you have the balance you like.

Pour the mixture into a freezerproof container. You want it to freeze quickly so pick a container that will hold the purée at a depth of no more than 4cm.

Freeze the fruity purée until it's really solid – at least 5 hours for most mixtures. Bring it out of the freezer 20–30 minutes before you want to serve it.

When the granita is just starting to soften around the edges, use a fork to scrape away at the surface, creating lots of icy shards. Quickly spoon into chilled glasses and eat immediately, before it has a chance to melt.

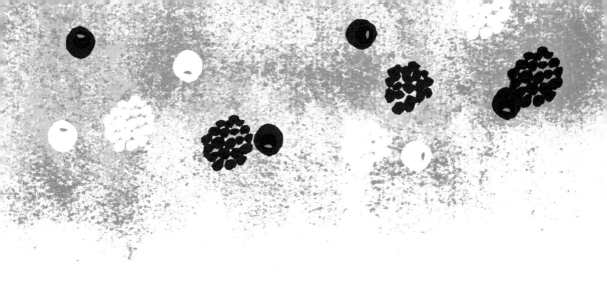

Fruit-on-the-brink lollies

If you don't yet have a tray of lolly moulds, it's an investment I'd recommend. You can freeze all kinds of sweetened fruit purées into lollies (see tips and swaps, below), and I find it's such a useful way to deal with fruit on the brink that our freezer at home is almost never without a mixed medley of lollies standing by to delight all comers. In fact I usually forget what flavour they are – so the only clue is the colour. Which is very often some shade of pink... MAKES ABOUT 6

500g soft ripe strawberries or raspberries, crushed and sieved

150g caster sugar

Juice of ½ lemon

Crush the fruit in a bowl with a potato masher, then pass it through a fine-meshed sieve to remove any seeds.

Put the sugar and 250ml water into a pan and heat gently, stirring, until the sugar is fully dissolved. Increase the heat and boil for 3 minutes.

Remove from the heat and allow to cool completely. (This simple sugar syrup keeps sealed in a jar in the fridge almost indefinitely, so it's worth making up a bigger batch to see you through the summer.)

Stir the lemon juice into the fruit purée with about half of the cooled sugar syrup. Taste and add more sugar syrup until you get the perfect tart/sweet balance. (Remember the sweetness will be muted slightly when it's frozen.)

Pour the mixture into ice-lolly moulds, leaving about 1cm at the top for the mixture to expand as it freezes. Place in the freezer.

Check the moulds after an hour or so. If the mixture has begun to freeze, try putting a lolly stick in. If it is not firm enough to hold the stick upright, try again an hour later. Once all the lollies have sticks, leave them to freeze solid for several hours.

To unmould the lollies, dip the moulds into a bowl of hot water for 10 seconds, then gently remove the lollies.

Tips and swaps

You can transform any smooth compote or purée of cooked fruit into lollies – Bramley apple, gooseberry, rhubarb, blackcurrant all work well. Just sweeten to taste with sugar syrup, clear honey or by whisking in icing sugar.

Yoghurt lollies You can freeze your frozen yoghurt (see page 254) into lollies. Or make a simple yoghurt lolly mix by mixing about 50g jam with about 150ml yoghurt (or cream or crème fraîche).

Striped lollies Try freezing your lollies in fruity stripes (as shown), using a variety of fruity purées and/or frozen yoghurt. Part-freeze the first layer for about 45 minutes before adding the next and don't forget to add your lolly sticks after the second or third layer, depending how thick the layers are.

Apple peel and orange salad

If you have children who are more likely to eat a peeled and portioned apple than a whole, skin-on specimen (I have one out of four who still insists), then a good recipe that uses the peel is very handy. This quick little salad fits the bill very nicely – it's delicious with some thick yoghurt for breakfast, and makes full use of all the sprightly flavour that remains in the often-discarded skin. SERVES 1

1 orange

Freshly pared peel of 1 eating apple

½ teaspoon clear honey

A few grinds of black pepper, or a pinch of ground cinnamon or cardamom (optional)

To serve

Thick yoghurt

Pumpkin seeds or toasted flaked almonds (optional)

Stand the orange on a board and cut off the top and bottom so it sits upright. Now work your way around the orange with a sharp knife, cutting away the peel and pith and exposing the flesh of the orange segments. (Save the peels for preserving in salt, see page 269; or crystallising, see page 270.)

Then, working over a bowl, slice out the segments from between the membranes until all that is left in your hand is the fibrous 'core'. Give that a squeeze to release as much juice as possible. Strain off the juice and set aside.

Finely shred the apple peel and place in a bowl with the orange segments.

In a separate bowl, whisk the reserved orange juice with the honey and the pepper, cinnamon or cardamom, if using. Trickle the spiced juice over the apple peel and orange segments and toss to combine.

Serve the fruit salad with a generous spoonful of yoghurt, trickling over any dressing from the bowl. Finish with a scattering of pumpkin seeds or toasted flaked almonds, if you like.

Tips and swaps

Dried fruit version Add some raisins if you like, or some finely chopped dried Hunza apricots or prunes. Leave in the juice to plump up for at least half an hour if you can.

Apple peel tisane

Put the pared peel from a smallish eating apple in a pan with about
300ml water and a couple of bashed cardamom pods, cloves or a
small piece of cinnamon stick, and bring to a gentle simmer. Heat
for a minute, then leave to infuse off the heat for a couple of minutes
before drinking – with a little honey and lemon added if you like.

Clafoutis

This classic French pudding is simplicity itself to throw together and a great way to turn surplus fruit into a generous pud. Cherries are the most traditional choice but you can use any seasonal fruit you have to hand. SERVES 6–8

Knob of butter, to grease the dish

400–450g cherries or other fruit (see tips and swaps)

75g plain flour

Pinch of salt

50g caster sugar

3 large eggs

300ml whole milk

½ teaspoon vanilla extract, a few gratings of nutmeg or a good pinch of ground cinnamon (optional)

To finish

Icing sugar, for dusting

Preheat the oven to 190°C/Fan 170°C/Gas 5. Lightly butter a ceramic oven dish, about 25cm in diameter. Scatter your chosen fruit in the dish; leave the stones in cherries, if using, so none of the juices or flavour escape.

Sift the flour and salt into a bowl and whisk in the sugar. Make a well in the centre.

In a jug, whisk together the eggs, milk and vanilla or spice, if using. Gradually whisk the liquid into the flour mixture to make a batter.

Pour the batter over the fruit and bake for about 35 minutes until golden and puffed up.

Clafoutis is best eaten warm or at room temperature, rather than hot, dusted with icing sugar. Serve just as it is, or with a jug of thick cream to pass around.

Tips and swaps

The following fruits work well in a clafoutis:

Whole gooseberries.

Sliced, peeled peaches and/or nectarines.

Halved plums (as shown) or greengages.

Pears, cut into fat slices, with a scattering of chopped hazelnuts or walnuts if you like.

Poached rhubarb or quince.

Fresh figs, with a cross cut in the top, squeezed slightly to open them up and placed in the dish facing upwards.

Prunes, soaked in hot black tea for 20 minutes or so to plump them up.

Whole blueberries, strawberries (thickly sliced or quartered if huge) and raspberries, alone or in combination.

Oaty banana drop scones

I'm a big fan of drop scones served buttered, with fat slices of banana and a sprinkling of cinnamon on top. We often have them for weekend family breakfasts or cosy Sunday teas. But when I have some brown, speckled, softening bananas that aren't quite up to being showcased in that way, I like to fold them into the scone batter so I can still capitalise on all their lovely, fruity flavour. SERVES 4–6

100g plain flour

1 teaspoon baking powder

Pinch of salt

80g rolled oats

1 large egg, lightly beaten

150ml milk

40g butter, melted

1 large, very ripe banana (the skin should be flecked with brown)

2 tablespoons clear honey

A little sunflower oil, for frying

To serve (optional)

Butter

Caster sugar, to sprinkle (optional)

Pinch of ground cinnamon (optional)

Slices of banana (a perfect specimen, if you have one!)

Sift the flour, baking powder and salt into a large bowl. Add the oats and mix well, then make a well in the centre.

In a jug, beat together the egg, half the milk and the melted butter.

Mash the banana and honey together in a separate small bowl.

Gradually pour the egg mixture into the well in the flour and oats, whisking to combine.

Using a large spoon, fold in the banana and honey, then gradually stir in some more milk, stopping when you have a batter with the consistency of very thick cream. You may not need all the milk.

Heat a large non-stick frying pan over a medium heat and add a little splash of oil. Rub with a thick wad of kitchen paper to lightly oil the pan.

You'll need to cook the drop scones in batches. Pour some batter into the pan – to form discs about the size of a digestive biscuit, spacing them apart. After a couple of minutes, bubbles will start to appear on the surface. Flip them over and cook for a further 3–4 minutes.

Transfer the cooked drop scones to a warm plate and cover with a clean tea towel. Keep warm while you cook the rest, greasing the pan a little more if necessary and adjusting the heat if they're browning too quickly. You should get about 20 drop scones from the mixture.

Serve while hot, spread with butter and topped, if you like, with a sprinkling of sugar, a little cinnamon and slices of (your best) banana.

Tips and swaps

Spicy/zesty drop scones Add a pinch of ground cinnamon, a few gratings of nutmeg or some lemon or orange zest to the batter.

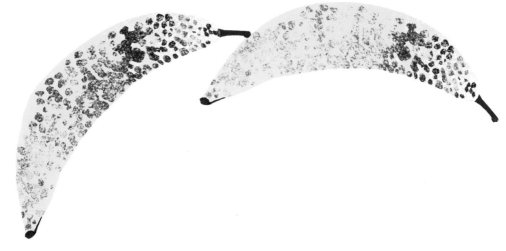

Banana, peanut butter and raisin bread

This great tea loaf is inspired by fond memories of childhood banana and peanut butter sandwiches. It's very quick to throw together. MAKES 10–12 SLICES

40g raisins or sultanas, soaked in hot black tea for 10 minutes

80ml sunflower or rapeseed oil, plus extra to grease the tin

160g light muscovado sugar

2 large eggs, lightly beaten

1 teaspoon vanilla extract

3 ripe bananas (about 300g peeled weight)

100g peanut butter (smooth or crunchy)

200g plain flour, plus 1 tablespoon

1 teaspoon bicarbonate of soda

1 teaspoon baking powder

1 teaspoon ground cinnamon

½ teaspoon ground nutmeg

Pinch of salt

2 tablespoons demerara sugar

Preheat the oven to 180°C/Fan 160°C/Gas 4. Grease and line a 1kg loaf tin, about 11 x 22cm.

Drain the raisins or sultanas from the tea and put to one side to cool.

In a large bowl, beat the oil, muscovado sugar, eggs and vanilla extract together.

In a separate bowl, mash the bananas with a fork, then add the peanut butter and mash together. Stir the mixture into the eggy batter until well combined.

Sift the flour, bicarbonate of soda, baking powder, cinnamon, nutmeg and salt over the mixture and scatter the raisins or sultanas on top. Fold everything together with a spatula.

Pour the batter into the prepared loaf tin and sprinkle the demerara sugar over the surface. Bake for 50–55 minutes, or until a skewer inserted into the centre comes out clean.

Leave the tea loaf to cool in the tin for about 10 minutes, then transfer to a wire rack to cool completely before slicing. It will keep quite well in a tin for 4 or 5 days.

Salted lemon peels

I use lemons so much in my cooking that I have lots of fleshy 'shells' left over once I've squeezed their tangy juice into whatever dish I'm making. They're too acidic to add to the compost heap in great quantity, so I needed to find other things to do with them. I've discovered that the fleshy skins can be given the Moroccan salting treatment very successfully, just as whole lemons can. (When you use preserved lemons, you often scoop out and discard their salty flesh anyway.) Use them in tagines, salads – in fact anywhere you would use conventionally preserved lemons. It's best to use unwaxed fruit.

Squeezed-out lemon halves: at least a dozen

Juice of 1 lemon per 5 or 6 squeezed-out halves (approximately)

Flaky sea salt

First sterilise a large, Le Parfait/Kilner style jar: wash thoroughly in hot soapy water, rinse well and place in a low oven at 100°C/Fan 80°C/ Gas ¼ for 10 minutes. Remove and let it cool slowly to room temperature.

Scrape out any excess bits of membrane from the lemon halves, then cut the remaining peel and pith into pieces, about 1.5cm wide.

Put a layer of sea salt, about 2cm deep, in the sterilised jar. Scatter on some of the lemon peels and cover with 1cm salt. Repeat until you run out of peel, then finish with another 1cm layer of salt. Pour over the lemon juice.

Seal the jar and leave for 4 weeks, shaking every week or so, before using the lemon peels.

To use the salted lemon peels, fish them out with a fork. Rinse under the cold tap and pat dry on kitchen paper before chopping and stirring into your salad, tagine, rice dish, etc.

Citrus sugar

This is another excellent use for citrus fruit skins left over from recipes that only call for the juice. Obviously it's easier to grate fruit before you've squeezed out the juice, so remember to do this first.

Spread some caster sugar out in an even layer on a sheet of baking parchment. Using the finest holes on a sharp grater, grate over citrus zest, being careful not to include any white pith. Leave to dry out for a couple of hours then use the paper to funnel the sugar into an airtight container. It will keep for several months and is very good used in baking or to sweeten tisanes.

Tips and swaps

Salted orange peels This technique works well
with orange skins too. Use them as you would
salted lemon peels.

Crystallised citrus peels

It's virtually impossible to stop nibbling at these, either plain or dipped in chocolate (see tips and swaps, below). They are good with a cup of coffee, make a great gift, and, chopped up, can be added to fruit cakes and biscuits. MAKES ABOUT 600g

About 500g citrus peel: pink grapefruit, oranges, bergamots and lemons all work well

1kg caster sugar

Granulated sugar, for dredging (optional)

Trim any remaining fruity membrane from the inside of the peel and thin out the pith a little by cutting some of it away with a small, sharp knife – this is especially worth doing with grapefruit, where the pith can be quite thick. Be careful not to cut all the way to the zest. Cut the peel into strips about 5mm wide.

Put the strips of peel into a stainless steel or cast-iron saucepan and cover generously with cold water. Bring to the boil and boil for a minute, then drain in a colander. Repeat twice more – this helps to remove some of the bitterness and makes it easier for the strips to absorb sugar later.

Rinse out the pan, then add the sugar and 1.3 litres water. Heat gently, stirring, until the sugar has completely dissolved and the syrup is clear, then bring to the boil.

Add the citrus peel strips, lower the heat and simmer until they're very soft and the pith is translucent – this will take about an hour or so.

Take the pan off the heat. At this point, you can refrigerate the strips in the syrup for several days before moving to the next stage if you like.

Set a wire rack over a tray lined with kitchen paper to catch the drips. Scoop the citrus peel strips out of the pan with a slotted spoon and lay them on the wire rack. Allow the syrup to drain off and pat the strips with kitchen paper to make sure they're not too sticky.

You can chop up the peel at this stage, if you like – to use in cakes, puddings, etc. It will keep for a few weeks in an airtight container, or you can freeze it for several months.

Alternatively, to coat the peels with sugar, heap a layer of granulated sugar on a plate and use two forks to toss the strips, a few at a time, in it, making sure they're coated all over. Arrange on a clean wire rack and leave for 3–4 hours to dry out. Thereafter they will keep sealed in an airtight container, for a month or so.

Tips and swaps

Chocolate dipped peel Dip the strips of peel (non-sugar-coated) in melted chocolate so that it covers half of each strip. Shake gently to remove any excess chocolate then lay on a sheet of baking parchment and leave to set completely. Once set, store in an airtight container in single layers, separated by sheets of parchment. They will keep for a couple of weeks, although the chocolate may lose its gloss after a few days.

Bashed-up-blackberry cordial

The recipe here is from my friend Pam 'The Jam' Corbin, River Cottage's preserving guru. I nearly always make it with blackberries because there are so many in the hedgerows near me and it's a great way to use any slightly mangled (though not mouldy) specimens, but you can follow the same basic technique to make other fruit cordials. MAKES ABOUT 750ml

1kg blackberries

Granulated sugar

Brandy (optional)

Put the blackberries in a saucepan with 100ml water. Bring slowly to the boil, crushing the fruit with a wooden spoon or potato masher, and cook gently until the fruit is very soft and the juices are flowing. This should take 15–20 minutes. Remove from the heat.

Set up a scalded jelly bag on a stand over a bowl (dipping the bag in a pan of just-boiled water for a minute first will help the juice run through). Or scald a large piece of muslin (in the same way) and use it to line a colander placed over a bowl. Tip the fruit mixture into the bag or muslin.

If you're using muslin, pull up the corners, tie in a bundle with kitchen string and suspend over a bowl: to do this, tie the bundle onto a long wooden spoon with the string, place the bowl in a deep stockpot and hold the bundle over the pan by balancing the spoon across the top of the stockpot. Leave to drain overnight.

Sterilise one large (about 750ml) or two smaller (375ml) bottles (see sterilising instructions on page 268).

Measure the juice and put it into a clean pan: you should have about 700ml juice to play with. For every 500ml juice, add 350g sugar. Heat gently, stirring, until the sugar has dissolved, skimming off any scum as it rises to the surface.

Immediately, pour the hot cordial through a funnel into the hot bottle(s), leaving a 1cm gap at the top. At this point, you can add a teaspoon of brandy if you like. Seal the bottle(s) with a cork, screw cap or levered closure seal.

The cordial will keep in a cool, dark place for several months.

Tips and swaps

Check your fruit This is a good way to use up any fruit that is too ripe to serve raw or to use for jam making, but look over it carefully for any sign of mould, as even a little can spoil the whole batch. With plums and damsons, as long as they're not too far gone, you can simply cut out any bad parts and discard them.

Other fruit options This works well with red- or blackcurrants, plums, damsons and all kinds of berries. Adjust the cooking time to ensure the fruits are simmered until they're soft and have given up as much of their juice as possible.

Serving options This cordial is very good as a long drink with ice and tonic or soda water, but it's great in cocktails too. Mixed with a little very cold sparkling wine, it makes a lovely aperitif.

Fruity vinegars

Vinegar has been used for centuries to preserve the bounty of summer. The sweet-tart combination of fruit and vinegar is a tremendous one, and these gorgeously coloured condiments can be used in both a sweet and savoury context (see right). This is another recipe from my friend Pam Corbin.
MAKES ABOUT 750ml

500g raspberries

300ml cider vinegar

Granulated sugar

Put the raspberries into a bowl and crush them gently with a wooden spoon. Pour over the cider vinegar, cover and leave in a cool place to steep for 4–5 days, stirring from time to time.

Set up a scalded jelly bag on a stand over a bowl (dipping the bag in a pan of just-boiled water for a minute first will help the juice run through). Or scald a large piece of muslin (in the same way) and use it in a double layer to line a colander placed in a bowl.

Tip the fruit mixture into the bag or muslin. If you're using muslin, pull up the corners, tie in a bundle with kitchen string and suspend over a bowl: to do this, tie the bundle onto a long wooden spoon with the string, place the bowl in a deep stockpot and hold the bundle over the pan by balancing the spoon across the top of the stockpot.

Leave to drain overnight; you can squeeze the bundle from time to time if you like.

Measure the liquid – you should get at least 500ml – then pour it into a saucepan. For every 250ml fruit vinegar, add 200g sugar.

Place over a low heat and bring gently to the boil, stirring until the sugar has dissolved. Then bring to the boil and boil for 8–10 minutes, skimming off any scum as it rises. Remove from the heat and allow to cool.

Meanwhile, sterilise two 375ml bottles (see sterilising instructions on page 268).

When completely cold, decant the vinegar into the cold, sterilised bottles and seal. The vinegar will keep in a cool, dark place for a year.

Tips and swaps

Check your fruit You can use berries that are slightly bashed or squashed, but avoid any that are showing signs of mould, as this can taint the flavour.

Other fruit options You can use this recipe to make vinegar flavoured with strawberries, blackcurrants or blackberries... all delicious.

Using fruit vinegars Trickle over everything from soft goat's cheeses to vanilla or fruit-based ice creams (as shown). Use them in salad dressings, marinades, sauces and gravies, or try mixing them with lots of ice and soda to make a long, refreshing drink.

Pickled watermelon peel

In the summer, there are few things more refreshing than cubes of icy cold watermelon, sweet and full of juice. And, after you've tucked into the pink flesh, I hope you'll have a go at making this tasty pickle. It's based on a classic condiment from the American South and is very good with ham, cheeses, pork and practically anything that you might serve at a barbecue. It's also great straight out of the jar, as a quick snack. MAKES ABOUT 1kg

About 500g watermelon rinds

3 tablespoons fine sea salt

For the brine

250ml cider vinegar

210g caster sugar

2 tablespoons flaky sea salt

1 red or green chilli, deseeded (unless you like the heat) and sliced

Thumb of ginger, peeled and thinly sliced

1 teaspoon black peppercorns

¼ teaspoon mustard seeds

4 cloves

3 allspice berries

2 star anise

Using a strong vegetable peeler, pare off and discard all the tough outer green skin from the watermelon rinds. Cut the inner white peel into 2 x 4cm pieces.

Pour 2 litres water into a large saucepan, add the salt and bring to the boil, stirring to dissolve it. Remove from the heat, add the peel and stir. Cover and set aside at room temperature for at least 8 hours, or overnight is fine too if that's more convenient.

Drain the watermelon peel and rinse under the cold tap. Return the pieces to the pan and add enough water to cover. Bring to the boil and simmer for 15 minutes. Drain.

To make the brine, put all the ingredients into a large non-reactive saucepan with 200ml water. Place over a medium heat, stirring to dissolve the salt and sugar.

Add the watermelon peel and bring to the boil. Lower the heat slightly and simmer for about 5 minutes until just tender. Remove from the heat and leave to cool – place a plate on top to keep the pieces of peel submerged in the brine as they cool down.

When cold, decant the pickled peel and brine into a plastic container, cover and refrigerate overnight. The pickle will keep in the fridge for up to 2 weeks.

Pickled pineapple core

I love pineapple, with its unpromising, prickly brown outer layer protecting all that sharp-sweet juice within. If, like me, it galls you to chuck the chewy, woody core into the compost bin, try this simple pickle. The method is similar to the one used to pickle ginger. Indeed, the pineapple core shares a similar texture to ginger, though the flavour is very different. This preserve is good with all sorts of things, from cheeses and oily fish to curries and stir-fries, and it's particularly delicious with thick slices of ham. MAKES ABOUT 250g

About 200g pineapple core

About 1 tablespoon flaky sea salt

150ml rice wine vinegar

1 tablespoon golden caster sugar

1 teaspoon mustard seeds

Juice and finely grated zest of 1 lemon

Juice and finely grated zest of 1 lime

Using a mandoline or very sharp knife, slice the pineapple thinly – coin-thin if you possibly can. Place the pineapple slices in a colander, sprinkle on the salt, give them a quick stir and leave to stand in the sink for 20–30 minutes.

Rinse the pineapple slices very quickly under cold water and pat dry with a clean tea towel.

In a small saucepan, gently heat the vinegar, 100ml water, the sugar and mustard seeds together, stirring to dissolve the sugar. Add the citrus zests and juices and immediately take off the heat.

Place the pineapple in a large sterilised jar (see sterilising instructions on page 268) and pour on the hot pickling mixture. Seal, cool and refrigerate for a couple of days to allow time for the flavours to develop.

This lovely pickle will keep in the fridge for a month or so.

Tips and swaps

Hot and spicy version Add a good pinch of dried chilli flakes to the pickling mixture.

CHRISTMAS LEFTOVERS

In this chapter, I've tackled the unique leftovers challenges presented by Christmas. During the festive season, many of us lay down enough food to feed a ravenous army, and our kitchens can accumulate a huge volume of cling-filmed and be-foiled foodstuffs. But this is a thing to be celebrated – and not just because leftovers symbolise the abundance and generosity of the season.

It's also the case that, once the big performance of producing Christmas dinner is over, leftovers provide us with several days of relatively low-stress fridge-foraging. We can tuck into sandwiches, slabs of cake and wedges of cheese without a second thought, leaving us with lots of time for the important tasks of watching films and sneaking afternoon naps, undertaking family walks and games, or reading novels, cosied up in amusing festive knitwear.

Most of us already know that, with a little relatively stress-free coaxing, the remains of the big bird (or joint of beef) can be transformed into a tasty curry (see page 284). However, I've discovered that with the addition of a spoonful or two of jar-end mincemeat, you can also whip up a fragrant turkey tagine (see page 286) to fuel a crowd through a day or two of delightful seasonal indolence.

Doorsteps of Christmas pudding, meanwhile, can be crumbled into a pretty sophisticated parfait (see page 296),

or simply fried and served with leftover brandy butter for
a once-a-year breakfast treat. I've also got ideas for those
cupboard-crowding ingredients we so often over-buy at this
time of year: why not transform your excess salted nuts into
a hasty satay sauce (see page 288), olives into tapenade
(see page 282), or those fancy biscuits into toppings for
gratins or crumbles?

There are recipes in other parts of this book that have
relevance at Christmas and I make no apologies for
drawing attention to them here. Scan my chapters on
leftover roots and leftover greens and salad to find ways to
turn excess roast parsnips and potatoes into something
special and give new life to tired leaves. There are even
ways to make cold gravy glorious again.

This is also a time of year when many of us give free rein
to our passion for cheese. If you find yourself with more
fromage than even the most generous cheese board can
accommodate, turn to the dairy chapter and check out my
recipes for potted cheese (see page 230) and ultimate
cheese drawer straws (see page 226). Fantastic for low-
input lunches, they're also a great addition to a New Year's
Eve party, combining seasonal thrift with gastronomic
indulgence – a marriage I'm very happy to celebrate.

THINGS TO DO WITH CHRISTMAS LEFTOVERS

Olives Turn leftover black or green olives into a tasty tapenade. Halve and stone about 150g olives. Put into a food processor with 2 tablespoons drained capers, a couple of anchovies, 1–2 garlic clove(s) and a handful of chopped herbs, such as basil, oregano, parsley and/or thyme, if you have them. Pulse until fairly coarse but evenly combined (or simply chop the ingredients together on a board). Transfer to a bowl and stir in a squeeze of lemon juice and enough olive oil to get the consistency you like. Taste and season with salt and pepper if required. Serve as a dip with crudités, crostini or hunks of bread.

Nuts, crisps and pretzels Whiz together in a food processor to coarse crumbs and store in a jar in the fridge, ready to use as a topping for gratins, pasta bakes etc.

Use chopped nuts to add texture to breads, cakes, muffins and biscuits, or incorporate them into tiffin (see page 310).

If you have some leftover walnuts, hazelnuts or almonds, use them the next time you are making pastry for a tart. Toast the nuts lightly, blitz until fine and replace about 20 per cent of the flour with the nut mix to add texture and flavour to the pastry.

If you have lots of leftover herbs as well as nuts, blend them together with some garlic and olive or rapeseed oil to make a quick pesto – great for an easy pasta supper or tossed through seasonal roasted veg.

Smoked salmon A small amount of smoked salmon (and other smoked fish) can add character to all manner of dishes. If you have enough left, try making potted fish (see page 108) or coarsely blitz trimmings with a few spoonfuls of cream cheese to make a spread.

For a quick supper, layer flakes of smoked salmon or trout into a potato dauphinoise, or fold through a creamy sauce for pasta with steamed broccoli, or fork through kedgeree, or add to omelettes and frittatas (see pages 43–5).

Stuffing Crumble any leftover stuffing into omelettes and frittatas (see pages 43–5), scatter it onto pizzas, or add to chicken, turkey and/or ham pies or cobblers.

Crumbled stuffing also makes a good filling for baked mushrooms – just top with a little grated cheese and breadcrumbs, dot with a scrap of butter and bake until golden and bubbling.

Cranberry sauce Tangy, sweet and delicious, a few spoonfuls of cranberry sauce can elevate humble ingredients into something special. Use it in a toasted sandwich (see page 42); most hammy, cheesy combinations work well. And of course, it stars in many a turkey sandwich. Cranberries are great with pork and venison too – try serving some with a porky meatloaf or pork or venison burgers.

Thin a spoonful or two of cranberry sauce with some orange juice and warm it gently to make a quick syrup to serve on pancakes, spoon over vanilla ice cream, or even stir into porridge.

To create a lovely seasonal fruit fool to serve as a light pud, swirl cranberry sauce and chopped clementines into a mixture of half yoghurt, half lightly whipped cream. Or, fold a spoonful of cranberry sauce and some orange segments through your breakfast yoghurt.

Clementines and satsumas Use excess fruit to make marmalade and curds, stir the zest into cakes and puds, and whisk the juice into dressings (adding a dash of cider vinegar too, for that essential burst of sharp acidity). Sliced clementines are particularly good atop an upside-down cake.

——

For a refreshing fruit salad, try a combination of clementine slices with some Medjool dates and chopped mint, sprinkling some orange flower water over the top, if you have it.

Mincemeat To add an extra dimension to an apple pie, spread over the base of the pie dish before you add the apples.

——

Or use mincemeat as a stuffing for baked apples: score the circumference of the apples with a sharp knife then scoop out the cores from the stalk end. Stuff with mincemeat mixed with a little soft brown sugar and soft butter. Bake at 190°C/Fan 170°C/Gas 5 for about 40 minutes until the apples are soft.

Brandy butter Don't leave a jar of brandy or rum butter hidden in the back of the fridge. Dollop some onto rice pudding, use to make luxurious cinnamon toast or spoon onto crêpes or eggy bread (see page 174).

——

Or, for a boozy bread and butter pudding, spread it onto the bread – this is a good way to use up any dried fruit left over from making your Christmas pudding or cake too.

Christmas cake or pudding Cut into slices and remove the marzipan and icing from cake. Fry the slices in butter, then dust with icing sugar and serve topped with dollops of brandy butter for an indulgent Boxing Day breakfast.

Panettone To make a luxury bread and butter pudding, thickly slice the panettone, butter lightly, then cut the slices in half. Arrange in a buttered shallow baking dish and pour over a creamy custard (see page 176). Leave to soak for half an hour. Stand the dish in a roasting tin and surround with hot water to come halfway up the sides of the baking dish. Bake at 160°C/Fan 140°C/Gas 3 for 40–50 minutes until just set and starting to caramelise a little around the crusts. Dust with icing sugar to serve.

Christmas biscuits If you have lots left over in the tin, bash them up a bit into coarse crumbs. Use as an 'independent' topping for fools and fumbles (see page 63), or incorporate into a chocolate tiffin (see page 310).

Dried, candied or crystallised fruits Chop and scatter over a puddle of melted chocolate spread on a sheet of baking parchment, then leave to set. Break up the set chocolate into shards and slivers and enjoy as a treat with coffee. This works with nuts too.

Chocolate truffles If you find yourself with an embarrassing excess, there are several things you can do with them: roughly chop and add to brownie or cookie batter instead of chocolate chips; halve and add to tiffin (see page 310); or stir one truffle into a cup of hot chocolate to add a luxurious touch.

Turkey curry

To my mind, the lull between Christmas and New Year loses some of its savour if it isn't fuelled at least in part by bowls of fragrant curry made from meaty leftovers. If turkey isn't your thing, you can, of course, make this curry using chicken, lamb or beef. SERVES 6–8

2 tablespoons rapeseed or sunflower oil

2 onions, diced

3 garlic cloves, halved and sliced

2–3 tablespoons home-made curry paste (see page 57), or a favourite ready-made curry paste

Up to 400g roast carrots or parsnips (or use fresh ones), in chunky pieces

400ml tin coconut milk

200–300ml chicken stock (see page 28, or from a stock cube is fine), or gravy

1 bay leaf (optional)

400–500g roast turkey, white and/or dark meat, torn into large chunks

Juice of ½ lime

Generous handful of coriander and/or mint, tough stalks removed and roughly chopped

Salt and freshly ground black pepper

Toasted cashews or flaked almonds, to finish (optional)

Heat the oil in a large, heavy-based casserole over a medium-high heat. Add the onions with a pinch of salt and sauté quite vigorously, until they are softened and golden. Add the garlic and fry for a further minute.

Reduce the heat a bit, add the curry paste and stir for a minute, then toss in the vegetables and stir until they're well coated in the fragrant, oniony curry mix.

Pour in the coconut milk and stock or gravy and stir well to combine with the spicy veg. Add the bay leaf, if using. If your pan is very large, you may need to add a bit more stock or water to cover, but don't make it too soupy. You want the final mixture to be quite rich and thick.

Simmer for 10 minutes. If you're using fresh rather than roast roots, simmer for an extra 5–10 minutes at this stage.

Now add the turkey and cook until thoroughly heated through, about 5–10 minutes. Stir in the lime juice and about half of the coriander and/or mint.

Scatter over the remaining coriander and/or mint, and the toasted nuts, if using. Serve with basmati rice, naan or flatbreads and your favourite chutneys.

Tips and swaps

Curried turkey pie This curry makes a great pie if you have any left over. Follow the instructions on page 46.

Curried turkey parcels Small amounts of leftover curry can be wrapped into wontons (see page 49) or enfolded into a pasty (see page 48). Make sure they are baked until the filling is piping hot.

Turkey and mincemeat tagine

Bear with me. This sounds just a bit too cute to be true. But it is actually really good. The cinnamon, fruit and nuts contained in a good mincemeat are reminiscent of the ingredients you might find in a Moroccan tagine. And, of course, a tagine is a very good way to use up leftover roast turkey. So this dinner of festive leftovers, featuring a cracking combination of sweet, savoury and spicy flavours, turns out to be sophisticated, sultry and very delicious. SERVES 6

Knob of butter

1 medium onion, very finely chopped

4 carrots, cut on the diagonal into 4cm pieces, or leftover roast carrots

1 garlic clove, finely chopped

1 teaspoon ras el hanout (North African spice blend)

½ teaspoon ground ginger

Pinch of saffron strands (optional)

3 tablespoons mincemeat

600ml turkey, chicken or veg stock (see page 28)

400g cooked chickpeas, drained and rinsed if tinned

About 100g pitted prunes

Small bunch of parsley, tough stalks removed and tied into a bundle with kitchen string, leaves roughly chopped

300–500g roast turkey, torn into large chunks

Trickle of clear honey (optional)

Salt and freshly ground black pepper

To serve

Some toasted sesame seeds

Couscous, made with well-flavoured stock

Heat the knob of butter in a large, heavy-based saucepan over a medium heat. When it has melted and stopped foaming, add the onion and cook for a few minutes to soften slightly.

Now add the carrots, garlic, ras el hanout, ginger and saffron, if using. Stir for a minute until the carrots are well coated in the spices.

Stir in the mincemeat then pour in the stock and add the chickpeas, prunes and bundle of parsley stalks. Season with salt and pepper. Bring to a simmer and cook for 15–20 minutes, until the carrots are tender (or just 10 minutes if using roast carrots).

Add the turkey and simmer for 5 minutes or so, until the meat is piping hot. Add a trickle of honey, if you like, then taste and season with more salt and pepper if necessary. Remove the bundle of parsley stems.

Serve the tagine scattered with the chopped parsley and sesame seeds, with couscous on the side.

Tips and swaps

Add roots Leftover roast parsnips or sweet potatoes, cut into chunky pieces, can be added to the tagine if you like.

Swap the meat You can also make this with leftover roast chicken or lamb.

Christmas nut satay turkey

This is another great pairing of inevitable Christmas leftovers: leftover roasted salted peanuts – or cashews – made into a tangy satay sauce to serve with leftover roast turkey or chicken. **SERVES 4-6**

Up to 500g roast turkey, pork or chicken

Sunflower oil, for frying

Salt and freshly ground black pepper

For the satay sauce

About 100g salted roast peanuts, cashews, almonds or a mix

1 teaspoon honey or brown sugar

Good pinch of dried chilli flakes

1 garlic clove, chopped

About 50ml coconut milk

About 2 tablespoons lime or lemon juice, plus a little grated zest

About 1 tablespoon soy sauce

Dash or two of fish sauce or Worcestershire sauce

To finish (optional)

Grated carrot

Coriander leaves

First make the satay sauce. Pulse the nuts in a food processor with the honey or sugar, chilli flakes and garlic – you are aiming for a coarse, crumbly paste.

Mix together the coconut milk, citrus juice and zest, soy and fish or Worcestershire sauce. Add very gradually to the nut mixture, pulsing between each addition, until you get a nice creamy paste, with a bit of nubbly, nutty texture too (you might not need every drop).

Taste the sauce and adjust as necessary, adding more coconut milk or soy or chilli or lime and so on until you have exactly the balance you like. You can then store the sauce in a jar in the fridge until needed.

Tear the turkey or other meat into strips. Heat a thin film of oil in a pan over a fairly high heat. Add the strips of meat and fry hard, shaking or stirring occasionally, until sizzling hot and crisping nicely at the ends and edges.

In a small saucepan, warm the satay sauce over a low heat, stirring occasionally. If it looks too stiff and pasty, loosen with a little warm water, or coconut milk. It should be thick and creamy and almost, but not quite, pourable.

Place the fried meat on warmed plates and generously spoon over the hot satay sauce. Scatter over some freshly grated carrot and a few coriander leaves, if you like, and serve with plain boiled rice.

Turkey rissoles

For many, Christmas isn't Christmas without turkey, and Boxing Day isn't Boxing Day without the conundrum of what to do with the inevitable mountain of cold meat. Of course, it's very good in a curry or tagine, or stuffed into enchiladas (see page 72), but here's another good solution. Make these easy rissoles for a tasty family brunch with any kind of eggs – fried, poached, scrambled – or serve for supper, with mash and any leftover gravy poured over the top. SERVES 4–6

About 400g roast turkey, white and/or brown meat, diced quite small

About 50g breadcrumbs

Generous handful of parsley, tough stalks removed, leaves finely chopped

2 tablespoons soft thyme leaves, finely chopped

1 garlic clove, finely chopped

Grating or two of nutmeg (optional)

1 large egg, lightly beaten

Plain flour, for dusting

2–4 tablespoons rapeseed or sunflower oil, for frying

Salt and freshly ground black pepper

Put the diced turkey into a large bowl with the breadcrumbs, herbs, garlic and nutmeg, if using, along with a generous seasoning of salt and pepper. Use your hands to mix everything thoroughly. Trickle the egg over the mixture and work it in evenly so it binds everything together.

To check the seasoning, break off a small piece of the mixture and fry it until cooked through. Taste it for seasoning and add more salt or pepper to the main mixture if necessary.

Divide the mixture into 8–10 pieces and form into shallow patties. Put on a plate, cover and refrigerate for at least 30 minutes, or for several hours if that suits you better.

Gently dust the rissoles all over with flour, shaking off any excess. Heat 2 tablespoons oil in a large, heavy-based, non-stick frying pan over a medium heat.

You will probably need to cook the rissoles in batches to avoid crowding the pan. Fry for 4–5 minutes per side or until golden and hot right through. Remove and drain on kitchen paper. Keep warm while you fry the rest, adding more oil to the pan as necessary. Serve hot.

Tips and swaps

Add sage leaves If you have any fresh sage to hand, fry a handful with the rissoles (as shown) and serve as a crispy garnish.

Add piquancy A spoonful or two of cranberry sauce or even a bit of chutney stirred into the mixture, will give your rissoles a piquant edge. Bread sauce can be a nice savoury addition too.

Toss in stuffing If you have any left over, chop it up and add it to the mixture – but ideally don't use more stuffing than meat!

Pork rissoles Use roast pork instead of turkey, add a little chopped sage to the other herbs and moisten the mix with a dollop or two of apple sauce if you have it, as well as the beaten egg.

Sprout, ham and chestnut gratin

Lover of Brussels sprouts that I am, even in my house I confess there are often some of the little fellas left after Christmas dinner. Luckily, they team up exceptionally well with other festive leftovers, to make a delicious crisp-topped gratin. SERVES 2

Large knob of butter

About 250g cooked Brussels sprouts (but not over-cooked!)

Up to 100g cooked ham and/or bacon and/or chipolatas and/or stuffing

Up to 100g cooked chestnuts, roughly crumbled

Splash of chicken or veg stock (see page 28), white wine or water (about 50ml)

2–3 tablespoons crème fraîche or cream

About 30g well-flavoured hard cheese (or cheeses – including blue cheese), grated

About 30g fairly coarse breadcrumbs

Salt and freshly ground black pepper

Thyme leaves, to finish (optional)

Preheat the oven to 180°C/Fan 160°C/Gas 4. Use some of the butter to grease a gratin dish.

Roughly chop or slice the cooked Brussels sprouts. Cut the meat and stuffing, if using, into bite-sized pieces.

In a large bowl, combine the sprouts, meat and stuffing, if using, and the chestnuts. Season with a little salt and pepper. Add the stock, wine or water, and the cream or crème fraîche and stir through.

Transfer the mixture to the prepared dish and spread evenly.

Combine the cheese and breadcrumbs and sprinkle over the surface. Cut the remaining butter into slivers and dot over the topping.

Bake for 15 minutes, or until the gratin is hot right through. If the cheesy topping is not golden brown, finish off under a hot grill.

Serve scattered with some thyme leaves, if you like, and grind over some pepper.

Tips and swaps

Add extra veg Other leftover veg, such as chopped roast parsnips or carrots.

Saucier option If you have a batch of white or cheese sauce in the freezer (see page 228), use it in place of the stock/cream to add richness.

Crumby cheesy Crimbo wafers

Who would have thought leftover cheese and stale bread could be turned into something so delicate and delicious? You can serve these wafers as a canapé with drinks, but they also make great croûtons to finish soups and salads. MAKES ABOUT 16

A little oil or butter, for greasing

100g grated hard cheese (see page 227)

35g fine breadcrumbs

1 teaspoon thyme leaves (optional)

Salt and freshly ground black pepper

Preheat the oven to 220°C/Fan 200°C/Gas 7. Lightly grease a large baking sheet or two smaller ones.

Put the cheese, breadcrumbs and thyme, if using, in a food processor with a few grinds of black pepper and a pinch of salt. Pulse a couple of times to combine.

Pile spoonfuls of the mixture onto the baking sheet(s), leaving space between each pile for them to spread out. Bake for about 8 minutes until pale golden brown.

Take out of the oven and leave to firm up on the baking sheet for 3 minutes.

Use a spatula to lift the wafers onto a wire rack to cool completely, or straight onto a plate if you're serving them warm.

Once cooled, the wafers can be stored in an airtight container for 2 or 3 days.

Tips and swaps

Spice them up Add a pinch or two of cayenne or grated nutmeg to the basic mixture.

Prep ahead Make a big batch of the mixture and keep it sealed in a bag in the freezer, then bake the wafers straight from frozen, simply heaping the frozen bits on to the baking sheet. Up the cooking time by a couple of minutes.

The mix also makes a very good instant gratin or pasta bake topping.

Christmas pudding parfait

This is an elegant way for Christmas pudding to end its days – the fruity, spicy chunks embedded in a luscious, snow-white ice cream. SERVES 8

125g caster sugar

5 large egg yolks

½ vanilla pod

250ml double cream

250g leftover Christmas pudding, crumbled into small nuggets

Line a 1kg loaf tin (about 10 x 20cm base measurement) with 2 or 3 layers of cling film (or you can use baking parchment if you prefer).

Put the sugar and 100ml water in a small heavy-based saucepan and heat gently, stirring, until the sugar has fully dissolved. Increase the heat and bring the syrup to the boil. Put a sugar thermometer in the pan (if you have one) and boil until the syrup reaches 120°C, i.e. the soft ball stage; this will take at least 10 minutes. If you don't have a thermometer, test by dropping a little syrup into a glass of chilled water: it should form a soft, flexible ball.

While the syrup is boiling, put the egg yolks into a large bowl. Slit open the ½ vanilla pod and, using the tip of a small, sharp knife, scrape the seeds out onto the egg yolks. Beat lightly with an electric whisk.

As soon as the sugar syrup is ready, take the pan off the heat. Whisking constantly, trickle the hot syrup in a very thin thread onto the egg yolks. Keep moving the whisk around so the syrup is incorporated immediately. The idea is to 'cook' the egg yolks with the hot syrup.

Once the syrup is fully incorporated, whisk for several minutes more, until the mixture is very pale – almost white – and thick enough to hold a trail when the beaters are lifted. Leave to cool (this should only take a few minutes).

Meanwhile, lightly whip the cream. Carefully fold the whipped cream into the whisked mixture, then add the crumbled Christmas pudding and fold in lightly.

Tip the mixture into the prepared loaf tin and flip the overhanging cling film over the surface to enclose the parfait. Freeze for at least 8 hours, preferably overnight, until firm.

The next day, when you're ready to dish up, peel back the cling film (or parchment) from the top, invert the parfait onto a board and peel off the cling film (or parchment). Cut into thick slices and serve immediately.

Tips and swaps

Alternatively, you can use Christmas cake in the parfait – just remove all the icing and almond paste first. Even a few really good mince pies can be chopped up and added in place of the Christmas pudding.

STORECUPBOARD LEFTOVERS

For this final chapter, I've directed my now-finely-tuned leftover laser into every dark corner of the kitchen. I'm peering into cupboards, reaching to the back of shelves and digging out packets, bottles tins and jars, in my quest to make the most of each last morsel.

Half a bottle of beer or cider? How about a soup (see page 304) or soda bread (see page 302)? That cupboard crammed with near-empty boxes of cereal? Make a batch of flapjacks (see page 308). Pastry trimmings in the fridge will be turned into turnovers (see page 49), which can of course encase other leftovers, or rolled into biscuits (see page 49) to serve with drinks.

I've also included River Cottage head chef Gill Meller's ingenious recipe for transforming random half-empty jars of chutney into a delicious tangy brown sauce (see page 306). Sometimes the whole is mightier – or at least spicier – than the parts.

I'm even putting already-brewed coffee and tea to work in spice rubs (see page 312) and second-time brews (see page 314). We are a nation of tea-drinkers and coffee-fiends – and that means vast mountains of tea bags and coffee grounds being consigned to the rubbish bin, or at least the compost heap. However, as it turns out, both can be put to further gastronomic use. If you have a real surfeit, they have non-edible uses around the house and in the garden too (see pages 316–7).

Eating up everything you've got isn't just thrifty, it's time-efficient too. Whether you're using up accidental leftovers – the ends of packets and bottles, jars and tins – or transforming 'planned-overs' into quick, tasty dinners, a little extra effort on one day reduces the work required the next – by really quite a lot. And having time left over, for you and those you love, is perhaps the sweetest, most delicious luxury of all.

USING UP STORECUPBOARD LEFTOVERS

Anchovies

Finely chop a few anchovies and beat into softened butter with some finely chopped garlic, a squeeze of lemon juice, a little salt and pepper, and some paprika, if you like, to make a delicious anchovy butter. Serve with crusty bread and/or radishes, or spread on thinly sliced, toasted baguette and flash under a hot grill to melt for a canapé.

Stud a leg or shoulder of lamb with anchovies, garlic slivers and small sprigs of rosemary, then leave to stand for a few hours before roasting to allow the flavours to develop.

Use to make a batch of salsa verde, to serve with fish, steak, roast pork and chicken, roast veg, etc. Chop a big handful of parsley leaves, plus some basil and mint with some garlic, capers and anchovies. Combine with a dab of mustard, a squeeze of lemon and a good splosh of olive oil.

When making a tomato-based sauce, add chopped anchovy to the sautéeing onions at the start – even one or two will lift the flavour. Try sautéeing the onions and garlic in the oil from the anchovy tin too.

Sauté some chopped shallot or onion in the oil from the anchovy tin (or olive oil or rapeseed oil, if using salt-packed anchovies) with a couple of chopped anchovies until soft, then toss in some finely chopped garlic, dried chilli flakes and some lightly blanched broccoli or purple sprouting broccoli. Cook for a few minutes then toss with hot pasta and grate over some Parmesan or other hard cheese.

Capers

Add capers to tartare sauce to serve with fish dishes, such as the crispy fish skin 'bacon' sandwiches on page 106 and freewheeling fishcakes on page 102.

Fry capers in a generous amount of browned butter until crisp and spoon the caper butter over simply cooked fish.

Make a quick piccata-style pan sauce to go with fish, pork or chicken. Fry the fish or meat, remove from the pan, then gently sauté a finely chopped shallot in the pan juices. Deglaze with white wine and stock, then simmer to thicken a bit. Add some capers and a knob of butter at the end, heat to melt the butter and then spoon over the fish or meat.

Create a tasty Russian salad: chop cooked carrots and potatoes into small cubes and toss with cooked peas, finely chopped cornichons and capers, in a little good mayonnaise with a squeeze of lemon and some salt and pepper.

Cornichons

Use chopped cornichons in the same way as capers to add tang to a tartare sauce.

Fold chopped cornichons into a simple potato salad, or a classic celeriac rémoulade.

Slice cornichons and add to an egg salad sandwich with a little chopped tarragon.

Add some finely chopped cornichons to a cheese (and ham, if you like) toastie.

Use the vinegar from the cornichon jar to make a mustardy vinaigrette (see page 38) and add some very finely chopped cornichons, capers and shallot. Use this to dress lightly steamed veg such as French beans or even asparagus, toss with just-cooked new potatoes or Puy lentils, or spoon over thick slices of tomato.

Olives

Make a batch of tapenade (see page 282) to use as a dip or spread on toast.

Toss some chopped olives with crisp-fried new potatoes and lots of finely chopped parsley.

Toss chopped olives into a salad with shredded radicchio and sliced oranges (blood oranges look particularly dramatic).

Try a salad of olives, cubes of feta and chunks of watermelon or halved ripe strawberries.

Fork a handful of chopped pitted black olives through herby couscous.

Mix some chopped olives with diced, ripe tomato(es), shredded basil, a splash of good olive oil and some salt and pepper, then pile onto toasted sourdough to make bruschetta. Or toss the same combination through pasta for a quick supper.

Stir a few olives into a Mediterranean-style chicken or rabbit casserole. Add some salted citrus peel too (see page 268); it goes very well with olives.

Pesto
Stir a generous spoonful of pesto into some thick yoghurt to make a quick dip for crudités.

Work a bit of pesto into the mix for meatballs or a meatloaf, to add a nice hit of herby flavour.

Stir a small amount of pesto into the beaten eggs for a summer garden frittata (page 44) or a simple omelette (page 43) for a piquant lift.

Tomato ketchup
Stir even small amounts of ketchup (or brown sauce) into barbecue sauces or marinades, to add sweetness and acidity.

Stir ketchup into a meatloaf or meatball mix. Spread ketchup on top of the meatloaf before you bake it too – for a delicious crust.

Mix ketchup with a dab of honey and a splash of soy sauce and toss chipolatas in the mixture, before roasting at 220°C/Fan 200°C/Gas 7 for 20 minutes, or until cooked through and sticky.

Biscuits and cake
Fold bits of broken biscuits into tiffin (see page 310) or crush and use to make the base for a cheesecake. Mix up whatever you have – digestives, gingernuts and shortbread all work.

Use slices of past-its-best, plain-ish cake (Victoria sponge, Madeira cake, Swiss roll, etc.) as the base for a trifle (see page 60).

Jam and marmalade
If there's only a little bit of jam or marmalade clinging to the inside of the jar, shake in some soy sauce and rice vinegar, add some finely chopped garlic, chilli and grated ginger and shake to emulsify. Use as a dipping sauce, glaze or marinade.

Mix marmalade with mustard and use to glaze a ham before baking.

Spread a small amount of jam or marmalade on the slices of bread for a bread and butter pudding (see page 176), also the panettone version on page 283.

Heat leftover jam with some water until boiling and pass through a sieve. Use as a sauce to trickle over pancakes, waffles or ice cream, or fold into lightly whipped cream and yoghurt as part of a trifle (see page 59) or fumble (see page 62). You can add a splash of liqueur to this for a grown-up version.

Stir a spoonful or two of jam into natural wholemilk yoghurt for a treaty snack or quick-fix pud – top with a sliced banana and some flaked almonds or granola if you like.

Soda ale bread

A soda loaf is always a good idea when the bread bin is empty and you want something to go with soup or with cheese – you can have it on the table in an hour or less. However, what I really love about this particular version is the way it neatly absorbs those half-bottles of beer or cider I occasionally find – for example, under a bush the day after we have friends over for a barbecue. The brew gives the bread a distinctive, deliciously yeasty character. MAKES 1 LOAF

Butter or oil, for greasing

350g plain flour, plus extra for dusting

250g wholemeal flour

1 teaspoon bicarbonate of soda

1 teaspoon light brown sugar or honey

1 teaspoon salt

Dash of rapeseed or olive oil

300ml buttermilk (see page 214) or thin yoghurt

200ml beer or cider

Preheat the oven 220°C/Fan 200°C/Gas 7. Lightly grease a baking sheet and dust with a little flour.

In a large mixing bowl, whisk together all the dry ingredients. Make a well in the middle and quickly stir in the oil, buttermilk or yoghurt and beer or cider with a knife, working just enough to bring the dough together into a rough ball. The quicker you work, the better the texture will be. If it seems dry, add a dash more beer or water – the dough should be quite soft but not too sticky.

With floured hands, turn the dough out onto a lightly floured surface and knead very briefly – just enough to bring it together into a rough round, about 7cm high.

Transfer to a baking sheet, sprinkle generously with flour and use a sharp knife to cut a deep cross in the middle of the loaf.

Bake for 15 minutes, then lower the oven setting to 200°C/Fan 180°C/Gas 6 and bake the loaf for a further 20–25 minutes, until it sounds hollow when tapped on the base. It's best eaten warm, with plenty of butter, but it's also good toasted the next day.

Tips and swaps

Oaty loaf Substitute 100g of the plain flour with porridge oats.

Fruity nutty loaf Add a couple of tablespoons of raisins and/or pumpkin or sunflower seeds, and/or a small handful of chopped walnuts, for a great texture.

Celeriac soup with cider and blue cheese

Increasingly, it's not unusual for me to crack open a bottle of good cider but not finish it all. Admittedly, it's usually the second bottle I don't finish... or was it the third? Luckily, cider has a uniquely complex, fruity, sweet-tangy character that makes it a superb cooking ingredient – even if it's lost any fizz it might have had. It pairs beautifully with root vegetables, particularly earthy celeriac, as this lovely soup demonstrates. It's also a great way to finish up some oddments of blue cheese. SERVES 4

Generous knob of butter

1 large onion, chopped

1 bay leaf

1 large sprig of thyme

1 large or 2 small celeriac, trimmed, peeled and cut into 2.5cm chunks (about 400g prepared weight)

1 medium-sized potato, peeled and cut into 2.5cm cubes

250ml dry or medium cider

600ml chicken, veg or ham stock (see page 28)

50ml single or double cream, or crème fraîche (optional)

Salt and freshly ground black pepper

To finish

Soft thyme leaves

Chunk of blue cheese

Heat the knob of butter in a large saucepan over a medium-low heat. Add the onion with the bay leaf, thyme and a good pinch of salt and sauté gently, until soft and translucent, about 15 minutes. Add the celeriac and potato and sauté for a further 5 minutes.

Pour in the cider and stock, bring to a simmer and cook for 20–25 minutes, until the celeriac and potato are very soft. Remove the bay leaf and thyme stalk.

Let cool slightly, then blitz the soup in a blender until smooth, adding a splash more stock (or water) if you think it needs it.

Return the soup to the pan, stir in the cream or crème fraîche, if using, and adjust the seasoning to taste. Reheat gently – don't let it boil.

Ladle into warm bowls and serve sprinkled with the thyme leaves and with a little blue cheese crumbled on top.

Tips and swaps

Blue-less version If you're not a big fan of blue cheese, serve the soup sprinkled with croûtons (page 39), bits of crisply fried bacon or some small slices of apple fried in butter.

Nippy version This soup is very good made with parsnips added to the mix too.

Celeriac salt

This is an excellent, delicate seasoning for white meats, fish
and root veg. Scrub the whole celeriac very well before peeling,
to remove every last trace of dirt. After peeling, dry the peels, and
any other trimmings from prepping the root, very slowly in a very
low oven (about 3 hours at 70°C/Fan 50°C/lowest Gas should do
it), or even on a cake rack immediately above a radiator, overnight.
Then blitz in a food processor with some good flaky sea salt:
about 50g celeriac per 100g salt. Store in a screw-topped jar.

Many chutney brown sauce

If you like to make chutney, and/or you have friends who like to make chutney (and these are among the best kind of friends to have), then you may find that your fridge accumulates more half-full jars of interesting, spiced and fruited preserves than you can shake a spoon at. River Cottage Head Chef Gill Meller came up with this inspired idea to transform a chutney glut into a tangy brown sauce.

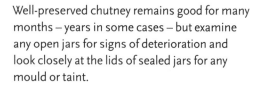

500ml or more of leftover chutney from an assembly of jars

Salt (optional)

Sugar (optional)

White wine vinegar or cider vinegar (optional)

Freshly ground black pepper

Well-preserved chutney remains good for many months – years in some cases – but examine any open jars for signs of deterioration and look closely at the lids of sealed jars for any mould or taint.

Sterilise one large (about 750ml) or two smaller (about 375ml) bottles ready for when the sauce is cooked (refer to the sterilising instructions on page 268).

Once you're satisfied that your chutneys are in good nick, use a rubber spatula to scrape every last scrap of them into a large saucepan. Stir everything together well and add enough boiling water from the kettle to create a fairly loose mixture.

Bring to the boil, lower the heat and simmer gently for 10 minutes, stirring now and again to make sure the mix is not sticking. Taste and correct the balance of flavours by adding salt and pepper, sugar and/or vinegar, no more than 1 tablespoon at a time, until you get just the balance you like.

Now purée the mixture in a blender or food processor until very smooth – you may need to do this in batches.

Return the sauce to the cleaned pan and boil for 5 minutes, again stirring so it doesn't stick and burn. Taste and season with more salt and pepper if necessary.

Pour the sauce into your sterilised bottle(s) and seal with a vinegar-proof lid(s). The sauce will keep for up to a year.

Serve with full English breakfasts, spread in cheese sandwiches, dab on pork pies and, above all, always have handy for a bacon butty.

Tips and swaps

Feel free to add the last spoonfuls of redcurrant jelly from the bottom of a jar to this mixture.

Some mango chutney, if you have it, adds a real brightness of flavour to the end result.

Cupboard flapjacks

Most families like to have a selection of breakfast cereals, mueslis and granolas on the go – and that can sometimes lead to having several almost-empty boxes taking up masses of room in the cupboard. The following recipe is a fantastic, sweet-treat solution to just such a proliferation situation. It will also happily embrace variable quantities of dried fruit, seeds and nuts (whether leftover or prime). MAKES 12

175g butter, cut into cubes, plus extra for greasing the tin

50g honey or golden syrup

125g sugar (preferably light brown or demerara)

150g sundry cereals, from muesli to cornflakes or Rice Krispies – whatever you have left over

100g porridge oats

About 25g unsulphured dried apricots or prunes, chopped

About 25g raisins or sultanas

About 25g pumpkin, sunflower or other seeds, or nuts

Pinch of salt

Preheat the oven to 170°C/Fan 150°C/Gas 3. Lightly butter a baking tin, about 25 x 20cm, line with baking parchment and lightly butter the parchment.

Put the butter, honey or syrup and the sugar into a medium-large, heavy-based saucepan. Heat gently, stirring frequently, until the butter is melted and everything is well combined. Remove from the heat and stir in all of the remaining ingredients.

Tip the mixture into the prepared tin and level out with the back of a spoon or a potato masher, pressing down to make sure everything is quite firmly packed in.

Bake for 25–35 minutes, until golden around the edges. The longer cooking time is for those who (like me) like their flapjacks quite dark, toffee-ish and chewy.

Remove from the oven and run a knife around the edge of the tin to release the flapjack. Leave to stand for 5 minutes, then mark out into bars – don't cut into it yet.

Leave the mixture in the tin until it's nearly cold before cutting into pieces and transferring to a wire rack to cool completely.

Once cold, the flapjacks will keep in an airtight tin for a week or so.

Tips and swaps

Dairy-free coconutty flapjacks Replace the butter with 150g coconut oil (and grease the tin with it too). Add 1 tablespoon desiccated coconut, if you happen to have some.

Spread a spoonful of nut butter onto a piece of flapjack for a really energy-boosting snack.

Recycled chocolate tiffin

One Easter a few years ago, there was so much chocolate in the house that I created this tiffin recipe to use it all up. It's so simple to make, even the youngest members of the family can have a go, though they certainly won't be the only ones who eat it. You can also have a bit of a biscuit and dried fruit clear out with this recipe. MAKES 16 SQUARES

350–400g milk or dark(ish) chocolate egg, broken into pieces

150g unsalted butter

3 tablespoons golden syrup

About 150g biscuits (shortbread-type, gingernuts or digestives, or a mix), broken into pieces

About 300g Easter egg chocolates (mini Mars, caramels, mini eggs, mini Crunchies, white chocolate buttons, etc.), roughly chopped if large

About 150g raisins or chopped prunes or unsulphured dried apricots

70–100g white chocolate, chopped (optional)

Line a 23cm square baking tin with cling film.

Put the chocolate into a large, heatproof bowl with the butter and syrup. Set the bowl over a pan of barely simmering water, making sure the water doesn't touch the bottom of the pan. Leave until melted then take off the heat and stir to combine.

Add the broken biscuits, sweets (saving a few for decoration) and dried fruit to the melted chocolate and stir until well coated.

Tip the mixture into the prepared tin and level with the back of a spoon. Scatter the reserved sweets over the top. Melt the white chocolate, if using, in a heatproof bowl over a pan of barely simmering water (as above), then flick and drizzle it over the tiffin.

Allow to cool completely, then refrigerate for 4 hours or overnight.

Lift the tiffin out of the tin and remove the cling film. Cut into 16 squares, using a sharp knife dipped into boiling water.

Tips and swaps

To make an adult version of this chocolate extravaganza, soak the raisins in a couple of tablespoons of brandy for a couple of hours before stirring into the tiffin mixture.

Coffee spice rub

Coffee is an ingredient in many American barbecue marinades and rubs, lending depth of flavour and perky acidity, especially to pork. This is my take on the idea, using grounds leftover from a cafetière-ful of coffee, although you could use grounds from a filter too. It's important to dry out the grounds completely (see tips and swaps, below). This rub has delicious – and rather surprising – liquorice notes.

2 tablespoons very dry, once-brewed coffee grounds (see below)

1 tablespoon freshly ground black pepper

1 tablespoon light muscovado sugar

2 teaspoons flaky sea salt

1 teaspoon fennel seeds

Pinch–¼ teaspoon chilli flakes

Pinch–¼ teaspoon ground cardamom (optional)

Put all of the ingredients into a spice mill or mini food processor and whiz until well combined. Alternatively, pound them together using a pestle and mortar.

The rub will keep sealed in a jar in a cool, dark place for a couple of months.

Tips and swaps

Drying coffee grounds Spread the coffee grounds thinly and evenly on a plate and let them dry naturally. Or, to speed up the process, line a baking sheet with baking parchment, scatter the coffee grounds over it and place in a low oven for 10 minutes or so. Take out of the oven and leave for at least an hour, until the excess moisture has evaporated.

Coffee-spiced pork belly Rub some of the spice rub into the scored skin of a 1–1.5kg piece of pork belly (as shown), making sure you get it right into the cracks. Leave to stand for an hour, to allow the flavours to penetrate. Give it a hot blast at 220°C/Fan 200°C/Gas 7 for 30 minutes, then turn the oven down to 160°C/Fan 140°C/Gas 3 and cook for a further 2 hours, until the juices run clear and the crackling is puffed up (you may want to flash the crackling under a hot grill if it's not puffed up enough).

Garlicky version You can add some finely chopped garlic to the spice rub for use on meat – mix it in just before you want to use it.

Tweaked brownies Add a teaspoonful of this blend to chocolate cake, brownie or biscuit batters to deepen the flavour.

Masala chai

Black tea doesn't generally take very well to being brewed more than once (though some green and white teas are quite happy to be re-infused two or three times). The exception is the classic Indian masala chai – where the tea leaves are boiled fiercely for a couple of minutes with a little spice. These days, my second or third cuppa of the morning is often a masala chai made from the recycled leaves of the previous brew(s). Here's how I do it:

Spent tea leaves: either 2 used tea bags, or 1 tablespoon loose tea leaves from the bottom of the pot

Milk

Couple of cardamom pods, or a pinch of ground cardamom

Fingertip of fresh ginger, or a pinch of ground ginger

Pinch of ground cinnamon (optional)

Tiny twist of black pepper (optional)

Sugar

Place the tea leaves in a small saucepan, with about ½ mug of water and ¼ mug of milk. You can use the remnants of a previous cup of tea (from the same day!), or tea from the bottom of the pot (as well as the leaves) if you didn't finish it. Bash the cardamom pods and ginger nugget and add to the pan, along with the cinnamon and black pepper, if using.

Place the pan over a medium heat and bring to the boil. Add a pinch of sugar, or more if you like (travellers to India will know that chai wallahs add *a lot*). Boil hard, swirling the pan or stirring the tea occasionally – in India the boiling tea is poured from one pan to another, sometimes from a spectacular and dangerous height.

When the tea has been boiled hard for a good couple of minutes, and is a deep nutty brown, strain it into a small cup or mug. It should be strong, spicy, milky and piping hot (sip it with care). Just half a cup of this intense brew is a generous portion.

Tips and swaps

If you have leftover brewed tea in the pot, there are a few other things you can do with it:

Soak dried fruit in hot black or fruit teas to plump them up before using in baking, casseroles or adding to your breakfast muesli or compote. You can store tea-soaked fruit in the fridge for a couple of days.

Use chilled green, white, fruit or mint tea as a refreshing alternative to water, milk or fruit juice in smoothies.

Use brewed, chilled tea as an alternative to water in baking.

Other uses for leftovers

The following household tips may seem just a bit quaint and old-fashioned, but they are genuinely effective. And when you think how much we spend on the cleaning products and garden treatments that these kitchen leftovers can replace, it soon seems mad not to. In fact, squeezing the maximum value out of each and every ingredient that crosses your kitchen threshold should be a matter of pride. When you're down to the last inedible rinds and remnants, shells and scrapings, there are many uses they can be put to. Let those ingredients take one more satisfying step before their final goodbye...

Citrus peels

Don't discard lemon (or orange/grapefruit/lime) halves when you've squeezed the juice, or the pared peels of these fruits. Their acidic nature and essential oils can be put to good use:

To get rid of an unpleasant lingering aroma – if you've been cooking oily fish, for example, put some spent citrus peels in a pan with a few cloves and/or cinnamon stick, cover with water and simmer for a minute. Turn off the heat, but leave the pan with its lid off. The essential oils of the lemon (or other citrus) and spices will gently neutralise any smells. Or leave some peels on a saucer, balanced on a warm radiator – their scent will permeate the room.

Dip a squeezed lemon half in salt and/or bicarbonate of soda and use it to scour, clean and deodorise wooden chopping boards – a great treatment if you've been chopping garlic or onions. Simply rub the lemon all over the board, leave for 5 minutes, rinse and dry.

Rub a squeezed lemon half over fabric stained with turmeric or other curry spices to help lift the mark.

Put some chopped lemon rinds in a spray bottle with white vinegar or cider vinegar. Use as a grease-cutting cleaning spray in the kitchen.

Dip a squeezed lemon half in bicarbonate of soda and rub over taps and other places where limescale has formed. Leave for 10 minutes, then rinse and dry. Repeated applications will help to remove really stubborn deposits.

Use squeezed lemon halves to help clean the oven. This won't lift really burnt-on grease but it will help to stop build-up becoming the sort of problem that takes strong chemicals to shift. Heat the oven as hot as you can get it. Put some lemon halves in a roasting tin, put the tin in the oven and carefully fill with boiling water. Heat for 15–30 minutes then turn off the oven. Leave for 30 minutes, by which time the citrusy steam should have helped lift a lot of the grease. Wipe the inside of the oven with a soft cloth, dipped into hot water with a splash of mild detergent or washing up liquid added, then rinse well.

To clean the microwave, put a lemon half in a glass bowl filled with water and heat on full power for 5 minutes or until the microwave is good and steamy. Wipe the inside of the oven dry with a clean tea towel or kitchen paper.

Nutshells (and other shells)

The tough sharp-breaking shells of pistachios, walnuts and hazelnuts can, like egg shells, all act as a slug and snail deterrent when used as a mulch in pots and beds. Collect them up, put into a cloth bag and bash with a hammer to break them up a bit. Scatter their spiky shards around delicate plants. Leftover mussel shells can be used in the same way. And you can mix your egg-, mussel and nutshell shards to accumulate quite a stockpile of slug-barrier.

Egg shells

Don't throw away the shells when you crack open your eggs. Deploy them as garden and cleaning aids:

Put empty eggshell halves back in their box and fill with soil to make little 'seedling pots' – a nice bit of windowsill growing to do with children. You can also plant mustard and cress in your little carton garden.

Dry out eggshells to make a slug deterrent – either in a warm place or in a low oven for about 15 minutes – then whiz in a blender to course fragments. Scatter this sharp, gritty mixture around tender young plants: slugs don't like moving over the rough surface. You will need to collect a lot of eggshells to have enough of this, so get saving through the winter and stockpile your 'eggshell gravel' for your spring seedlings.

Use coarsely bashed-up eggshells for cleaning out the insides of bottles or narrow-necked vases. Just put some in the bottle, add the smallest drop of washing up liquid and some water and give it a good swirl, letting the eggshells scour away any marks. Drain and rinse. You can use uncooked rice or lentils in the same way.

Save the calcium-rich water from hard-boiling eggs. Once cooled, you can use it to water houseplants or vegetables from the nightshade family, such as tomatoes, peppers, potatoes and aubergines.

Mayonnaise

If you have a jar of mayonnaise past its use-by date, write 'DO NOT EAT' on the jar and keep it for the following:

To remove sticky stuff, such as labels from jars and bottles or chewing gum from shoes. Rub the mayonnaise on the surface, leave for a few minutes and it will begin to lift the label or gum so you can prise or scrub it off effectively.

To remove crayon and some pen marks off smooth surfaces, such as painted walls, vinyl and oil-cloth type tablecloths. Rub some lightly on the mark, leave it for a minute or two and wipe off with a damp cloth.

Coffee grounds

The coarse texture and acidic nature of coffee grounds means they have no end of reuse potential. If you'd like even more to play with, many coffee shops will happily give you their spent grounds at the end of the day if you ask.

Deploy them for any of the following:

Generously scatter coffee grounds around tender plants to help deter slugs and snails.

Add coffee grounds to the soil around acid-loving plants. If you have alkaline soil and would like to try turning a pink hydrangea blue, mix in a couple of tablespoons of coffee grounds around the soil at its roots. It doesn't always work, but it's impressive when it does!

Worms love the nitrogen in coffee grounds, so do tip the remnants of your daily grind into a wormery if you have one – or onto the compost heap if not.

Use dry coffee grounds as a good scouring powder. Dab some on a sponge and rub away at any burnt-on bits on pans.

If you're brushing out a fireplace, scattering on some coffee grounds before you start makes it easier to collect up the dust without engulfing yourself in a cloud of it.

Dry coffee grounds are very good at absorbing odours. Keep a small dish filled with grounds in the fridge to keep it smelling fresh.

Tea

Don't discard spent black tea leaves, or any tea left in the pot. Both can be used in the garden:

Scatter spent black tea leaves around the roots of roses – they like the tannic acid.

Cooled, leftover brewed black tea, in a fairly diluted solution, is a good feed for acid-loving houseplants, particularly if you live in a hard water area.

Storecupboard essentials

One's ability to work magic with leftovers – which, by their very nature, can be rather random and unpredictable – is greatly enhanced by having a stand-by stock of trusted basic ingredients. The following is a list of the storecupboard stalwarts I try to make sure I rarely run out of – a combination of the sort of staples that can reliably form the beginning of a dish, and the flavour-packed condiments and seasonings that can finish it off with aplomb.

Anchovies, capers and olives I try to ensure I always have these salty, flavour-packed ingredients to hand. Either added alone or in combination, they are very often all it takes to lift a dish out of the doldrums. Look for sustainably fished anchovies, such as those from Fish4Ever.

Biscuits Good quality, shop-bought, all-butter shortbread, digestives and gingernuts are great standbys for quick puddings and treats. It pays to bear them in mind as potential ingredients, as well as elevenses.

Booze Red and white wine, beer and cider, are all splashed about routinely in my kitchen. Unfinished bottles go into the fridge and usually get called upon within a day or two. They give complexity to all kinds of recipes. My go-to spirit is Somerset Cider Brandy made by Julian Temperley – a sprinkle or a slosh is good for all kinds of things – from heady game stews to grown-up chocolate puds and trifles.

Bread My wife Marie makes wonderful sourdough bread regularly, but we also love checking out artisan bakeries to see what they are up to. And we usually have a loaf or two of bought or home-made bread in the freezer for back up.

Breadcrumbs I often turn any stray crusts, ends or slices of semi-stale bread into plain or seasoned breadcrumbs (see page 39). You can freeze them in fairly small batches to crumb fishcakes and other patties, create a topping for gratins, or fry into pan grattato (see page 204) to add flavoursome crunch to pasta dishes. Or, if dried out completely in a low oven, they can be stored in a jar and kept in the larder for a couple of months.

Chocolate I find a good quality dark chocolate with around 70% cocoa solids the most versatile for cooking, but my kids prefer milk chocolate, which often gets used to make things like the tiffin on page 310.

Coconut milk Having a few tins of coconut milk in the cupboard means I can make creamy curries, soups and dressings in minutes.

Dried fruit Raisins, sultanas, prunes and unsulphured dried apricots are the ones I reach for most often. I will often soak these – in hot tea or apple juice – for half an hour or so, to use as fruity 'juice bombs' in salads or quickly improvised puds.

Dried herbs I don't use a lot of dried herbs, as I'm lucky enough to have a productive herb garden, but I find it quite useful to have some

dried bay leaves, oregano, sage, thyme and herbes de Provence on hand when I'm low on the fresh stuff. Check use-by dates from time to time – or simply use your nose to assess the potency of your dried herbs. Their flavour will fade as they age.

Flour These days I mostly use light brown flour in place of plain white in my daily baking and pancake making. My wife Marie keeps a range of flours for her bread making and I plunder them from time to time. Spelt flour has a pleasing complex flavour that I like in some savoury and sweet recipes. Rye flour is even more distinct, holding moisture – and spices – particularly well. Both flours can be used in improvised crumbles, or added to pancakes and drop scones, especially those destined for a savoury outing.

Honey I wouldn't be without a good, fragrant, runny honey – I get mine, raw and minimally processed, from local beekeepers.

Mustard I use hot English mustard more often than any other kind. I also keep a milder Dijon mustard and a wholegrain variety, for when I fancy its lovely seedy texture in a dish or dressing. I've bought and been given many 'fancy' mustards down the years but never found one that came close to displacing these dependables. I keep mustard in the fridge, as it retains its true flavour much longer.

Nuts and seeds I always have walnuts, pecans, cashews, pine nuts and almonds to hand, along with pumpkin, sunflower, poppy and sesame seeds. To me, a bit of nutty or seedy crunch (particularly if those nuts or seeds have been lightly toasted in a pan first) absolutely transforms a simple salad. I'm never without

a jar or two of nut butter, either – peanut is classic, of course, but cashew butter is also a favourite. Nut butters thicken up sauces and curries a treat. They are great binders in baked dishes too.

Oils When I'm frying or sautéeing and I don't want the oil to contribute any taste to the dish, I use a flavourless sunflower oil. Otherwise, I use extra virgin rapeseed oil. I also employ this lovely, golden oil for roasting and dressings. For finishing dishes such as soups, roasted vegetables and salads, where the flavour can really shine, I turn to a good, peppery extra virgin olive oil.

Pasta I always try to have three different kinds of dried pasta on hand: long pasta such as spaghetti or linguine, pasta shapes such as farfalle, fusilli and penne, and small, rice-shaped risoni or orzo for soups and salads.

Pearled spelt or pearl barley These are both terrific for stretching a small amount of leftovers into tasty soups, stews and salads. I often cook extra, as 'planned-overs'.

Pepper Freshly ground black pepper has an astonishing ability to lift flavours, and I make sure there's a pepper mill always in reach when I'm cooking.

Pulses Dried pulses are better value for money, but you can't beat tinned ones for speed and convenience. I use chickpeas, cannellini beans, borlotti beans, kidney beans and lentils all the time – you can build a substantial meal around any one of them.

Rice Basmati, both white and brown, and long-grain brown rice are my go-to grains, for accompanying curries and other saucy dishes.

I tend to prefer brown rice, for its nutty texture, in dishes (hot or cold) where the rice is mixed through with other ingredients. I also keep arborio rice for 'true' risottos, and pudding rice – for rice puddings!

Salt I use ordinary table salt or fine-grained sea salt for salting cooking water and general seasoning. But I go for a flaky sea salt such as Maldon or Cornish for a final, sprinkled seasoning when its delicious crunch will really add something to the dish, for example on open sandwiches, creamy soups and salad-y assemblies of leftovers.

Soy sauce Soy and tamari (a Japanese-style soy sauce that usually doesn't contain wheat) add intense, savoury flavour to leftover veg, fish and meat, whether in stir-fries, salads or broths.

Spices Of course it's fantastic to have dozens of spices to play around with in the kitchen, but it's suprising how often I come back to my small cabal of dependable friends: For heat, I use cayenne pepper for an all-pervasive background heat, dried chilli flakes (including seeds) when I want the heat 'speckled' through a dish (and visible), and smoked paprika for a smoky, sweet warmth. For their winning, heady aromas, coriander, cumin, fennel and caraway seeds are the other spices I turn to most often. If I have time, I'll toast and grind cumin and coriander seeds myself, but I use the pre-ground versions and ground cinnamon too. And I always have cinnamon sticks and whole nutmegs for grating; these spices lend their spicy warmth to both sweet and savoury things. And I wouldn't be without cloves, for bread sauce and the Christmas baked ham.

Stock cubes I use a lot of home-made stock, but I regularly use organic stock cubes too. The ones I reach for most often are Kallo's organic, yeast-free veg stock cubes.

Sugar I use fine golden caster sugar and light muscovado sugar more than other sugars.

Tomatoes (tinned) I much prefer whole rather than chopped, tinned tomatoes – they are just more substantial and generous. It's quite easy to locate and remove any bits of skin, along with the hard pale tops, which I routinely do. I also like to have some bottled passata (sieved tomatoes) on hand for quick soups, sauces and stews.

Vanilla extract Just a splash of this sweet, sexy, intensely fragrant liquid lifts the simplest of biscuits, cakes, pancakes and custards. Get a pure extract, or a seed-flecked vanilla bean paste, rather than vanilla 'essence'. I always have whole vanilla pods too. Ndali vanilla from Rwanda is the best I've ever come across.

Vinegars The bottle of organic cider vinegar in my kitchen is in pretty much constant play. I use it in dressings, quick pickles and to add a balancing acidity to things made with sweet root veg. I also like the rich apple balsamic vinegar made by Aspall for doctoring sauces and gravies. I have almost given up using wine vinegars, although I have no strong objection to them.

FRESH ESSENTIALS

Butter We use a good salted local butter for daily spreading and off-the-cuff baking. But I do like unsalted butter too. It has a higher burning point than salted butter, so it's good for gentle frying, though a dash of sunflower

oil will raise the burn point of salted butter. If I'm buying butter, especially for sweet baking, I will also choose unsalted. It's more creamy and lactic, which just gives it the edge for special puddings, cakes and tarts.

Cheese My capsule 'cheese wardrobe' usually includes a mildish, firmish goat's or ewe's cheese for crumbling onto salads and soups, a mature organic Cheddar (not *too* strong) and a hard, Parmesan-style cheese for grating – either the real thing, Parmigiano Reggiano, or a hard, mature goat's cheese called Capriano. A luscious, tangy creamy blue, such as Dorset Blue Vinney or Cornish blue is useful too.

Chillies Medium-sized, medium-hot red chillies are the ones I use most frequently. Red jalapeños and fresnos are great, all-rounder chilli peppers.

Citrus fruit Because I hate to waste the zest, I always buy unwaxed citrus fruit. Lemon juice is almost as essential to me as salt and pepper, but I use a fair amount of orange and lime juice and zest in my cooking too.

Cream and crème fraîche Both double cream and crème fraîche are very useful, even in quite small quantities, for rounding out flavours and enriching dishes.

Eggs When our hens are taking a break from laying, we buy local free-range eggs. Why wouldn't you?

Garlic This is a must-have for me. Stale garlic is worse than no garlic, so I buy it regularly.

Herbs I'd be stuffed without my bay tree – its leaves are essential for stocks, sauces and soups, and brilliant with fish. But dried bay leaves are great too, if you have no space for

a bay tree. I grow lots of lovely herbs, but common thyme and flat-leaf parsley are the ones I pick and use almost daily; rosemary, mint and sage are the next in line.

Mayonnaise I often make my own, but I keep a jar of good ready-made in the fridge too, for adding to quick dips, salad dressings and sandwiches. There's an organic one I really like called Laydilay.

Peas or petits pois Frozen peas hold their flavour and sweetness brilliantly, making them a highly acceptable alternative if you can't get hold of the very freshest of fresh ones. And, of course, they can be used all year round.

Puff pastry Fresh or frozen, this is brilliant for the swift transformation of leftovers into tarts and pies. I always buy all-butter pastry – organic if possible.

Salted/cured pork Bacon, pancetta, chorizo, and cooked and air-dried ham are all incredibly useful for bumping up the flavour of a dish, even when used in quite small quantities. I make my own, but also buy good local products from outdoor-reared pigs.

Stock vegetables I always have onions and carrots on hand – celery too, when the English crop is in season (autumn and winter). I also think of parsley as a 'stock veg' and as it's available all year round the thick stalks go in almost every fresh stock I make. These are the essential building blocks of stocks, soups and stews.

Yoghurt I use natural wholemilk yoghurt even more frequently than the richer alternatives, double cream or crème fraîche, in savoury and sweet dishes. For puds, I'll often swirl yoghurt and cream or crème fraîche together.

Index

ACKNOWLEDGEMENTS

Leftovers cooking, as I hope this book makes clear, is not dull or do-goodish. It's immensely creative – and I could not have completed the project without the support of an immensely creative team.

First, thanks must go to Debora Robertson, who has been my sounding board for the whole project, and worked so hard to help me develop and test the dishes herein. And to Gill Meller, my River Cottage right arm, who suggested, tweaked and honed many of the recipes, and made all of them look so tempting in the photographs. Louise Tucker did wonderful work on the photo shoots too.

Simon Wheeler and I are well into our second decade of collaboration, and with each book I marvel anew at his gift for bringing my kitchen exploits to fresh and immediate life on the page. Yet again, he has done a magnificent job, for which (yet again) thanks Simon. And thanks, as ever, for additional photography under unreasonable time pressure, to my wife Marie.

Huge thanks also to our illustrator Tim Hopgood, whose vibrant and colourful drawings add an extra layer of deliciousness to the book.

More plaudits go to designer Lawrence Morton who has met the considerable challenge – often under-appreciated, I think – of making words, images, illustrations and recipes come together in one seamless and elegant whole.

At Bloomsbury, I am indebted to Natalie Bellos, my very gifted editor, who has overseen the entire undertaking with her usual charm, energy and good humour, and to her highly efficient assistant editor, Alison Glossop, for all her hard work.

The incomparable Janet Illsley has project-managed the book into the tempting and tidy package that it now is. And production manager Marina Asenjo has ensured that it looks good enough to eat.

A big thank you, as always, to Nikki Duffy, for her invaluable advice and guidance, some cracking recipe ideas, and a whole new level of punning in e-mail subject boxes.

And to my agent Antony Topping, for his unfailing enthusiasm for the Leftovers project, as well as all the usual stuff.

A book like this comes together, not only in the office and the studio, but also at home, in the kitchen, around the table. This is where ideas (and leftovers) are born, discussed, trialled, tested, occasionally found wanting, but (I'm delighted to report) much more often enthusiastically received – with a tweak or two helpfully suggested for next time around. For this unending and invaluable contribution I am hugely indebted to my loving family. Marie, Chloe, Oscar, Freddie and Louisa, you inspire and cheer me every day. Thank you.

Bloomsbury Publishing
An imprint of Bloomsbury Publishing Plc

50 Bedford Square   1385 Broadway
London   New York
WC1B 3DP   NY 10018
UK   USA

www.bloomsbury.com

BLOOMSBURY and the Diana logo are trademarks of Bloomsbury Publishing Plc

First published in Great Britain 2015
Text © Hugh Fearnley-Whittingstall, 2015
Photography © Simon Wheeler, 2015
Photograph on page 197 © Marie Derôme, 2015
Illustrations © Tim Hopgood, 2015

British Library Cataloguing-in-Publication Data
A catalogue record for this book is available from the British Library.
ISBN: HB 978-1-4088-6925-3
ePub: 978-1-4088-6926-0

2 4 6 8 10 9 7 5 3 1

Project editor: Janet Illsley
Designer: Lawrence Morton
Photographer and stylist: Simon Wheeler (simonwheeler.eu)
Illustrator: Tim Hopgood (timhopgood.com)
Indexer: Hilary Bird
Printed and bound in Italy by Graphicom

To find out more about our authors and books visit www.bloomsbury.com. Here you will find extracts, author interviews, details of forthcoming events and the option to sign up for our newsletters.